Building B

BUILDING BRIDGES INTO WORK

THE ROLE OF THE COMMUNITY WORKER

Edited by: Paquita McMichael,
Bruce Lynch & Daniel Wight

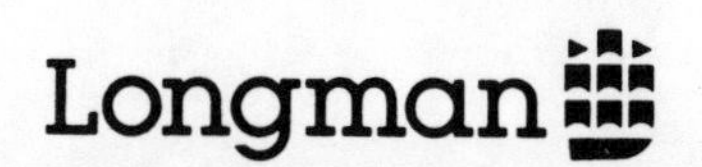

Building Bridges Into Work: The Role of The Community Worker

First published in 1990

Published by Longman Group UK Limited,
Industry and Public Service Management Division,
Westgate House, The High, Harlow, Essex CM20 1YR, UK.
Telephone: Harlow (0279) 442601

British Library Cataloguing in Publication Data
McMichael, Paquita
Building bridges into work: the role of the community
1. Great Britain. Community business enterprise. Role of community work
I. Title II. Lynch, Bruce III. Wight, Daniel 338.6

ISBN 0-582-07115-1

Typeset by The Setting Studio, Newcastle upon Tyne.

Contents

Acknowledgements

Finding community workers involved in community enterprises posed us with a number of problems at the outset of this project but our eventual success in tracking them down has been amply rewarded. We are therefore particularly grateful to the eleven who contributed their accounts - with all their ups and downs - to this venture. We hope that their honesty will contribute to helping others who follow them. Some of the accounts read rather like television serials and we wonder if there isn't a future for a new brand of 'soap' hanging on the adventures of everyday community businessmen.

A large number of other players have entered the cast, many of them one-time community workers, now in administrative positions. Throughout we have been impressed by the fact that those we interviewed were both highly active in the field and reflective on their practice whatever their current position. We thank them all for giving us the benefits of their experience.

We should offer our thanks to the Scottish Education Department for their financial support for the Scottish studies included in the text. Without their funding and that of Moray House College we could neither have begun nor completed this project.

We are much indebted to the Centre for Leisure Research, Cramond, Edinburgh for allowing Daniel Wight to work on the second (English) stage of this study while in their employment. We realise this was a considerable financial contribution to completing the project.

A number of accounts were first published in Scotland. We have now added four English projects to our original Moray House publication and widened our discussion. It has been our good fortune to have the help of John Armstrong from The Community Work Training Unit, Leicester as our collaborator in this. His eye for extension of our initial chapter to the UK context has been invaluable. We greatly appreciate his contribution made while under pressure from other demands on his time.

We have been sustained through the preparation of this book by the unfailing good cheer, willingness and inventiveness of Carole Jackson and Laura Boath who have typed and retyped a text which has not only been edited by us but also by those whom we consulted. The eleven community workers have each read our presentations of their account and amended them where necessary. We hope that this publication will repay them to some extent. As the authors we remain the debtors.

Paquita McMichael   Bruce Lynch   Daniel Wight

Part One: Community Enterprise and Community Work Approaches

1 A Rationale and Some Definitions

Look out there. (Govan dockside). That's an area of 50 per cent unemployment, huge poverty, lots of social problems, drugs. You name it, it's there... You get guys who do placements in youth clubs. That's great, but there has to be more.

The big difference I can detect between now and four years ago is, we don't have this animosity about community business that there used to be. So many community workers now see this as being totally relevant in their area, an exciting area to work in, and something that is much more challenging than the mundane everyday parts of their job.

Glen Buchanan, Strathclyde Community Business

The Development of Community Enterprise Initiatives in Scotland and England

Community Education and the training of community workers stress the responsibility for identifying community needs and enabling members of the community to find ways of meeting those needs. In the late 1970s and during the 1980s a paramount need has been for employment. As large manufacturing plants have closed in every Region, from British Leyland and coal mines in the central lowlands, to British Aluminium and Wiggins Teape in the Highlands, and, as smaller businesses have suffered from these losses, unemployment has risen to wholly unacceptable levels. In England the same process of de-industrialisation has led to a decimation of jobs in traditional industries. Sunderland, the location for two of our accounts of community workers' experience, has seen the complete run down of its traditional shipbuilding and heavy engineering industries, with little sign of the large scale new investment necessary to replace the many thousands of jobs lost. Furthermore, unemployment does not affect social classes and communities equally. The damaging effects of unemployment are concentrated amongst working class communities, with black people being particularly likely to face long term unemployment and few job prospects.

Given this background of community decline there has been a steady growth in interest during the late 70s and 80s, in the extent to which smaller scale community based enterprises can provide vitally needed job and training opportunities for residents. This growth in interest has brought the concept of community enterprise to the attention of a much wider audience, with consequent interest in the principles that lie behind the work.

Recent central government legislation may well expand the scope for community enterprise. The 1988 Local Government Act has introduced the principle of compulsory competitive tendering for a wide range of local authority services. The Griffiths Report on community care and the ensuing White Paper in 1989 also envisage a change in role for local authorities, from direct providers of services to that of case managers designing an appropriate care package for a client. To do this they will need to draw on services operated privately, by the community and by informal carers.

Whilst these changes may provide business opportunities for community enterprises there is also considerable scope for difficult conflicts of principle. For instance, what will be the reaction of a local authority which has supported the establishment of a community business, when that business starts to bid to provide services in direct competition with the local authority's own workforce? Is there a likelihood that such bidding will lead to job substitution rather than job creation? Will the need to provide a guaranteed standard of service over a specified time period add to the tension between achieving results and maximising process, learning and community development? The Ruchill account illustrates the dilemma. Will it be possible to retain the community focus?

Community enterprise initiatives in both Scotland and England have received considerable support from local authorities, often through the establishment of specialist development units to provide advice, support and development assistance. However, there have been some differences of approach between Scottish and English local authorities which have led to a difference of emphasis in the development of community enterprise. This difference is related to the differing structures of community work employment in the two countries.

English local authorities have tended to develop community enterprise initiatives as one part of a wider initiative to restimulate the local economy. Central units have often been established within the Chief Executives' Departments and have focussed on the objectives of job creation and economic viability. This centralised approach within the wide ranging objectives of economic development has on occasion led to a top down rather than bottom up approach to stimulating community enterprise. The differences of approach and priority of a central local authority unit and a local community enterprise project are revealed in the two Sunderland case studies. The participants in the Town End Farm project clearly felt that the central unit, Sunderland Common Ownership Enterprise Resource Centre, gave a higher priority to economic viability and demonstrable expertise than to local community needs and development processes.

Several Labour controlled authorities in the larger cities have been influenced by the concept of local socialism and have sought to develop wide ranging policies to use the resources of the local authority to remodel the local economy as a counter to the adverse effects of central government policy and industrial rationalisation. In these circumstances community enterprise has tended to be a small part of the wider local authority strategy geared to economic re-growth. In turn this tends to place the emphasis on economic viability rather than the wider contribution of community enterprise to programmes of community development and education.

In Scotland there appears to have been a stronger tradition of developing community enterprise as a technique of community development and education, rather than solely as a means of job creation and economic viability. This may have been influenced by the use of community enterprise approaches in more rural areas, such as the Highlands and Islands, where wider community development concerns required consideration as an integral part of the process. The account of Ferguslie Park reveals the tension, often inherent in community enterprise initiatives, between economic viability and community development as prime concerns, despite the size and success of the project. As the worker comments:

> I saw community business as a means of keeping unemployment on the political agenda, and I saw the concept of community business as being like a tenants' association. I saw it as a place where people who had experience of this area, who knew the problems in this area, would get together and create employment that would be different from working for a private business.

The differences between England and Scotland in the employment location of community workers also help to explain the differing emphases on community business. In Scotland community development and education are very firmly located in the policies and provision of many local authorities. In the areas of social work, community education and leisure and recreation, there are examples of long established commitments to community development. This is partly explained by differences in enabling legislation between the two countries. The result is the presence of community workers in fairly large numbers and often in organised teams within local authorities which provides the opportunity to develop a departmental community development approach to new issues such as community enterprise. Strathclyde Regional Council employs more than 300 community workers, a figure far in excess of comparable English authorities. Scotland also has a tradition of developing community education provision which in turn has helped to increase the emphasis on the educational, personal and community development aspects of community business.

Community workers are therefore far more firmly located in the Scottish local authority structure than is the case in England. Within England the employment of community workers is far more diffuse, with local authorities generally playing a less prominent role in their employment. There is also considerable variation between English authorities in their involvement in community development. In turn this means that English community workers are much less likely to be organised in large teams within local authorities, and therefore much less likely to be able to develop team policies which in turn might influence the authority's policy on community enterprise.

The Urban Programme and the Inner Area Programme have been important sources of funding within many English cities, and through these programmes non-statutory agencies have been able to obtain funding for usually small scale community based projects, thereby becoming an important element in English community enterprise provision. Over the last eight years central government has increasingly tied this funding to economic rather than social objectives. In turn this has led projects seeking funding to concentrate on quantifiable economic returns such as the number of jobs created, rather than wider social benefits and community development. Again, the tension between process and product becomes evident. At various points in a project's development choices have to be made between process/educational objectives and product/economic viability/job creation objectives. In the long run success tends to be judged by quantifiable results, jobs created and economic viability. Most of the accounts reveal problems of seeking to resolve community development objectives and economic viability, and the demands this makes on the residents involved.

The employment location of the community workers and the demands of funders therefore have a significant bearing on how community enterprise is approached and what outcomes are sought and prioritised.

Both the English and Scottish accounts provide a wealth of examples of the tensions and choices confronting the community worker engaged in community enterprise. Among the tensions identified are those created by pressures for top down as against bottom up development, for commercial profitability as against community development and for obtaining expert business skills from outside the community as against developing these skills within the community. While dealing with these issues community workers must also decide whether to act as enablers or more directive organisers, and whether to stress a development role or a role as expert manager/entrepreneur. Many of these tensions are compounded by the difficulties of breaking down the traditional employee culture. Should these tensions not provide problems enough, community enterprises also have to face continuous uncertainty about funding and income generation which can undermine long term planning and the hope and commitment of the participants.

These tensions make severe demands on workers and their training. They also make demands on the employing agencies and the community groups involved. Community enterprise is clearly a complex and taxing process which may often show only limited success if measured solely in terms of jobs created, rather than wider benefits to the personnel and communities involved.

The Purpose of this Book

In 1984 we began a project on community workers' experiences in this field. For us, the questions in our inquiry were whether, and to what extent, community workers had made a response that took account of the fundamental need of the unemployed: to have a job.

In planning the research we were conscious that few community workers had the confidence to tackle unemployment head on. They had, we surmised, a number of skills and resources that enabled them to offer personal or social skills training to prepare the unemployed for re-entry into work: for interviews and for successful self-presentation. They were also likely to have a variety of adult education and leisure and recreation programmes in which the unemployed might enrol. We believed that they would be less uncertain of their potential role in social and economic development if they had the guidance of those who had already trodden the path of community enterprise. We therefore planned to present accounts of their experiences given by these workers. Readers should note that the case studies, which we designed to act as guides and which form the majority of the text, do not always illustrate 'successful development' in terms of financial profit. Social and educational development in personal and community terms plays a large part in these workers' definitions of success.

The goal of this project was, therefore, to provide case studies of community workers for community workers, so that they might gain from the experiences – both good and bad – of those who had already attempted to confront the unemployed's most fervent desire – Gi'e us a job. From the studies of individual workers, scattered throughout Scotland and England, told largely in their own words, we have drawn a number of conclusions. These we have integrated with the views of officials in their own and other organisations whom we saw as having important contributions to make. We have used both types of source to construct an appropriate role for community workers in developing community employment initiatives.

It should be noted that the study began in Scotland. This was largely due to the higher profile of community businesses there and the established tradition of community co-operatives in the Highlands and Islands. The research has been extended to cover community enterprise projects in England in order to make the study applicable to community workers throughout Britain.[1]

Definitions to be Used

It is important to clarify our use of definitions of community employment initiatives and community enterprise.

Scottish agencies have developed a series of very specific definitions for community business, community co-operatives and workers' co-operatives. The Scottish case studies are closely based on these definitions, and we have used them for our analysis.

In England there is much less consensus about definitions, and terminology used may vary from project to project. In the English case studies we have explained within the study any variation in definition used by the project, otherwise it can be assumed that the Scottish definitions hold good. The Salford study is the main English case study where locally derived definitions have had to be explained.

We have used the terms community employment initiatives and community enterprise to include community businesses as well as community and workers' co-operatives. Community Programmes, funded by the MSC, have also been included in our conception of community enterprise. This is because we have discovered that they have frequently been used by workers to provide a financial and motivational starting point for later business initiatives.

Our definitions are as follows:

Community Business

In 1982 LEAP (the Local Enterprise Advisory Project) produced this definition of a community business:

> A community business is a trading organisation which is owned and controlled by the local community and which aims to create ultimately self-supporting and viable jobs for local people in its area of benefit, and to use any profits made from its business activities either to create more employment, or to provide local services or to support local charitable work. A community business is likely to be a multi-purpose enterprise which may be based on a geographical community or a community of interest.

The Community Business Scotland 1986 Directory adds to this.

> Membership of any individual Community Business is open to anyone who lives or works in that locality, and also to 'outsiders' provided their representation never exceeds 49 per cent. It is the Members who pay an annual subscription, who elect the Board of Directors, who in turn guide the direction of the Company and appoint the staff and workers.

From this description it is clear that community businesses are under the control and management of the local community and accountable to it. Local links are specified through the community business's legal structure, with company articles specifying that membership is to include a majority of workers and/or residents drawn from the local areas. The members elect a Board of Directors to oversee the everyday management of the business. A number of these companies are limited by guarantee and many hold charitable status due to their aim of alleviating poverty. Increasingly community businesses act as holding companies from which subsidiaries develop separate, fully owned projects.

Most community businesses try to make use of local labour exclusively. However, because of the skills required for some jobs, that requirement is occasionally waived. Workers as well as managers and the Board of Directors (management committee) are typically involved in joint consultation for the day to day running of the business through the use of regular business meetings. In many instances the employees also act as the selection committee for persons applying for managerial posts.

Community Co-operatives

Community enterprise may well take other forms. Indeed community co-operatives in the Highlands and Islands preceded the notion of community businesses which arose in response to the needs of urban areas. Community co-operatives were initiated in rural areas where public transport and other amenities are limited, the cost of living high, land resources poor, and where there is little or no private sector commercial interest or investment.

> A Community Co-operative is directly owned by the community in which it operates and has economic and community objectives. Membership is open to all adult residents of the area served, but in a slight variant of the Community Business model, these members subscribe to shares in the co-operative. Voting however is the same: on a strict one person one vote basis. Dividends can be paid by the co-operative.
>
> This locally raised share capital is matched on a £ for £ basis by the Highlands and Islands Development Board, providing a pump-priming capital injection into the business. The HIDB can also make available Management and Establishment Grants over a limited period to assist the community enterprise to become established, rather like the way the Urban Programme and other grants are used elsewhere. In addition, the Board's normal business grants and loans can be available and have been used by the co-operatives primarily for new buildings such as community halls.
>
> Community Business in Scotland, 1986 Directory, p58

In both of these types of enterprise social as well as commercial objectives play a large part.

Workers' Co-operatives

Finally, a workers' co-operative, of which we have one example amongst our case studies, is a business owned and managed by the workers within it. Phoenix co-operatives are usually set up when a large firm is closing down a local branch. Sometimes the parent companies are willing to contribute to the development of a new enterprise. Though these businesses may have conventional management structures they are accountable to the workers.

Intended Readership

This book is intended for three main audiences.

First, and possibly most importantly, for workers in the field and students training for work in the community.

Second, for local authority personnel concerned with local economic development.

Third, for voluntary organisations concerned with local economic development.

We hope that they will find, in these experiences, a wealth of ideas, pointers towards difficulties that might be avoided, and guidance towards solutions. Very often, they will also find a clear portrayal of the dilemmas which face community education in the field of employment initiatives. Nowhere in these pages is the process of community workers' involvement made to look easy.

Layout of the Book

The book is in three sections:

Part One – Community Enterprise and Community Work Approaches – a short review of community enterprise in Scotland and England and the response made by community workers.

Part Two – Community Workers' Accounts of Community Enterprises – eleven case studies[2] describing and analysing projects in Scotland and England. These case studies are organised according to the size of the project, and to a certain extent by the emphasis on process, which tended to be stronger in the smaller projects. The studies come from a wide diversity of geographical location, urban and rural, and are based on a variety of communities, illustrating a range of enterprises at differing stages of development and success.

Part Three – Drawing the Threads Together – we analyse key issues arising from the case studies and relate these to an appraisal of community enterprise and its outcomes.

Design Features

Since this publication is intended to give easy access to points of interest and to be used for reference we have included a series of specific design features.

1 A matrix of the case studies and the characteristics used for their selection is provided.
2 Each account is introduced by a list of the particular aspects of community work involvement in employment initiatives which it illustrates; and concluded with Points for Reflection – of use for study groups.
3 At the end of most accounts the individual community worker's views on his or her role and its potential are outlined.
4 Reference is made in the concluding chapters to the case studies which illustrate particular points.
5 A list of acronyms with the organisations for which they stand is provided.
6 We have used the feminine (rather than the more common masculine) pronoun to refer to community workers in generic terms. This is for shorthand purposes and is not meant to imply that women are more involved in community enterprises than men.
7 The Five Ks Questionnaire – has been devised as a set of questions for community workers thinking of embarking on community enterprise or already well launched. These questions are meant to be prompts to reflection, not barriers to action.

Notes

1 Unfortunately we were unable to find examples of Welsh community enterprises in which community workers were involved.

2 We are most grateful to the community workers who have contributed their accounts to this volume and who have agreed to act as resource persons to those who wish to draw further on their experiences. Their names and addresses will be found at the end of the book.

2 Responding to Unemployment: the Role of the Community Worker

> At the end of the day we are talking about building viable communities, and to do that there has to be an economic basis as well as a social basis and social infrastructure. (Ex-worker with Easterhouse Festival Society, Glasgow)

In this chapter we shall outline three approaches that may be used in community work with the unwaged or unemployed. We shall draw attention to the development emphasis that we have adopted and which has guided our choice of personal accounts. We shall also raise the ideological questions posed by many community workers, before we launch upon the accounts of particular initiatives. In so doing we hope to indicate the ways in which community enterprises (businesses and co-operatives, and even Community Programmes) have been used as a means of achieving educational goals as well as employment opportunities and financial success[1] We therefore respond to the question of whether they can fulfil the aims of community education and community development.

In 1968 the Younghusband Report identified community work as 'primarily aimed at helping people within a local community to identify social needs, to consider the most effective way of meeting these needs and to set about doing so, in so far as there are available resources present'. It follows that community work is an interactive process in which the choice of strategies and approaches to be taken by the worker and the community group(s) reflects the features of the community in which changes are proposed or already taking place. An outstanding feature of nearly all the communities in which our case studies are located is the high level of unemployment, creating a situation which affects not only the individuals in the locality but all the organisations which serve them and to which they contribute. Community Education through its neighbourhood teams provides one such organisation.

How do they react to the pressing needs of the unemployed? They may select one of a number of approaches (Development, Service and Action) with which to tackle the problem. Each approach has a different emphasis and a different outcome for the community. If the workers who are allocated by the team leaders to work with the unemployed respond most strongly to the need for social and economic regeneration in their communities, they may well choose to adopt the third approach that we describe- the 'Development' approach. This would not rule out, however, responses drawn from the 'Service' and 'Action' approaches.

Which approach is chosen is likely to be determined by (a) the workers' assumptions about the causes of these problems, (b) the political framework they adopt, (c) their notion of the 'community', and (d) their analysis of the role of the worker and the client group (Barr, 1982). In the following descriptions of the 'service', 'action' and 'community development' approaches we will briefly touch on these factors affecting the worker's choice.

The 'Service' Approach

In working with the unemployed the approach very commonly adopted is that of offering a service. This is the most traditional and widely used response to their needs though relatively few resources have been made available to implement it, despite widespread devastation to individuals and communities. This is in spite of the fact that, for example, the Thompson Report (DES, 1982) and the Minister of State for Education (DES, 1983) have both emphasised the need to prioritise work with the unemployed.

The 'Service' approach aims to meet the needs of the unemployed who are excluded from leisure pursuits by poverty, either because local facilities are too expensive or those in neighbouring areas are inaccessible, due to expensive transport. Following this approach community workers, either within their own centres or in specially commissioned 'drop-in cafes' or 'Unemployed Centres', provide free or cheap pool table facilities, games, free newspapers, and opportunities to acquire new skills in, for example, photography and local history, and sometimes in do-it-yourself activities.

Over and above this provision community workers may offer counselling to those seeking help, provide vocational skills training sessions for individuals or groups, and offer help with the skills required for job re-entry. This may involve help in completing job applications, in interviewing techniques and in communications skills. Increasingly, centres for the unemployed are turning into information centres, covering questions on welfare, employment opportunities and adult education.

Detached work with unemployed groups centering on issues identified by members of a group, but which may or may not be immediately tied in with employment, may also be provided. Projects of this type have taken place in, for example, an Edinburgh housing estate. The worker there has been concerned to use the group experience as a vehicle for personal learning and change. However, the way in which the issues are generally viewed, that is as personal and localised, means that it falls under the 'service' approach to community work.

Much of the community work mentioned so far involves responses to individuals (although the individuals may be part of a group). In making these responses community workers may be accused of viewing the unemployed as the focus of intervention and therefore perceiving them as victims of their own weakness and inadequacy.

More community oriented activities within the 'service' approach have involved the unemployed in projects related to their immediate environment, for example, clean-up campaigns or environment improvement projects funded by the MSC or Urban Aid. The significance of these projects for the community worker lies in their potential for involving local people in devising and managing the project themselves and in the educational opportunities that the project affords. Furthermore, such work involves individuals and groups with external local government and government agencies and with local voluntary associations in addition to their immediate peers and community. As a consequence understanding of community structures and management may grow and new perspectives develop on a potential role in making the administration responsive to local community needs and interests.

The 'Action' Approach

The 'service' approach may appear partial in analysis and impact to many community workers. Head (1975) argues that 'the inability of community workers to tackle the tasks of defining the type of society required for human well-being and to attempt the difficult task of achieving human liberation in a post-industrial society represents a failure of extreme proportions'. The challenge is therefore to find means of redressing this situation. An 'action' approach to community work may offer a solution. The concept of 'action' and the interpretation of causes and situations are more radical and politically centred. Thus an 'action' approach is more politically sensitive and is the least common community work strategy, since it is apt to place the worker in the front line of controversy, often in conflict with the employing authority. It is therefore less likely to attract funding for the various programmes undertaken by the neighbourhood team.

In the area of unemployment, the community worker engaged in an action approach would begin by raising awareness of the nature of the problem facing a group and go on to locate its causes. The emphasis would be less on alleviating the situation than on radically altering the conditions which create the problem for the group and for society. The approach entails politicising the issue by 'helping people appreciate the reality of unemployment' (Smith, 1983).

One strategy that community workers following an 'action' approach might adopt would be to engage the group in an educational process designed to examine the mystification of unemployment and the stigma attached to it. The aim of such a strategy would be to destroy the group members' sense of guilt and undermine their belief that they have themselves created the problem of their unemployment. Following their new understanding of the social and economic position the group would be helped to take up an action stance in accordance with their new set of beliefs.

Finally, the approach would be based on a class analysis, and would attempt to break down artificial barriers between the employed and the unemployed working classes. The issue of unemployment would be placed in a wider context in which it has meaning for all the working population as well as the unemployed. A large pool of unemployed labour depresses wages and conditions of employment amongst the employed themselves and also acts as a real threat to their attempts to tackle such issues independently with their employers. As a result of this analysis the community worker, using an action frame of reference, would seek to establish and strengthen links between the unemployed and the employed, trade unionists, local government and political figures who identify with a class-based analysis of the issue. By widening and deepening the power bases and developing local and national pressure groups the community worker would hope, in the short term, to bring about social and economic changes through government action. In the long term, the aim would be to effect a more equitable distribution of wealth and power in society as a whole. However, since this aim is unlikely to be achieved unless the capitalist economic system on which society rests is significantly modified, such a removal would be the ultimate if far off vision of the 'action' approach. Towards this end, in small but incremental steps, the community action worker hopes to travel, campaigning on housing and welfare rights on the way.

The 'Community Development' Approach

The essential features of a community development approach have been documented by McConnell (1982). He defines them as being:-

1 holistic, in that the emphasis is on the relationship between person and environment;
2 responsive to needs, rather than imposing viewpoints or strategies;
3 emphasising the process of defining needs and finding appropriate ways to meet them in such a way as to strengthen local community organisation and power as well as to achieve the goals sought;
4 creating pressure to improve local participation in the planning of services central to the community's life and well-being;
5 using activity-based learning centred on an issue or project as an educative device for raising individual and group awareness of their own dignity and liberty and of the importance of social justice and equality in a democratic society.

We shall interpret these five points within the framework of the social and economic regeneration of a community; in this way we distinguish the 'development' approach from the 'service' and 'action' approaches. It seeks to involve and benefit as large a 'community' as possible and looks to both social and economic outcomes. It does not have the campaigning emphasis (particularly obvious in welfare rights work) of the 'action' approach.

To quote Colin Roxburgh, Senior Development Worker for Strathclyde Community Business:

> Community economic development implies not merely the developing of the 'what' but also the 'how'. It is the process by which people create the structures and institutional arrangements needed to adapt or respond to changing economic and social conditions in a manner that creates lasting benefit to a community. (The First Ten Years p.49.)

Consciousness Raising

A community worker adopting a 'development' approach pursues the same initial strategy as the 'action' oriented worker and concentrates on awareness raising, focusing attention on unemployment in ways that may hitherto have been unfamiliar to the unemployed. Typically, this may be done by considering such things as the scale of the problem as well as its impact and meaning for the lives of individuals and groups, and for the community and society as a whole. This would require knowledge of the rate of unemployment in the locality, of the social groups affected and of the types and adequacy of service provision made for each group. To the extent that the information culled from census figures, the district planning department and job centres as well as from local groups themselves indicates a level of need requiring responses from the community then to that extent the worker has reasonable grounds for acting.

Sometimes, however, local groups will themselves have arrived at a sense of disquiet over the problems in their community, and will themselves have solicited help. Which form the help will take is dependent on other considerations.

The Community Worker's Political Values

These considerations include the community worker's own values – her own political framework. While the worker would try to increase the group's awareness and understanding of unemployment through social and political education and would endeavour to support individuals' acquisition of the social and political skills necessary to further their objectives, the emphasis would remain on the group's own determination of their needs and objectives. For the community worker to attempt to convince or persuade the group of the rightness of her values and goals would be to replace one kind of dependency with another. Inevitably, there will be occasions when the worker will not be in sympathy with the group and at these times she should be prepared to be forthright as to her political stance. If need be she should be ready to withdraw if the group's views and strategies are in conflict with her professional and ethical position.

The 'Community' in Question

A further consideration which will determine the role adopted by the community worker lies in her definition of the community. Rarely does the total community however defined, form the clientele. Nor indeed would that be practicable, given the many needs to which she might be expected to respond.

Within the local community there will be a variety of groups and individuals concerned with unemployment. Their concern will have a number of explanations which may stem from their roles as unemployed persons themselves, or as relatives of the unemployed, or as people providing them with services, or as community activists, community agencies, trade union and religious groups or simply as local members of the community with an interest in the community's welfare. In addition to these groups there will be individuals with personal or private needs which may be met by getting involved in social issues, of which unemployment might be just one. In the case of community employment initiatives, however, the term 'involvement' is both a central concern and a problematic one.

A major difficulty in practice is with gaining broad based community support and interest in community enterprise initiatives. To begin with, whether the initial interest in a development project comes from groups or individuals in the community or whether it is a product of the community worker's own analysis and reflection, the community itself must be informed. It is typically in small group meetings that the matter is broached. Frequently this leads to a public meeting on the topic of unemployment and responses to it. It is often from such meetings that a sub-group is formed with a particular interest in pursuing a strategy for generating employment. The sub-group which may later become a steering group and management committee is likely to form the central group with whom the community worker collaborates and to whom most of her time will be allocated.

Style of Work – Preparing for a Community Enterprise

To claim that any group learning experience is non-directive is, of course, naive. No matter how learner-centred, 'empowering', 'enhancing' or 'self-actualising' the approach, it is rarely argued that educational encounters can be purged of their hidden values – whether it be to thrust people onto their bikes or to create a strong dissident action group. Within a 'development' approach, a worker is expected to declare her hand and indicate how she prefers to operate. She would need to make it clear that she would use a participatory style and expect the group to undertake central tasks in the project, albeit with appropriate help and support. Not only would members of the group have to carry out these tasks they would also have to share in decision making and accept accountability for those decisions to the group as a whole and to the community. In short, with a 'development' approach the enterprise would have to involve the group and, through its members, the community. For this to happen the group must first learn to believe in themselves and the potential for change within themselves and the community.

The working style outlined above reflects an attempt to engender confidence through experiences within the group and in interaction with others, whether they be district and central government agencies, politicians, schools, colleges or other community groups. In order to assist group members the worker seeks to present a model of appropriate behaviour. A statement, however, detailed, of the 'development' approach and its aims given to the group at the outset of the venture will not be enough.

Educational Aspects of Development

Educational objectives permeate the 'development' approach. The aim is not so much that the solution to a particular problem be found, but rather that the group explore ways of dealing with the issue as creatively as possible.

In the case of employment initiatives, there are the educational benefits to be derived from the acquisition of new ideas, new perspectives and new skills as succeeding aspects of a business venture are encountered and explored. Members of the group will pursue a wide range of self-developing activities in pursuit of success. Here the community worker has a major influence through enabling the group members to tackle new learning with confidence and enthusiasm.

Identifying Problems and Notifying the Group

Finally, the worker is expected to act directly. Community employment initiatives have been set up to achieve a number of objectives, some of which relate to individuals and others which relate to the enterprise itself. Most community businesses (or cooperatives) experience real difficulties in getting established and becoming economically viable. For those community enterprises which deliberately or unwittingly fail to fulfil the basic expectations of community businesses – such as involvement of the wider community as well as good business practices in marketing, accounting and auditing, then the worker has a responsibility to draw the group's attention to their failure. If the fault is serious enough, and the group decline to rethink their position, the worker may well consider withdrawing from the project or informing the community of the problems she has detected. This is important since the venture is not owned by the group but by the community of which the community worker and the group itself should be representatives.

Reservations

In the ways outlined a community development approach with an emphasis on social and economic regeneration may be seen to be a suitable way for the social services to address unemployment. Clark (1987) suggests that it has the advantage of combining social welfare work at local level with attention to wider political issues, for the social services needs of the unemployed are closely linked with the operation of the political system. We may go on to suggest that as the community with which the worker is engaged develops its analysis of the economics and politics of unemployment, so it becomes aware of this interlocking system. This may, however, lead to discouragement rather than action. Indeed there are many arguments against community work involvement in this field. Barr (1988) summarising the opinions of many workers who have expressed their doubts has listed nine sources of ambivalence about community business. The hostility he met we have also encountered and found in similar forms. Barr mentions the history of community education which in no way predisposes towards economic interventions. Rather has it responded to the consumers' needs in terms of welfare rights, leisure and recreation pursuits and counselling. In short, the history is such as to support a 'service' approach.

He remarks on the ideological assumptions of community education, built upon socialism and even the overturn of a capitalist society and certainly dubious of the notions of competition and profit. Indeed community businesses may set one section of the community against another as elusive employment forms a battle ground between, for example, council employees and a community enterprise seeking local contracts. Can the 'enterprise culture' be supported by workers who are fundamentally opposed to the politics of the new right and unwilling to collude with an oppressive state, he asks.

Our own inquiries revealed a reluctance to support the development of a successful elite. Community workers argued that only a few ventures were likely to be financially viable and unemployment only marginally affected. They might find themselves in the uncomfortable position of supporting the strong while the weak were 'whittled out'. This reservation led on to the reflection that failure – a frequent accompaniment of business start-ups – was not necessarily beneficial. Though learning might occur, they asked, what were the costs? They would be getting into an area of high financial and high psychological risk for themselves and their communities. If they offered sufficient support to the group to avoid failure would they be developing a new form of dependence?

This doubt raised the question of the community education worker's knowledge and competence in fields with which they were unfamiliar by inclination and training. Nothing had prepared them for direct participation in the economy or for appropriate planning for others in this field. Furthermore, Barr continues, there may be considerable ambivalence in the hierarchies of community education and consequently inadequate support for their involvement. Other areas of need may have a higher priority, or, even within programmes for the unemployed other approaches may seem more worthwhile (job loss prevention campaigns, pre- and post-redundancy support services, information centres or job creation programmes).

Barr made three other distinct observations:

1 that community organisations often lack confidence in community business since 'in communities characterised by economic marginality and poverty, scope for business development in the local setting is highly unpromising...' Limited disposable incomes reduce the number of potential customers;
2 that the methods and processes of community work are incompatible with the methods and processes of community enterprise; and
3 that community business may merely become a vehicle which is exploited by more powerful vested interests, being a low cost, marginal but high profile activity and consequently of value to a cost-cutting, image building Conservative government.

Rather than attempting to demolish these arguments (indeed some of them are telling and not easily countered) we shall reiterate that a development approach, handled with skill and foresight, may prove crucial to communities seeking to establish their right to a place in the sun. We should emphasise that no practitioners think community education will solve widespread unemployment. Rather it must be seen as a matter of empowering individuals and communities, reducing dependence on central and local government, and on employers, and giving outlets to both social and economic creativity.

The accounts which follow display to what extent this may be accomplished while opening to public gaze the dilemmas for the community worker who embarks on enterprise initiatives.

Notes

1 We should point out that financial success is achieved with difficulty and our case studies do not necessarily illustrate it.

Part Two: Community Workers' Accounts of Community Enterprises

Introduction

We present the accounts of eleven community workers who have ventured into the field of community enterprise, sometimes at considerable personal cost. On the whole, however, these reports are invigorating and illuminating. They show that a community development approach is a suitable way to encourage local communities to acquire the skills of participation, negotiation and decision-making which underpin the democratic process. They also show the painstaking progress to economic viability and, in some cases, the fragility of that achievement. In the detailed descriptions of fund raising, management committee struggles, searches for premises and educational disappointments and triumphs we hope that there is something new and interesting for everyone.

For the sake of encouraging the use of these accounts for training purposes we have included a number of 'Points for Reflection' at the end of each one.

In these accounts you will read the reflections of community workers who have struggled long and hard to enable the groups of unemployed men and women to gain control over their own lives and to develop an economic future for themselves and for others. We have let them speak for themselves with the minimum of interference. We have edited the accounts to reduce their length but not the meanings which their authors wished to convey.

We have included:

a some background information supplied by the workers themselves on their previous experience and on their perception of the area and the local economy. Where possible we asked each individual to comment on the state of community activity when they arrived;

b information on how the community enterprise developed - the initiation of the idea, the formation of the group, the planning, funding and finally trading;

c reflections on the role of a community worker in establishing a community enterprise, the skills and knowledge necessary and the criteria of success.

MATRIX OF INITIATIVES

Initiative	Contact with	Source of Initiative	Nature of Enterprise	Funding	Stage of Development
Bingham: Community Products Initiative	An unemployed group of centre users	Centre Users	Community Business Playgroup Furniture	Community Ed Innovative Youth Project: John Watson's Trust: Craigmillar Festival Society/ESF; Lothian Regional Council	Jan 85 First proposals - Trading April 87 Closed down Jan 88
Musselburgh: NUmac	Trade Union: AEUW	Trade Union, Shop Steward and Community Worker	Workers' Co-op Light to medium engineering	Regional Council	Jan 87 First Proposal Nov 87 - Trading
Armadale: Armcraft	Targeted group pre-redundancy British Leyland	ex-BL workers	Community Business: Wrought Iron furniture	Community Chest Urban Aid MSC - CP	Jan 87 First proposal Feasibility Jul 88
South Aston: Park Lane Garden Centre	Parents' meeting at local school	Community Worker	Commercial Garden Centre within Community Project	Birmingham City Council, MSC, Wimpeys, Barclays Bank, UK 2000, etc	1978 South Aston Adventure Play Centre initiated 1987 ideas for Garden Centre developed Dec 88 - Trading
Ferguslie: Flagstone Enterprises Ltd	Tenants' Assoc	LEAP	Community Business Stone Cleaning	STEP, Urban Aid MSC, SCB	1979 - Proposal 1981 - Trading
Shetland: Mossbank & Firth Community Co-op	Residents' Assoc	Residents' Association	Community Co-op Retailing and Bank, Laundry and Dry Cleaning Agency	Own share capital	1980 First Proposals 1983 - Trading

Town End Farm Estate - Sunderland North Community Business Centre	Unemployed groups and Centre Users	Turning Point Unemployed Workers Centre	Workers Co-op: Joinery Co-op Food Co-op Community Cafe Photography Enterprise Forum	Urban Programme Enterprise Allowance Enterprise Allowance Enterprise Allowance Wearside Opportunity	 1989 - trading 1989 - trading 1989 - trading Jan 1990
Renton: Renton Regeneration	Renton Housing Action Group	Community Worker	Community Business Work-spaces; Building renovations Taxi Firm	SCB, ESF MSC - CP	Aug 86 First Proposals Aug 87 - Work-spaces Trading, Renovations
Little Hulton Community Enterprise Project Ltd	Various community activists	Community Worker	Community Co-operative: Clothes re-cycling, Launderette, Printing, Credit Union, etc	Tudor Trust, RIBA, Start Up, Clothworkers' Foundation, Glynwed Trust, Urban Aid, etc	Sept 1986 idea initiated April 87 Clothes re-cyling started April 88 Launderette opened
Ruchill	Ruchill Community Project and the Community Council	Community Council Community Worker	Community Business Security Service G20 Decor	Urban Aid	1984 Food Co-op 1987 - Community Business Trading
Sunderland Common Ownership Enterprise Resource Centre (SCOERC)	Housing Co-op Local Unemployed people	Banks of the Wear Co-operative Housing Services Ltd	Over 11 workers' co-ops set up 1986/7	Urban Programme Calouste Gulbenkian Foundation EEC Social Fund	SCOERC 1983 Only one of the workers' Co-ops set up by SCOERC has ceased trading

3 Bingham: Community Products Initiative Hazel McLeod

This account is given entirely in the words of Hazel McLeod, and is of particular interest because of:

1 the maintenance of the group through adverse physical and social situations;
2 the knock-on effects into the community of the employment initiative: Community Products;
3 the flexible response shown to each new need the group expressed;
4 the variety of funding;
5 the determination to widen the educational input.

Starting Work with the Unemployed

I am a community worker at Bingham, that's in the Craigmillar part of Edinburgh. There was 41 per cent unemployment in the area when I arrived as the new community centre worker back in January 1985. No unemployed clubs were running when I came here. In fact, nothing was going on. There had been a young unemployed group going, but, that had fallen away. The community had the view that the unemployed group was a waste of time. Some unemployed people still used the centre, but, not as an unemployed group. In January of 1985 I met with the unemployed users to find out what they wanted and how they wished to make use of the centre. Their immediate response was 'Can you give us a job, Hazel?' In fact they wanted my job, it seemed so easy to them. Under the banter, however, was this real need expressed for work and a sense of guilt in their not having it. We sat down to look at the skills people had within the group.

The Group

At this time the group consisted of people ranging from ages seventeen to fifty-five and I think that mixture was a good thing. The more mature unemployed person actually helped the younger person keep motivated throughout the project and I think that has been invaluable. There was actually eight who stayed the course. That was January 1985 and it is now July 1987. When you think of the initial idea, there is a long process to go through. We didn't envisage that length of time when we started. We thought it would be six months all cut and dry, a clear smooth path.

The original group of people I worked with were all men, bar one. There was a girl about twenty-two in the group who always maintained her contact with the group but didn't actually take part. The people that I had been working with on several occasions on a group basis were saying they wanted to work with wood. They fancied doing something with their hands. There were various degrees of abilities – some people were do-it-yourself fanatics. The younger ones wanted to try it all and there was one man who had been a skilled tradesman. He had been a cabinet maker, so from the very beginning he was the key to that project. He was quite happy to share his skills with the younger ones, but there were several problems still with them. There was nowhere for them to meet because the community centre has only two rooms. There was no workshop facility, no money for tools, no money for wood and a lack of expertise.

Aims and Objectives

The initial money we looked at came from community education and a youth project. In May, 1985, Community Education were offering money for innovative projects with the young unemployed. However, to get a hold of that money we needed to have aims and objectives. I met with the group and we sat down for an entire afternoon and worked out what they would like to do. That was the basis of the innovatory project. But, there was no doubt about it, that as the worker, I had to help the group focus on things that were realistic.

An Educational Input

The group decided that for the project they wanted to make wooden toys. The bits that I added in were the learning bits; the bits about looking at the philosophy of play and why children needed to play. Why was it important when making a toy to look at the many different facets of that toy? We visited nurseries, handicapped schools etc. to find out what children played with. At the end of the project the group said, 'We did it Hazel, because you thought we should. We didn't really think we needed it, but it all made sense now'. However, I must say there was a bit of resistance to doing that learning bit. But for me, that was the role I had to take, there was no point in getting money if there was no concept. The group needed to have some understanding of the place of toys in a child's development. They visited Moray House College's Play Resource Unit, nursery schools and a school for handicapped kids, to look at the special play needs of these children. That resulted in the group coming back and getting a disco going; raising £80 and donating half the proceeds for toys for the youngsters.

Raising Questions

To get the money to get a worker to work with the group had to be a priority. We didn't know whether we would get the money, we didn't know whether we would get a worker or not, it was a pie in the sky. So there was a couple of months when we didn't know where we were going. During that time, my role was helping the group learn to work together, offering support in helping the group think through their ideas, write letters, apply for funds, etc. I got them to do as much as possible. My job was to pose them the right questions such as 'Why should people give you money?' 'What are people giving money for?'

Finding Premises

We also had to find premises for the group to work in and we heard that the Jack Kane Community Centre had a workshop that was never used at that time. To get these premises we had to negotiate with the management committee of the Centre to get access to the workshops which were freezing cold and miserable. However, that took a management committee meeting which was another month away, so each time something cropped up there was a time gap. We got the premises in November 1985. We then heard we could have a worker through the Innovative Youth Project money and lo and behold here we were. But where were we going to get the money to make the stuff?

At that time the John Watson's Trust had put out some criteria for working with unemployed people in areas of deprivation, as long as there was an educational input to it. This project which was set up as an Innovative Youth Project also met the criteria as far as the John Watson's Trust was concerned. So we made an application to them for £1,000 and we got everything we asked for – which was like a dream.

Group Dynamics

That in itself was another phase, we had the money to buy tools. The group themselves bought the tools. I did none of that at all. I was at this point a support for the project. The worker hired to work with the unemployed group was a local chap who had been working with a voluntary organisation in the area and he took on the role of the worker. That was a difficult role for him because he was a quiet person and the dynamic of the group was also very quiet. The individuals within the group didn't communicate very much with each other so it was a case of individuals working together to make individual toys. That was something that was recognised could be a hassle if it was going to work.

I had largely withdrawn after the new worker was appointed, although the group still kept in contact when they came to the centre. However, after several weeks things were going badly within the group and I was asked to have a meeting to look at where it was going wrong. We added music into the workshop, in case the silence got on top of them, but we couldn't alter the dynamic of the group by expanding the group any more physically, because the workshop couldn't take any more, so enlarging the group wasn't possible. The person who has now taken over the community business was the one person who managed to motivate people in the group. When he was there, there was a totally different atmosphere.

Perseverance through Adversity

They had originally started doing three afternoons a week – Mondays, Wednesdays and Fridays, but they wanted to work all day because of the time spent in just getting into the workshop, getting everything out, working for a couple of hours and putting everything away again. So they eventually worked on Wednesdays and Fridays all day. I must say when I was looking at the diary (someone made a diary of the different days) it is really amazing some of the things they got through in the twelve week period. The place was freezing cold to a point where you had to have your coat on for the first hour and a half, there was a one bar electric fire and the snow was on the ground. These guys were not used to having to get up, so it was very hard, and to go to somewhere that was cold and miserable was yet another thing. When we looked at all these different things we realised if we were going to get anywhere, we would have to change some of these things. At the end of December 1985 the group almost packed up. They were still based in the Jack Kane Centre where the working conditions were very bad. However, it was the morale of the group which was the real problem. In December then there was a big meeting. The group were at an all time low and they didn't know whether they wanted to carry on and they were ready to pack it in because it wasn't worth it anyway. They couldn't take the toys any further because they had come across some technical problems they couldn't actually fulfil. There was no way they could do it without expertise.

Co-operation with the School 1985/86

Now back in January, 1985 I had tried to get them access to Castlebrae School to the woodwork classes but no-one would go and we came to this problem in December, so I said 'What is the answer, where do we get the expertise. I suppose we could go back to Castlebrae?' So I went as negotiator with the group project worker at that time for access to Castlebrae school from the technical department and they welcomed us with open arms. The chap met with the group and understood what they were trying to do and took them in as a group into the school on Friday and Monday morning. They all went as a group. He gave them access to tools and helped them with some drawings, the use of the bigger tools, cheaper wood and support while they were making something. He also got them to draw up plans, to make a catalogue of their work. He added some structure to what they were doing and they went back for six weeks. The youngest person had actually made a table and chairs, something he was not in a position to do before. I think that helped them to decide to go and complete the project.

The school have been very interested in the follow-up to that project. It gave them community status. Everybody has helped us; you just have to find the right folk.

The Role of the Key Individual

Throughout this time John, who is now the co-ordinator of the community business, had the vision to see a market for what they were doing. He was saying, 'My goodness we were visiting these nurseries and they can't get toys like this, they cost a fortune.' He looked at the toy catalogues and said the toys the group were producing were about 200 per cent cheaper than in the catalogue. So he was actually saying, 'I think we could do this full time. I think we could start a wee business.' The group threw around ideas such as working on the side whilst on the dole and everything. But he said they should look at something constructive.

Around about that time there was also a power struggle. 13 January 1986 was a very significant time because John, who had learned quite a lot from the project and added to his own do-it-yourself expertise, became quite difficult to cope with in the group. He had quite a power struggle with the group worker who was being paid for doing a job; but it was John who had actually gone further than the person who was leading the group. That became a very uncomfortable time for the group. But John was now saying it had potential. They were getting interest from local nursery schools for toys to be fixed and shelves to be built (not paid). However, it did give motivation to get started again and the group kept going even after the project money ended and the part-time paid worker had left.

Establishing Contacts – 1986

Another question in my mind at the time was: could we take the project further? Could we get more help from other people? Through my work I had contact with Craigmillar Festival Society and also the Housing Department and I knew that the European Social Fund had put a lot of money into Craigmillar which was specifically for retraining people over the ages of twenty-four years who had been long-term unemployed.

I contacted the local person dealing with the European Social Fund to look at their objectives in relation to our group whose motivation was again dropping off. John was the only one eligible to meet the criterion for employment by Craigmillar, because he was the only one in the group still living in the scheme. He was also the person with the ideas and the vision. I suggested to the group that Craigmillar Festival Society (CFSoc) see the Innovatory Project Report which was supported by the voluntary trust and the group said 'O.K. This is O.K. It might work.'

We set up a meeting with the European Social Fund coordinator, myself, John and the project worker to consider the possibility of John being taken on by the vocational retraining unit to learn about business i.e. community business, private business, cooperatives etc. At the time we realised that if we were to set up any kind of business venture we would need some new expertise in bookkeeping, administration, planning, projection and market research, all of which we would have to consider once we had an idea. We were actually very successful in that application because the C.F. Society have to justify their use of the cash spent on retraining somebody to the European Social Fund. Our proposal fitted the criteria and so it was set up as something which the C.F. Society would take on. John was employed in March 1986 and that was a full year after the initial idea was started at that workshop. Because of the type of person he is, an entrepreneur – he calls himself a con man – he has a lot of skill. He had been a printer by trade for twelve years before being made redundant and worked ten hour shifts, so he said he was not going back to that. He had a lot of sense. He was also able to take on the academic side of the training and gained access to Queen Margaret College's Small Business Course in April 1986. There were a lot of long lengthy discussions after some of the sessions he had been at and for some time he needed a lot of my support.

Throughout the time he was involved in that course he continued to work in the community centre with the voluntary helpers. The Management Committee were approached by myself and John to consider letting him have the use of one of the rooms in the community centre as a workshop. There was a cupboard which is 6 ft x 4 ft where they stacked all the tools. That was a major problem: space to work in. But, he was warm, he had a telephone, he had some support when he was doing the business studies course and it was more local than the Jack Kane Centre. The volunteers also came there easier than the Jack Kane Centre, so the local premises were booked. The Management Committee backed him all the way because they were more aware of the possibility of local people being employed at the end of the day if it was successful. So the European Social Fund, Craigmillar Festival Society, Bingham Management, Community Education, Local Regional District Councillors were all aware of what was going on and supporting it and we also had John Watson's Trust thanking us and asking for reports. So there were a lot of people involved, not just the community worker. You must use the networks around you. It would have been no good doing it ourselves. About fifteen or twenty local people were offered the chance of being involved in the scheme, but only three took it up. We are not talking about a large number of people.

Market Research: April – November 1986

From April 1986 right through to November 1986, John worked with local people to build up a stock of toys. However they quickly dropped toys because the channel for toys was far too narrow. John had found in his market research that people wanted existing equipment refurbished. No other organisation did this and he saw that as a development of the project. We have also found out that nobody really makes play equipment to your specification so that was another avenue that they started to look at. We had nursery teachers come down and actually said what they wanted built to their specification. They went out and told their colleagues.

Establishing the Company – 1987

The play equipment itself had to be good quality, it had to be durable and have all the safety aspects for children who are under five years. To that end he actually worked with children over the summer to a point where he had an Open Day, an exhibition, in November 1987. This was actually following market research and he had something like 69 per cent return on his market research to all nursery schools in Lothian Region. Queen Margaret College were astounded by that when he took the evidence back to them. Over 200 people were invited to the open day at the community centre where the toys were made and the press did a feature article on it. From that day he sold everything they had made and now has orders for lots more. He is at the stage now where he can't keep up with the demand. We have now taken on a full-time worker. John is going to share his business skill with him and he also has two volunteers who do work on a casual basis to help meet the demand. In January of this year he had a public meeting and that actually launched Community Products Initiative as a company. They are going for company limited by guarantee and there was another meeting to go to Register House and register the company.

There is a little dream, once you get past the problem area, get the money, get premises, then some of these things disappear. However, when we got to the point in January when the company was going to be launched, we really couldn't continue within the community centre. There is no good the community worker working with the group in isolation. Everyone around who could be a resource should be roped in. We contacted the housing department and they were very fruitful in as much as the Estates Department gave us a shop which was to be demolished in a year which cost the Company £4 a week rent. Because of the Company's charitable status the rates will be next to nothing. Craigmillar Festival Society gave us £400 loan because there was a cash flow problem in the demand for equipment and the amount of wood that we actually had to make things. Also at that time Community Education had sent round a piece of paper saying there was extra revenue grant folio money available at the end of the year. So on Thursday we got going and Friday we put the whole projection plan and the business plan in an envelope so they would get it on the Monday morning.

The company went for a loan of £2,000 to Lothian Regional Council in April 1987. because the projection indicated that we needed a loan of £2,000 for the first year. At the moment orders are coming in every day. We also managed to get on the Regional's 35 list, which is a bit of a triumph. The budgets for the majority of nursery teachers and groups in the Region that we have marketed for come out, as mine do, once a year and have to go through the Regional Purchaser. You never get cash in hand. It is applied for on a form. Now there are 'Contract' books for that. Ideally we would like to get on the 'Contract' books but the way round it is, if you cannot find anything in Lothian Region, you apply for it. You find a source: you put it on a piece of paper; you apply. The suppliers have now paid us our first cheque and we now have something to show in our books for the Region. So it is looking good. We have premises for a year; we have already had a meeting with the housing department to look at a workshop unit to be built on somebody's spare ground.

At the moment we have two workers on casual, and one person employed full time, and John, (in July 1987) so that is two full-time and two part-time people who work. One chap doesn't want any money at all because the whole supplementary benefit system is a nightmare. He can't accept any money at all. It would not be worth his while as he is a single parent. He comes every day solid and works continually. The other two people are doing community workshop and they are being paid casual. Already we are looking to next year. You continually have to look ahead and we have had a lot of support.

The Role of the Community Worker

I was looking at the role of the worker and I have been general dogsbody – 'Throw everything at Hazel.'

'How do you motivate people?' somebody asked me. In some sense the people motivate me. Seeing other people work through horrendous situations as they did, I wondered what I was bothering about. Their enthusiasm was the thing that kept me going for the majority of time. But to try to put it into one phrase, I saw my job as a facilitator of employment creation. People didn't want to come to a club just to play pool and darts. They wanted real jobs. They wanted mine for a start. But at the end of the day they wanted paid employment; they did not want to continue to do volunteer jobs. People want salaries. My job, therefore, when people were expressing that, was to bring groups together and help them in the early developmental process by having group discussions, by talking individually to people in the group, because that is what happened. So you have to make yourself available, help them explore the ideas, plan what they want to do, help them implement that in any way. That means make the contacts I had available to them and then start the process again, because the end of the Innovative Project became the start of the community business research,and we now have the community business established. But already we start another process of maintaining that and developing other stuff.

I am actually a centre-based worker, which was part of my problem. About July last year (1986), the work load that was given to me was too much. I asked a colleague at Castlebrae to set up the project and support it as opposed to myself. That actually never worked in practice. Whilst he did come down and see it, he would go away. I would end up spending half an hour with a person anyway because I was there on the spot. So I was asked by the group to continue. At the moment I think I am too easily available. They need to work it through for themselves. They are still coming back to me with problems so that I think that there will be a period over the next few months when I will continue to offer support. Also the team leader and the community education officer in the area have agreed to go on board the project. In my head I'm saying that I'll give it another year, and, as they say, if it all goes down the drain, a lot of people will still have learned a lot from the experience.

Perspectives on Success

Already there has been some knock-on effect. Bingham is a very small easily defined geographical area with a very old established community spirit. Everybody knows everyone else. A few local people becoming successful, being paid for doing something they really like has created a lot of 'buzz' in the community. Even district councillors are talking about it. It has given others incentive and they are getting ready to go themselves; so there is an energy about the place. There are local houses being built so there is more energy around in the community anyway, and workers trying to capitalise on that. Definitely, there is more enthusiasm. There is one group of 14 who have met every Monday night for weeks. They have something tangible to work on. At the moment there are three new business ideas being discussed by local community groups. One relates to local transport, a second to contract cleaning business and the third to a knitting company. These groups are not attached to the Community Products Initiative as I think that would fudge what is going on there. However, they will be able to draw on that expertise. However, I suppose I should also add that it hasn't been all smooth sailing. People who have been involved in the Community Products Initiative have also been getting some hassle from some local people: perhaps that is inevitable!

John, the mainstay of the business project, could have gone the private enterprise route, and for a while there was a big personal dilemma about his going out on his own and setting up privately. I think the Queen Margaret College training bit and the length of time it took and the discussions he had with different people in the community encouraged him to try and look at it either as a co-operative or community business. John didn't like the co-operative idea and so the community business evolved from that. By November, 1986, John was saying, 'I want to make sure there are people getting jobs like myself, people who are older and who want to do something else because my whole life has changed. I can't believe it, and I want other people to do that if they want.'

Points for Reflection

- How motivation was sustained
- The effect of introducing a new worker
- Links with other agencies
- The pursuit of the educational aspects of development
- The role of the key individual in the group
- The number of people involved in production
- Dependency on the worker

4 Musselburgh: NUmac Paddy O'Brien

Paddy O'Brien's role in establishing NUmac, a precision engineering workers' co-operative, is peculiar in this set of case studies for six different reasons:

1. Paddy O'Brien is employed as a community worker in the voluntary sector and has no formal qualifications;
2. he is not inhibited in 'leading from the front';
3. his involvement in the project was very brief, withdrawing from it only ten weeks after its conception;
4. NUmac is the only phoenix workers' co-operative in our study;
5. it is our only example of employment generation in manufacturing; and
6. thanks to a fortunate set of circumstances it has, so far, been remarkably successful in a very short time span.

From our brief study of NUmac it would be foolish to try and give a definitive explanation of its success, but it is valuable to note various contributing factors: there was a skilled and experienced workforce that had established good working relationships; the firm they had worked for had been financially viable and was only closed in the interests of the holding company; local politicians were committed to workers' co-operatives and local community workers were eager to promote them. Paddy O'Brien of the Musselburgh Unemployed Workers' Centre, East Lothian, had previously had experience of establishing both successful and unsuccessful 'secondary co-operatives' (where semi-independent businesses share premises and facilities) in Bolton and Birmingham.

The Liquidation of Morfax

Morfax Scotland Ltd. was a medium-to-heavy engineering firm in Prestonpans, East Lothian, making 'virtually anything from an engine to a roof rack.' Much of their work was subcontracted to them by much larger firms such as Ferranti, who would take a large order but would find it unprofitable to incorporate certain items into their production line and so would pass this manufacturing on to a smaller company. Morfax had a workforce of sixty-eight, but it was a subsidiary of the far larger firm Mac International. In January 1987 Morfax went into liquidation. The company was profitable, Paddy O'Brien explained, but:

> it was not making sufficient profits to justify the investment into the company, so it was virtually bankrupted ... The Management, in fact the directors, the owners, decided it was an advantage to the company as a whole to get rid of that one section. Now that company could have continued, but they were only going to make £5,000 a year.

Initially the workforce were left with the impression that the management would buy out the company and their jobs would be secure.

But the management of the place wanted full control and the funding agent who was going to help, the SDA (Scottish Development Agency), they wanted 51 per cent control and put one of their own workers in there to manage the company, because they said it was because of mismanagement that the company went into liquidation anyway.

Eventually the offer wasn't accepted by the Receiver, and by that time it was too late for the workforce to organise... So redundancy went in one day: at the end of the day... they were told to pick their tools up, that was the redundancy notice, and not to come back. But part of the workforce were kept on to finish the orders.

The reaction of the workforce to redundancy at such short notice was to be 'totally pissed off ':

I mean, you knew the company was in liquidation and you had got the impression that the management would buy it out. You'd got the impression that your job was secure. Then you walk into work and you were still under that impression, but when you go to leave work it's 'pick your tools up and don't come back'. That 'pisses' people off... A lot of the workforce were at the older end of the market, sort of forty plus, and, you know yourself, that if you are forty or fifty the chances of getting a job are limited or nil; and certainly the chance of getting a job in East Lothian because there is no industrial base... some people probably went on a bender for a couple of days. Other people went off fishing and other people wanted to consider this co-operative.

A Phoenix Co-operative Suggested

The Musselburgh Unemployed Workers' Centre became involved when they were asked to give advice about redundancies about three weeks prior to liquidation. Bill Lindsey, the shop steward, was on the Management Committee of the Centre and knew of their work in giving welfare benefits advice to people facing redundancy. Paddy O'Brien of the Centre immediately took the line that 'We should be going for a workers' co-op.' Bill Lindsey was interested in the idea and suggested it to the workforce: 'Let's at least look at the potential of getting the workers to co-operate together.'

The first meeting was held in the Unemployed Workers' Centre just as the men had been laid off. Bill Lindsey contacted everyone at their home addresses and three people turned up.

I put the idea that they could in fact control the company themselves. But you've got to understand, I think, that someone who has been employed for twenty or thirty years and then becomes self employed, taking responsibility for your own future is a big step. I mean I know it's not a big step but it looks it because you're responsible for your own tax system, you're responsible for the profit to the company, you're responsible for the buying and selling, you're responsible for everything and to some people that looks almost impossible, that's something that rich people, business people do, it's not something that a worker does.

It's certainly a class thing. When you go to school, and certainly with me and with the older generation, you're bred to accept authority, to go and do your job, to work from nine to five. The working man is shoved into employee. But you are never encouraged once to think of yourself, to become independent and that was probably the first barrier that we had to overcome. The way we did it was to show the advantages of self employment. Start hitting on things like, 'You want to go on holiday next year? Where are you going to go? Now how do you book your holidays there, you just go down to the holiday shop, you book your holidays and away you go. If you now think about it you arrange to meet a factory in Spain because you want orders. You get at the two factories, one at the beginning of the fortnight's holiday and one at the end. It is then a business trip so the company have to reduce their profits, so the company are paying for you to go on holiday. Quite legitimate.' There's all sorts of things you can do providing you know the system and unfortunately workers are never taught the system and that's a closed shop to most of them. So we encouraged the workforce to have confidence.

Assessing Feasibility, the Skills Needed, and Involving Outside Agencies

The three workers attending the first meeting were clearly encouraged enough to bring four of their mates along to a second meeting a week later.

I went through a thumbnail sketch of what they had to do to create the business from where they are now to where they want to be. The thing stressed more than anything else was: don't worry about finance. You must not worry about finance at this early stage because they're looking at sort of £100,000 to £200,000 to start – a lot of money where collectively between them they would be lucky to raise £40,000 if they put their houses on the market maybe £60,000.

A further reason why they could not consider the finance in detail was that their redundancy payments had not been calculated, and this was not to be paid for another three months. Paddy O'Brien was confident that if the business idea was feasible the money could be attracted from somewhere. He was not worried about raising expectations which could not be fulfilled:

I don't think that's a problem because if the idea is good, if the idea is financially feasible, and if you're committed to certain targets then you can get the money. That is never a problem because, I mean, with capitalist society, if you want, the bankers and the money controllers are looking to make a profit.

Even though an investor could not buy shares in a workers' co-op they could make a profit by giving a business loan.

There are also funds from the Regional Council or the District Council by the SDA or the SCDC (Scottish Co-operative Development Council) who could put money in and that would bring them over the 50 per cent level which in turn means the bank are more interested because they're not taking on the full responsibility. So the money itself, it's easier to get maybe £200,000 out of the bank than it is to get £2,000. If the business ideas had been on the low level, £2,000 to get started, then we would look at the money aspect in much more detail... but in that sort of business, I mean, looking at £100,000 plus, look at the business, look at what you want. Can you make it work? Is the commitment there? Have you got all the skills you need?

There was a whole list of things that they had to go and work on. . . It was after the following week's meeting that they all went away and discussed it and decided that they would go for it. From there it started to generate – they really started to put things together

Most of them realised that because of their age they weren't going to get employment. Most of them realised through the welfare rights that their redundancy payments were not going to take them far, and pretty soon they would have nothing left. So a lot of them realised very quickly that they weren't going to be better off, they weren't going to get a job, and this was going to be it. I think in many ways we'd given them a straw and they latched on to it, and the straw's developed into fruition but I mean that's not going to happen every time. It can happen quite a lot, but you need to get certainly a very small element of that workforce, and you need to talk the basic language, and you've got to instill confidence that they can do it, that they are as good as their bosses, that in fact they must be better than their bosses because their bosses put the place into liquidation.

At this time Joy Clark, another worker at the Unemployed Workers' Centre, organised visits for the group to several co-operatives in Fife. It was an enormous boost to the men's confidence to see that other workers had succeeded in establishing their own business when faced with redundancy. Two phoenix co-operatives particularly relevant to them were in engineering and leisure wear.

In the course of establishing exactly what preparation was needed to develop a co-operative the group soon realised the value of their own experiences. It was necessary to:

> identify the skills needed within the company, identify the area in which they are going to work, to identify if there was a market there. People started chipping in 'I've got a customer contact list', 'I can remember the customers I used to visit', 'I remember the customers that came to see me about these products', 'I remember this person from this department' and they started to accumulate this collective knowledge of people to contact again. It was obvious quite quickly to them that these people were still interested in that service, and I think that gave them an encouragement to continue.
>
> Through general discussion they identified the skills that were not available to them collectively. That's where we started to involve outside agencies.

Initially Paddy O'Brien contacted these agencies and arranged the meetings with them himself. He started by contacting the Economic Development Unit of the District Council, the employment initiatives section of the Regional Planning Department and the chair of the Regional Planning Department, Councillor Tony Kinder. 'Tony was quite supportive...almost to the point of instructing that Department to give any help and assistance required.'

Involving Tony Kinder at an early stage was part of Paddy O'Brien's belief in lobbying through the political structure: 'I have got a great belief that you use politics first.' In contrast with his experience in Bolton, in Lothian Region he felt that the most effective way of doing this was by contacting the councillors who would then influence the local government officers. In Lothian:

> The politicians control the officers, they lay down instructions... Had it been another authority then perhaps you'd need to encourage the officers who would then encourage the politicians.

Paddy O'Brien felt it was obvious that the agencies mentioned would have to be involved, as well as the Scottish Co-operative Development Council, and he had no hesitation in organising appointments for the group: 'Sometimes you need to take the lead...' He would arrange a meeting with an agency and then tell the group:

> This can happen if you want it to, and it could be beneficial to you if it does. You can arrange another time if it's not convenient. Now that happened a lot in the early stages because there was a need for it... From there on they just picked it up, and took the ball into their hands.

Having acted as a catalyst to get the group working, Paddy took a less directive role, mainly chasing them up to carry out the tasks they agreed to do in meetings.

Following the third meeting Paddy arranged for the group to have their own extension on the Unemployed Workers' Centre's phone, to use a desk and to have access to stationery and stamps. In retrospect he feels that free access to this office infrastructure was essential for the group's development at that stage. The costs incurred could be lost in the general expenses of the Centre. The group were now coming in to the building every day and established a corner of the office to work from, but it was soon clear that they needed their own independent base where they could be contacted without having to go through the Centre. The District Council provided them with an empty office conveniently placed across the road from the Centre, and about seven weeks after the initial meeting the group moved in there.

> From there really I withdrew a lot, virtually totally. But I mean there were little elements: the very mild or very silly things. They moved into an office with nothing. We arranged for them to borrow desks, chairs, typewriters, opened access to the computers, 'till they got their own computer and typewriter, and all these other elements as well. There was access to a telephone until the telephone was installed. All these little things were an immediate help that wouldn't have created much of a problem except sidetracking...

Although the group now had the professional assistance of agencies like the SDA and SCDC their advice was not always useful. Initially they tended to accept it, but they later realised it was not always best to defer to the experts. The SCDC set a timetable for the co-operative's development which the group felt seriously held them back, and they were also ill-advised about designing a logo. When producing a publicity leaflet they were encouraged to use a Glasgow advertising agency to design a logo. Paddy O'Brien dissuaded them:

> I said to them: 'What do you want your letterhead to say? Who is that letterhead to go to? Adopt a process of elimination, which is all the advertising agencies would do'. I said that if you do a lot of this work yourself first you're going to save a lot of money, and you're capable of doing it, and they came up with the idea of calipers. Now that idea appealed to them and I did a rough graphic, dead easy to do the outline at the time, and they presented it to the group. The group decided that was fine so they eliminated the advertising agency and they went to a graphic artist who actually did the complete layout for them; but it's little elements like that that the community worker can still be involved in...

In November 1987 NUmac Precision Engineering Ltd. started trading from an industrial estate in Tranent, employing twelve men and one woman. So far they have survived the difficult initial year of establishing contacts and a reputation, and their work has included machining, sheetmetal work, machine tool maintenance, and light fabrication.

The Community Worker's Role

When asked to reflect on the community worker's role in facilitating employment initiatives like NUmac Paddy O'Brien emphasised the importance of five points:

1 the need to encourage the group,
2 being prepared to take the initiative,
3 being ready to act politically,
4 having a basic understanding of what business involves, and
5 paying attention to group dynamics.

> I suppose the most important part of it is to develop and encourage the group that have got the potential to carry that idea through. But the other point is never, never believe that because the project is too big it won't work; because it hasn't got a model to work on it won't work. Because a model somewhere else hasn't worked doesn't mean to say that it won't work here; and not to be restricted. I mean people have made millions of pounds out of the most ludicrous ideas. I mean the Rubik Cube... Release your mind and take community business away from the idea that all you can do is recycle furniture or low-level community business. Community business

and co-operatives can be as big as you want and it is in fact the way you structure that community business or co-operative that will either allow it to be developed or hold it back.

... So you have to keep an open mind, you never put down the idea unless you know what you are talking about. You only encourage. Then you say to them it's through a full and comprehensive feasibility study that you tell whether the business is viable or not. So never, ever discourage somebody and it's just encouragement and people, you've got to take the lead, you've got to respond quick, you've got to sometimes take 'undemocratic' decisions by phoning somebody up, getting their advice and maybe get them to come along and talk, lead from the front sometimes – sometimes it needs it... I think it is a fault with a lot of community workers that in fact they try to lead from the back.

Leading from the front enables the community worker to set the pace of the project's development. Paddy O'Brien laid great emphasis on the need to achieve quick progress at the start in order to maintain enthusiasm. For instance, when Councillor Tony Kinder arranged for a grant of £1,000 to conduct a feasibility study it came just at a point when the group were at a low ebb, feeling they had pursued the project as far as they could.

You have got to work quickly. If not the confidence, the enthusiasm very soon dwindles, and you've got a hard job then to re-encourage. You need to encourage along and in the initial stages you need to be quick. But once they have established themselves to the idea that they are going to set up a community business and look at the feasibility, the time scale then alters. I think initially you need to be quick, you certainly need a lot of encouragement, a lot of information. Basically you just keep their head buzzing. Brainstorming is very effective. You can overdo it of course. Once you've got them to the point where they are thinking about it that much you can then start to level them out and get them working to consolidate.

After a few weeks of instigating ideas Paddy retired to a position of simply urging the group on to carry out the work that they were identifying for themselves.

Paddy O'Brien also feels strongly about the notion that a community worker cannot get involved in politics:

Our lives are controlled by bloody politics, and you need to use that political element wherever you can. If you can use it effectively then use it. I know that you are supposed to be apolitical, non-political and all the rest of it, but it controls your daily life so you've got to use that element, particularly if the project looks good and exciting.

So far as technical business knowledge is concerned Paddy did not think community workers need great expertise. However they need to have an idea of what creating a business means. At the minimum this must include knowing what a feasibility study is and knowing how to do a thumbnail sketch of a cashflow – what your income and outgoings are going to be. Community workers also need to know the appropriate individuals and agencies to contact for assistance. But beyond this they need to be able to pursue a community employment initiative with the agencies even though most economic development units within councils:

are not geared up to help community business with a new deal – because they've got no model to work round. NUmac was quite good because it was an engineering co-operative and there are in fact models to work on. If a community worker has a new initiative and there is no model to work from they will find difficulty in getting the projects right.

Group work skills were not discussed a great deal in relation to NUmac, not because Paddy O'Brien thought them irrelevant but because the group worked well together from the start. This was because of their long experience of interaction both in the workplace and in their social lives, which Paddy readily admitted was an advantage not often shared by unemployed groups trying to establish some collective project. Nevertheless, working together in a co-operative inevitably puts greater demands on one's interpersonal skills than does conventional employment.

> If you go into work in, say, Ferrantis, you may not like the people you work with but you go to work. Nine to five, brilliant, away you go, get your wages. They will probably turn up next week and the week after. You keep going. You don't like the people but you put up with them. Collective business: if you can get that sort of attitude of mind you can do it but you have got the added element that you talk to each other about how the business is developing, about work levels and all the rest. So you need to put a lot of work into group work, if you want. Reviving each person's skills.

A further reason why group work skills did not feature prominently in Paddy's account was a happy coincidence between the group's membership and the numbers needed in the co-operative. There was no point at which individuals had to be cut out from the project, and in fact another couple had to be recruited. (By that time the original management had set up a separate company and taken twenty of the original work force with them.)

One of the people encouraged to join was the original Sales Director of Morfax. Although it was recognised that his expertise was needed the group adopted a policy of collective responsibility towards management:

> They realised that management and money management and sales management wasn't the responsibility of one person: they had to discuss that as a group. One individual can't run that whole company, so they realise that they are all bosses and they are all workers. They have all got different elements of responsibility but at the end of the day decisions will be gone into collectively.

Paddy did do some brainstorming sessions early on with the group in order to assess how well they worked together.

> If you look at what happens at a brainstorming session you can identify rogues or possible problems, if you use it in the right sense. It's not so much the information coming out, although that's interesting, but you're watching what happens between the group... if there are quiet people you've got to tease them out

A Second Employment Initiative and Problems with Group Dynamics

Paddy O'Brien illustrated the importance of group work by briefly describing a second employment initiative at the Musselburgh Unemployed Workers' Centre. Five young unemployed people wanted to start a workers' co-operative doing silkscreen printing. On the face of it this seemed to have considerable potential, but the group dwindled down to two people and although a third then joined it, it was clear to Paddy O'Brien that the individuals were unable to work together. He said as much to two officers from the Regional and District councils who were thrilled at what they supposed were another five people about to be employed through a community employment initiative.

> In some ways they were trying to ride on the crest of NUmac... I said to them...' no matter how much money you put into this, and how much potential its got, it will never work with these people. What they need is some interpersonal skills developing first, and if you want this thing to survive and go ahead and become a reality we need to work on that element first'.

However the group was eager to proceed and tried to do a feasibility study. The outcome of this was its complete disintegration, and in May 1988 it no longer existed.

> What was happening was that within that group one person wanted to be the 'big boss', and in a collective that doesn't work. There was the same person who didn't really want to get their hands dirty, who wanted to do elements of work within the collective that others weren't capable of doing, that was in fact selling. They hadn't got the right approach, they hadn't got the art of talking to people. It was obvious that that was never going to work. Now what should have happened to that group was group work, so you develop interpersonal skills, relationships and developing the whole idea of a collective.

The project has not been totally abandoned, however. Paddy O'Brien is planning to start a community business, based in the Centre, which will incorporate silkscreen printing along with several other businesses: a recording studio, furniture renovation, light removals, certain building services and second hand computers. These enterprises would not be a secondary co-operative because they would not all be financially viable; a community business structure would allow for cross subsidisation between the projects.

> What we can do if it's set up right is to have six to eight people working who each have skills in at least two of the areas. If in one area business is low, they can help with another area of the business.

Points for Reflection

- The worker's responses to knowledge of impending redundancy
- Value of 'striking while the iron is hot'
- Knowing how to create a business
- Attitude to fund raising
- Use of the Network

5 Armadale: Armcraft
John McGhee

In the Armadale study a group of older men, in most cases laid off by British Leyland when the plant in Bathgate, West Lothian, was closed down in 1985, are at the heart of the initiative. This study, of a business in its early stages of development and some distance from trading in a formal way, draws attention to four main features of the community work involvement:-

1. the targetting of a particular group of the unemployed;
2. the use made of a local infra-structure of support groups;
3. links made into traditional education via the local school;
4. the importance of funding, development support and premises for advancing potentially viable ideas.

The Community Worker

John McGhee has been in Armadale for three years and fits comfortably into this West Lothian small town as he has lived and worked in the area for the past twelve years and has himself come from a similar mining community in Ayrshire.

His interest in working with the unemployed on economic regeneration and community development has not been a product of recent enterprise agitation in politics and the press. On the contrary, he was one of the first to be involved in the setting up of community businesses in Lothian.

> I actually helped to set up the Community Council in Stoneyburn. From there it's just gone on, first to the Beag Community Business and, through Urban Aid, to the building of Stoneyburn Workshops. Then West Calder saw that idea and took it up.

Although John was involved in the development of community businesses in this area he has since lost some of his enthusiasm for the direction they have taken.

> I'm quite disillusioned about the way the workshops idea developed. From being a sheltered environment for people to gain skills and develop their own business ideas it's turned out to be a sort of letting agency, and no real enterprises – just letting various premises.

Having seen his own father develop a small business idea during his retirement, he has shown an interest in the use of the existing skills of the men with whom he has been working and seen the potential for a production rather than a service company.

We will see in the following pages how the ideas of a number of Armadale groups have begun to take shape – none of them pursuing the Workspace approach except in so far as they themselves need premises for their own activities.

The account given below is derived from a number of discussions with John and from a talk he gave to student community education workers at Moray House College in Edinburgh.

The Setting

West Lothian, a district dotted about with small towns amidst the farming land, has been heavily dependent on the mining and car-making industries, though others such as Plessey, Levi-Strauss, British Steel, Golden Wonder Crisps and Steetley's brickmaking factory have contributed to the local economy. Most of these have suffered complete closure or much reduced production over the last few years.

> British Leyland at the peak of employment in 1981 had about 4000 qualified people from a radius of about twelve miles in West Lothian, so when they actually closed, it had a massive impact on the communities. And, to add insult to injury, the majority of people who were working in the early '60s when the plant opened were imported from Glasgow and were left stranded in an area with very low community provision, very low employment provision and with no family ties to fall back on. 64.8 per cent of the total work force was over the age of forty-five, when they were made redundant.

> In the space of six to eight months thousands of men were catapulted into the labour market which didn't exist, from engineering skills which were no longer in demand. The majority of the new engineering firms are based in Livingston New Town, which is a development area and invaded by microelectronics. The people whom they tend to employ are young school-leavers and married women with some experience of working on the assembly line and who work on a part-time basis... so the future for the forty to forty five age group is not very rosy, and for those over forty five is non-existent.

West Lothian has an economy that upsets many received opinions:

> One of the strange aspects of the employment market is that the majority of women who are looking for work in West Lothian get work, albeit on a part-time basis, and you find that in a lot of households where the male is unemployed the woman's got a part-time or full-time job – so the role reversal has to be dealt with as well. Furthermore, Livingston New Town attracts all these hi-tech industries by providing low factory rental. So any new industry that does come in is channelled towards Livingston which is about ten miles away, and would cost about £3-£4 a day to travel to.

With no major industries left there is also a relatively poor service base.

> Forty per cent of the employment used to be in service industries, compared to 62 per cent in the whole of Scotland, but if you haven't got money to spend on services, there's no point in having service industries.

> In Armadale, there's a high proportion of one- and two-man businesses who supply the mainstream service industries – one-man and two-man garages, for instance. There isn't a great base of firms employing more than twenty-five people locally ... One good thing is that the Regional and District Councils have adopted a policy of trying to have goods supplied from local companies, whereas before they would send to England if they got a better discount.

John is more than conscious of the economic weakness of West Lothian and, coming from his previous experience of community business, ready to make use of the restructuring of community education to make his own contribution in the field of unemployment.

The Community Education Neighbourhood Team

John, as part of a neighbourhood team, is aware that work with the unemployed is related largely to the priority it receives.

> It is a regional priority – one of the areas within Lothian Region that community workers should be working on. But, to be truthful, up until three or four years ago it was recreational, because of a lack of base knowledge that community workers had. They didn't have the necessary knowledge about the other employment initiatives that were going about. I had been to lots of conferences and meetings and I'd been involved with community enterprises before so I knew the basics and also knew quite a range of examples.

Since working with the unemployed on employment initiatives rather than on recreation, consumes time on an unprecedented scale, careful management of workload and of resources amongst the team members is needed, but even more important is the commitment to the work.

> Although the neighbourhood teams are supposed to be working as neighbourhood teams there's still a lot of people scared about letting go of their buildings. They sort of retrench back into their managerial role rather than getting involved in an issue-based workload, though they state at every opportunity that they would like to be released from these responsibilities. I think it's because administering the building gives them a cosy support structure with ancillary staff.

In John's case there was a senior worker ready and willing to take an issue-based approach and support his endeavours in the field of unemployment. John recognises that without him and the whole neighbourhood team's co-operation this work would have proved almost impossible to undertake.

First Links into Armadale – 1986

There are several threads to the development of what was to be Armcraft, one through the setting up of ACE (Armadale Community Enterprise), another through the Armadale Forum (a group of professionals which included representatives from the Academy, District and Regional Planning Departments, Community Education, Health and Housing) a third via the British Leyland pre-redundancy course and the fourth through the formation of Community Enterprise Lothian Ltd. (CELL).

The first step was taken through John's invitation to help an inter-church discussion group (to which community councillors also belonged) move forward in their plans to affect local employment.

> It was only a talking shop and they didn't know how to progress and to get funding and how to constitute themselves, so I was asked to go along and try to help the group. So I went along to the first meeting and asked the group what they themselves wanted to achieve and what objectives they wished to set themselves. They said they wanted to create employment locally and relieve unemployment because they realised there was no way we would get major employers back into the area. So anything that was done would need to be done locally on a small scale with local people, local involvement and utilising local firms or charitable trusts. So we sat down and drew up a constitution, set our objectives and got ourselves registered as a charity, and this did lead to funding from the local District Council.

ACE, as it was now constituted, wished to find something they could get off the ground quickly, creating a few jobs and having an impact on the town. In this way they hoped to raise their profile and establish themselves as a known and active group with an employment remit. After looking unsuccessfully for premises for setting up workshop spaces in which, under protected conditions and with an information centre, unemployed people could revive or develop skills before launching out on their own, ACE turned to the Manpower Services Commission for the funding of a Community Programme. Together with the Personnel Department of Community Opportunities, West Lothian (COWL –

the overall management agency of MSC programmes) members of the ACE committee interviewed local long-term unemployed applicants for a squad of forty men. These men went on to work on environmental improvements sub-contracted by the District Council.

> We advertised for our forty men through the Job Centre. The only person we recruited outside the area was the project manager, but he had previous experience on another project in Broxburn and Kirkhill (also in West Lothian) in an environmental improvement scheme. (He also was appointed by COWL and ACE jointly). This raised the profile of ACE, which had previously been regarded as a clearing house for ideas and talking shop. So we actually had jobs on the ground and something we could show the people.

ACE came into existence at much the same time as the neighbourhood team, and John remains as its secretary, while also being a member of Armadale Forum. ACE has close links with the Forum which acts as an information sharing network, with Regional and District Officials who advise ACE and also members of the Forum. There are therefore two associated groups concerned with employment initiatives – ACE, generated by local Armadale inhabitants and the Forum, the professional practitioners, whose interests are more diverse.

A Targetted Group – British Leyland Closure and a Redundant Workforce

Alongside the developments in ACE, and related to them, was another initiative. Community Education, together with Lothian Region Social Work Department, West Lothian College of Further Education and West Lothian Rights Association, responded to the imminent closure of the British Leyland plant in Bathgate with several two-day pre-redundancy courses held in the spring and early summer of 1986. John did not take part in these meetings which took the men through the College courses on offer, the financial consequences of unemployment and the welfare benefits available, the management of large redundancy payments and the range of responses they might make, whether as family members, members of friendship networks or as individuals facing a loss of identity and purpose.

He was, however, drawn in at the next stage.

> A follow-up to the pre-redundancy course was conducted by means of a series of recall meetings held throughout West Lothian at the end of January 1987. Those who had attended the course were contacted by letter and invited to nominate a suitable centre for further meetings. A total of twenty-five indicated they would be willing to come to Armadale Community Centre, but, in fact on the evening only thirteen people actually came.

We will now turn to look at the group of men with whom John began to work.

> There was a lot of feeling of hopelessness, because the men were in the forty-five to sixty age group. In fact, some of them had taken early retirement as opposed to redundancy and they couldn't see any light at the end of the tunnel. They didn't know what they were going to do... We found that maybe 125 people from Armadale worked at British Leyland, but they didn't work beside each other. It was a huge plant, and we discovered that people didn't even know people who stayed down the road from them, yet they knew people in other villages who worked in the same block as them.

It was a real problem to identify a need for the formation of a local group and to provide a mechanism to respond to their needs. In fact although eight or nine areas had recall meetings only about five of them decided to form groups. Those who decided not to were those who were so thoroughly sickened by their experiences of redundancy that the name of BL was forever burned into their memory, and they didn't want to have anything whatsoever to do with it in any shape or form.

The majority had got a sizeable sum as they'd served in Leyland since it was opened, so they were about to finish up Unemployment Benefit, and they'd no prospects of getting Supplementary Benefit with a capital sum. So they'd no income coming in, and they would all have to live off the resources they had. Quite a few of them had wives who were working part-time as well, which added insult to injury. They came from a kind of macho-minded background and felt it beneath their dignity to come out during the day and say, 'Look, I'm unemployed. What can you give us to do?

The thirteen men who had attended the first follow-up meeting, now six months into their experience of unemployment, were eager to discuss their situation. The group were led by two of the community workers who had participated in the pre-redundancy course and after reviewing the course went on to assert their continuing need to meet, with the topic of Welfare Benefits as their most pressing concern.

At the following meeting, to which staff from West Lothian Rights Association were invited, twenty-seven men attended. Members of the local Welfare Rights group also came to help resolve difficulties. At the end of this meeting the men raised the subject of the Enterprise Allowance Scheme, and this gave the impetus to the decision to continue meeting on Wednesday afternoons.

Introduction to the Enterprise Allowance Scheme

At the next meeting, members of the Community Business at Stoneyburn Workshops and of Bathgate Area Support for Enterprise (BASE), responded to the men's interest in the Enterprise Allowance Scheme and outlined the support and advice services which were offered locally to those embarking on self-employment.

Of the group that we had initial contact with there are about four altogether who have actually started up a business themselves, either on a sort of franchise basis, being self-employed, or starting their own business.

Once the rest of them had participated in a number of leisure time activities to get used to each other, working in a group, the men themselves decided that, since their employment prospects were virtually nothing they would need to look at alternatives. The work ethic is ground into their background and they felt they needed work. They had worked for forty-five years or so and they needed work to fulfil themselves. So since then (about October 1987) we have worked steadfastly towards achieving the aims of either setting up some sort of local community business or getting some sort of cooperative off the ground.

Visiting Other Employment Initiatives

John fostered this newly forged purpose – 'to make work for themselves' – and arranged a series of visits to community businesses and employment initiatives both in the local area and throughout the Central Scotland Belt.

We've been to the Buckhaven project which had a multiplicity of different strands of funding – mainstream, CP, YTS, Job Training Scheme and small business funding.

We took them there and the group was most enthusiastic about the type of projects they were doing, like wooden toy making, metal work, printing and pottery, because they too have skills that could be easily adapted to these enterprises.

We've been to Goodwill in Glasgow to see their furniture restoration workshops, because that was already an idea they had – and they had the skills as well.

We've been to Craig's farm in West Lothian, Stoneyburn workshops and West Calder workshops... anywhere where I felt they could get ideas.

John stressed that it was no good 'just telling them about it, you've got to take them and let them speak to people', so many of the early days were spent in garnering ideas from elsewhere, but also in building up a skills profile. In this they took part in a pilot survey conducted by ACE, which was trying to track down the range of knowledge and skills available within the unemployed population of Armadale as a whole.

They became involved in the local umbrella group (ACE). They came along and got involved in their meetings. They went and actually sat in on meetings of people who were trying to start up community businesses. They approached all the agencies that could give them help and looked for resources which they could use as a base for starting.

Problems with Premises

But the group ran into serious trouble.

The problem reached a crescendo when they discovered:

(a)that there was no surplus accommodation locally which could be used, so that if they wanted to start anything they would need to move out of the community:

(b)that the carpet was drawn from beneath them.

They had drafted an application for work space with a view to starting some sort of community business, and the Scottish Office in their wisdom, decided we didn't fit the criteria for Urban Aid, (because Armadale is too rural and not associated with a big enough town though it meets the criteria of deprivation on every other count). So they are still fighting...

Working with the Local School

In the mean time the group struggling to keep themselves together decided that they would like to get some new skills and improve on the skills they did have. West Lothian College of Further Education was some distance from Armadale and therefore costly to reach.

One of the features of West Lothian is that it is a very rural area and bus fares are astronomical, so if you provide a central resource in West Lothian, nobody can get to it because the transport costs are out of reach, so we were looking for some sort of local base for the men to use to improve skills, try out ideas and get some sort of professional support.

This led to the pursuit of instruction at Armadale Academy which was within easy reach and, furthermore was accessible to such an approach because of a peculiarly fortunate set of circumstances. A new Rector, Ralph Wilson, had recently been appointed who was one of the Scottish pioneers of community schools and had not long before been director of the Scottish Community Education Council (SCEC). His commitment to the involvement of the Academy in community concerns was immediately apparent. The Senior

Community Education worker was drawn into the school management committee and Ralph Wilson's Depute was encouraged as a member of Armadale Forum and an enthusiast for 'a coherent, upright and pluralistic curriculum' to enlist the help of the Craft, Design and Technology Department in offering facilities for a technical skills development course. This was initially organised by a team from West Calder Workspace who were funded to provide a post-redundancy programme, but moved on to a co-operative training scheme managed by the school and John on Tuesday and Thursday afternoons.

> Group members negotiated access to the Academy together with teaching-staff time to assist with skill development and production of prototype equipment which could eventually be marketed commercially.
>
> Funding for materials was met through Community Education's Disadvantage Budget, West Lothian District Council and ACE via the District Council's Community Chest.
>
> Those group members who were not particularly interested in community business were catered for and encouraged to develop woodwork and D.I.Y. as a hobby.

The group was fortunate in having the talents, both human and technical, of Hamish Donald the Principal Teacher of Craft, Design and Technology who threw himself into encouraging the men to make heavy playgroup furniture to be sold to the local nursery school and playgroups and garden furniture made of wrought iron to undercut in price and durability the more common wooden furniture available at the garden centres. The £600 allocated to Hamish for his work with the BL men covered the cost of materials and enabled him to buy equipment that would serve both pupils and men. In fact, this sum of money was a welcome bonus to a department that was allowed only £1,200 for the year's budget for the whole school.

Although John might have had qualms over co-operation with traditional teachers, in Hamish he found a colleague who clearly met the men's need for personal warmth, for technical guidance, and for appreciation of their wide knowledge and existing levels of skill.

The men's skills showed to good effect when the school got a new metal bending machine:

> It had just arrived prior to our Thursday afternoon session...(and by the time I got back) the men had the boxes all stripped down and built up, and the teacher hadn't a clue how to build it up, but some of the men had been working with that kind of machinery in the factory so they built it up and had it working for him before the end of the afternoon, so he was very pleased with that one.

A further spin-off for the school was the presence of adults who gave a sense of genuineness to the skill to be acquired.

> Our men are wandering from one workshop to another depending on what they are actually doing, so the kids are in their classes working away with minimal supervision and can actually see the men getting involved.

For the Community Education worker there were other advantages:

> We hope there will be spin offs in other places and that other departments will see in the school what extra things this adult participation and adult involvement have brought the technical department. Meanwhile some of the men have begun to work on SCOTVEC modules on working with wood etc. They will get a paper qualification to assist them and to give them background information on various skills.

Although the arrangements with the school were of mutual benefit, they were not without their difficulties at the outset of the scheme.

> A member of staff had been timetabled in the school specifically to work with these groups (evidence of commitment from the management structure), but we had a problem for a while. The fact is we had great difficulty in getting people. A lot of publicity went out but we had only one or two people who were interested, yet this one member of staff timetabled to do it. So, of course the other teachers saw him as having nothing to do. But there was a push and the interest grew again.
>
> We used word of mouth through the men who were actually doing it themselves and through the community newspaper which had a tear-off slip which told people the range of things they could get involved in. And there was another idea of a Tool Library for the unemployed men getting the skills in the woodwork class who would like to do some work at home or mend things at home but didn't have the tools or the money to go and hire. We have a commitment from the Technical Department to assist us with this.

Preparing for the Business Start-Up

By May 1988 approximately sixteen men were regularly involved in work at the school with about eight of these interested in pursuing the idea of a community business. They had already made a number of prototype products – wrought iron gates, wrought iron coach lamps and quality wooden toys such as wheelbarrows and rocking animals (dogs and llamas!), children's garages and a double rocking chair. On May 27 a day seminar, open to the public, was held with the co-operation of Community Enterprise Lothian Ltd. (CELL) and Bathgate Area Support for Enterprise (BASE), both enterprise support groups, to raise the profile of the Armadale group and to explore possible future developments. This was accompanied by an exhibition of the prototype products in the entrance hall of the community centre.

> The whole thing about the wrought iron work is we concentrated on a quality custom-built product. The people who build them will go along, consult with the customer and draft designs in conjunction with the customer and produce the finished article.
>
> We had a set of orders from the Methodist Church – that was just before the exhibition, and we have an order for another three sets of gates and an order for coach lamps and six orders for the wheelbarrows. We've actually turned down a few orders because we're not geared up to deal with them just now. We've taken names and addresses from the interested people.

Following the day seminar the group made contact with CELL:

> They agreed to allocate a development worker half a day a week initially, to look at the mechanisms of setting up a community company which would provisionally be called Armcraft.

A steering group was set up with office bearers from ACE and from the ex-BL workers who had been involved in producing the prototypes at the Academy. John went on to say:

> There is a fifty-fifty split. Then on the committee there are three members from ACE and five ex-BL workers. I am in it as secretary, and the CELL development worker is coming along to support us through the initial stages... He drafted a constitution for the Steering Group, and the committee is just planning a submission for Urban Aid funding again. We have just regained Urban Aid status, which is marvellous.

Despite this gratifying change of status and a grant from the Regional Council of £2000 to promote local industry, recruit local people into it and carry out feasibility studies, there is still a major problem:

> There is still the same old bugbear about premises. In our previous Urban Aid submission we asked for a new building to house five to six workshops, but they wouldn't wear any capital projects so we have to get money to refurbish existing premises. This is our biggest problem because there aren't any existing premises that we could refurbish.

> The units at the industrial estate are all full now and though the Regional Council has agreed to build three 1000 sq. ft. units at Bathville with associated yard space there are cutbacks in Regional spending so we don't know if they will get off the ground this or even next year. Meanwhile I have got the industrial manager for the Regional Council to agree verbally that, if and when these units are built, one of them will be identified as being a base for community business.

Maintaining Impetus during Delays

For the time being the men are prepared to 'guddle along at the Academy', but suffer from the limited time they can make use of the workshops, which, of course, hampers their ability to meet orders and develop a business. The immediate solution to this problem appears to lie in negotiating open access to the school. This seems possible since the staff of the Craft, Design and Technology Department are being cut back, thus releasing a classroom.

Maintaining the group therefore presents yet further problems. Over the summer a number of men have drifted off to jobs with the District Council. They are expected to return in the autumn since these jobs are temporary and often part-time. Other participants have been spurred by community education contacts to take up voluntary work and one member of the Steering Committee was felt to be so busy with his driving for Dr Barnardo's that his absence from a meeting could be accounted for by his many commitments.

One of the means of maintaining impetus has been splitting the tasks of the Steering Group so that they all remain involved. Two of the men agreed to search for premises, such as a vacant shop which had been lying empty for three years.

> They are going to find out the size of the place, who owns it and see if we could lease it. Some of the men are going to investigate vacant units we think might be available at Steetley's, the one-time brick works at the top of the town. The treasurer is getting together with someone from CELL to look at new accounting systems which would fit into the community business type of company.

> She's come through ACE, which was initially a council of churches thing and she became involved through the Methodist Church. She's very keen.

The group, having become rather despondent, is now much encouraged by the return to Urban Aid status.

> We were getting quite dispirited because we had two days at the Academy and we were getting on and producing but the men were finding there wasn't a next stage without somewhere to work away and do things in their own time and unrestricted by school hours. Now we have the Urban Aid thing, that has added a wee bit of momentum to it, and we are looking at development products as well. Some of the men are looking around to see what is on offer for sale, whether they can produce them either cheaper or of better quality.

We therefore leave the group regaining enthusiasm and members as they link in with CELL, establish a steering group with a constitution, progress on to a feasibility study, allocate tasks and explore the key issue of premises. The long period from January 1987 to June 1988 has had its doldrums but has nevertheless seen great progress amongst men who had written off their futures, were quite often on tranquillisers and desperate for something to occupy the seemingly endless hours.

The Role of the Community Worker

John, like other community workers in the field of employment initiatives, has had to find a way of working with a group which differed in age structure and in origin from anything for which he had been prepared.

In targetting the British Leyland workforce the West Lothian community education workers felt themselves to be at a loss.

> We were basically picking up the needs and aspirations of the unemployed people, and finding out how they were coping with unemployment. Nobody in the whole of Britain had written up anything whatsoever, so we were fishing in the dark, feeling our way.

> I think community education workers, like teachers and other professionals, like to speak to a group that is already in existence. The whole sort of time commitment of having actually to establish a group you can actually put your message across to is something which is very odd.

> Work with the unemployed is a very difficult area to work. It's making the initial contact, and trying to establish some sort of contact with people, some of whom in my case are old enough to be my father, and the time it takes before you have any sort of results, any sort of quality results. You will see that it is actually easier to get involved in something else than take up all that time in work with the unemployed. Community workers are like everybody else... if it's an easy option they'll fall in with it. They can occupy their time quite happily looking after mothers' and toddlers' groups and youth clubs and that, but if you're going to roll up your sleeves and get moving it's a different story.

In working with the recall groups they found the need to set themselves objectives:

> The objectives that were set at the outset were to identify any need for the formation of a local group and to provide some sort of mechanism to respond to any of the expressed needs.

These objectives were those of the community education workers but John saw his role as facilitating the expression of the BL group's own objectives. He found that they were articulate and ready to state their own needs, though they had clearly forgotten everything that had been told them in the pre-redundancy course.

John was clear that he also had an educational role and that this too might present problems.

> A lot of people make assumptions that the community education staff have the range of skills. Everybody doesn't have every skill, and it's very hard to be asked when you don't have any higher contact or prior knowledge of a particular area of work, to identify what skills the men really need to progress their ideas.

However, as we have seen, he used his professional network to enable the men to negotiate with the school for skills training and ultimately for the acquisition of SCOTVEC certification.

To pursue his educational role, he also stresses the need for a very personal contact.

> You've got to be prepared almost to take them by the hand and sort of say, 'We're going to the school today. We'll take you.' You've got to make them feel comfortable, and show them around. It's a lot of work doing that. It's got to be very much on a one-to-one basis.

This personal contact needed to be used also to counteract the overwhelming sense of depression.

> The first topic of conversation when the Armadale group meets any of the other BL groups is, 'Who has died?' And the incidence of strokes and heart disease within that particular group is really frightening. When you see people who have worked all their days and been healthy, within a year and a half of unemployment they have just disintegrated physically and mentally.

Skills for Working with the Unemployed: Groupwork, Expectations and Maintenance Demands

> I've certainly found that I've used groupwork skills more consciously than I've ever used them in any other group I've ever worked with. You can't go into a group of adults and say, 'We'll do this, this and this'. It is a constant process of negotiation – particularly in trying to maintain the group and make sure that I change the subject without being the front person.

Maintaining the group was achieved, given that the unemployed have quite clear personal goals of regaining work, creating work or simply being occupied, by setting weekly goals while at the same time making sure that the men's expectations were met but were not excessively optimistic.

> Nothing that we are doing just now will change Armadale overnight and we have to make people aware of that. It's all about changing attitudes. We know ourselves, and we say, right at the beginning, 'We're not here to provide jobs'. We laid that on the line and said, 'Look we're not promising anything'.

Yet there were other expectations with regard to progress.

> If the group expect to get somewhere at a specified time, if they don't get it in that time then they get quite upset about it. The problem that we had right at the very start was to keep up with the group. They were making demands all the time, and it was a problem that if you fail to meet a set of expectations then how does that set the group back, keeping in mind they didn't have much previous contact with community education (and didn't realise that we ourselves would not have all the knowledge and skills they were after). If you build up their expectations and you cannot fulfil them, they'll vote with their feet. It's exceptionally difficult to get a second chance.

We have seen that, in answer to these demands, John arranged consultations with the Rights Association, BASE. the school and with numerous other projects (as well as with some of the Regional councillors who were invited to talk with the men and see their work). This, the work at the school, together with a programme of social events, kept the group together, though the amount of servicing of the group gradually took up two days a week with the school and one day on social activities.

> One of my concerns when I first got involved was how much time we would be spending with the group. Initially it started off with only working with the group one afternoon a week, and then it built up to three afternoons and maybe a couple of mornings. And the concern I expressed to the group was, are they seeing too much of each other? And they said, 'No, we want to get involved and take up as much time as possible. We don't want to have spare time. And the more things that you can find to occupy our time the better.

John's attempts at maintenance were therefore successful, though the men went through a period of despondency initially when some individuals left to start up jobs on their own and later when financial support and the absence of premises handicapped them. The more recent drive with the assistance of CELL development workers has given the group more heart.

Three further issues are raised by these comments: firstly, the degree of responsibility taken by John, secondly the value of an extensive network to supplement his knowledge and skills and thirdly, the use of available financial resources.

The Centrality of the Community Worker

John was conscious of the need to meet the expectations of the group by drawing upon services with whom he had contacts, but also of the need to remove himself from occupying a dominant role.

> I'm working co-operatively with adults and operating within a sort of consensus model rather than a directive model. I feel that's important because you must allow the people you're working with to negotiate the speed that they actually progress at and the component parts of the project they want to be involved in.

With respect to his role in the details of the business start-up John is clear that he cannot take the group into the detailed planning:

> My function is really if people have the idea and they have the necessary skills to produce or develop a product then I'll look for an agency to take that on. I don't see that I should take people right through to start up in business for themselves, I don't have the skills for that. But intrinsic to that is you must really trust the people you're working with to be able to recognise that that's as far as you can take them.

Indeed, at this point, he has enlisted the help of the CELL development worker and is passing on lead roles to the steering committee of Armcraft.

> I am taking the Steering Group through the same sort of things that I experienced so that they know what it is all about and develop some expertise. A lot of the people in the group have been alongside when I have made contact, for example, when we went to Buckhaven and to other workspaces, then the group come along, ask the questions and meet the people in charge.

It has taken eighteen months for the group to reach the stage of setting up a Steering Committee and undertaking a feasibility study. This is not the speed at which John himself would have preferred to move. The lack of premises and the lack of funding for premises have slowed down progress. Meanwhile, however, the men have had the time to develop confidence, cohesion, interpersonal skills and purposefulness.

Networking

John's involvement with the unemployed drew on a considerable number of resources. The first strand of the network was his own profession:

> Prior to the BL recall a group of staff from community education throughout the area got together. These staff were based on neighbourhood teams in areas where a particularly high proportion of people who had been made redundant were concentrated. So these staff were brought together to look at skills, and to get an insight into the process the men had gone though prior to being made redundant. The group is still operating at present as a support and skill-sharing network for work with people forced into redundancy. It has helped us to learn from our experiences with BL and be of use when Steetley's and Golden Wonder closed down. We get together and we all put our reports in so we're all aware of what each other's doing, so if somebody's got a good idea and it's working, then we give it a try.

Most recently, he has been invited to be one of the Regional Community Education consultants to other workers involved in community employment initiatives.

Through his previous experience at Stoneyburn and contact with West Calder he was able to draw on members of these community businesses to advise the Armadale group, and, moving on from there via word of mouth and conferences he set up a network of contacts with other projects the men visited.

His connection with ACE from its inception, through its complex involvements in MSC funding for Community Programmes, to its participation in the Steering Committee of Armcraft, gave him a central view of the total Armadale approach to unemployment. His participation in the Armadale Forum added other useful strings to his bow. District and Regional councillors were accessible as also were the Academy and the District Planning Department. His contact with the industrial manager for the Regional Council has enabled him to put in a plea for premises, and most recently the establishment of CELL has provided the group with renewed impetus and a development worker.

Funding

As John has observed, working with the unemployed is time-consuming and often draining. Not only must the worker maintain the spirits of the group, keep up their momentum, give them access to various forms of education and training but also provide the funding for often quite expensive development costs. He has tried a number of different sources.

> We have managed to acquire some money from our own department, and also because of our close links with the Forum we have managed to acquire money from the District Council Planning Department – Community Chest money, disbursed to community groups for specific projects. We got £500 for a community newspaper and £1000 for opportunities for adults. It was applied for by ACE on behalf of the unemployed.

Here we see the use of a voluntary body to act as the holding company for employment initiatives:

> It's a tangled web. You use one group to get money to cross-fertilise things. ACE has been seen as the properly constituted voluntary group – the umbrella organisation – that we do everything under. If we go via Lothian Region's Education Department that automatically debars us from applying for anything, so we have to use a constituted legitimate body to make these applications, and ACE is the obvious one whose aims and objectives have been drawn up. In fact, ACE has had £1,500 of the £7,500 Community Chest budget for this year!

Further money was needed and other finances slowly acquired through a process of using the network and discovering the appropriate funding bodies:

> Our most successful thing is that we scrounge from our local councillor, who is chairman of the finance committee. It's knowing who to go and see or who to phone. We are getting quite good at getting wee patches of things from here and there and putting them all together – using one thing to spawn another.

> The ACE £1,000 was for materials for Adult Opportunities, but the application was framed in such a way as to pay for materials for this group, but also to promote the production of prototypes which could develop into some sort of feasible community business. At the same time, in order to get the money, we asked for it to go towards an information network in the area which would link into the community newspaper – typesetting for various things. This money allows us to offer courses free of charge and free of material charges.

ACE was also aware of the charities that could be tapped.

> There are quite a few publications on charitable trusts and we have a local group at present who keep tabs on these sort of things, called Bathgate Area Initiatives Team, which is an Urban Aid sponsored five year project, but the information they gave us, we have already through our various networks. We have actually passed information on to them.

The key often lies in framing the application for funding in such a way as to comply with the particular rules of each funding body. John was aware of inadequacies in this respect:

> We know where to go to get money and we know who to talk to but in terms of actually making applications I wouldn't say we were particularly successful... There could be three or four different organisations with different aims and objectives. Also making applications to the same body for different things is a difficult one.

There is therefore a complex range of activities in which community education workers are engaged if they become involved with employment initiatives. Can this be considered worthwhile? In terms of the worker's own development there are clear benefits in John's estimation.

> Even though you spend a great deal of time you are making a range of contacts, increasing your skills, building up better relationships within the community as a whole and establishing your base within the community in a way that is unusual.

Successes

If we turn to the benefits John observes for the men with whom he has worked, he is also sanguine. In spite of the fact that no actual business has yet materialised, and that relatively few of the original recall group are employed except through Community Programmes or, alternatively, within the informal economy – 'on the black' – he considers the long haul has been relatively successful in educational terms. This has been shown, firstly, in the growth of confidence and secondly in an increased range of interests.

> They were in a sorry state when I picked them up and were at a really loose end. Now they are much more confident. They have a lot of things to occupy their time, not just employment related things – hobbies such as local history. (We've been on a couple of visits to Perth and Pitlochry for this).

> Two have been away on a leadership course for outdoor education and every one of them went on a welfare rights course and learned about the benefits system.

> Frank is a voluntary driver with Dr Barnardo's because he has a mini- bus permit and he's tapped into that and now enjoys it. He's interested in what is going on at the centre and has done some jobs such as putting up goal posts and repairing bits and pieces.

They took an increasing responsibility for meeting their own needs.

> A lot of the work was done by them in gaining access to the technical skills course. All I did was bring in the Depute Rector of the Academy. He gave his spiel and they told him all the equipment they needed and what they wanted to do. He said he'd introduce them to somebody who'd pilot a do-it-yourself course, and from there the demand and whole thrust has come from the men. The demand is still coming from them because they have the confidence to demand facilities and negotiate them for themselves.

The men's ability to present a case also improved.

> I think they have become highly articulate. We had a group from the Region's Urban

Programme Committee out to have a look at the area when we were fighting to be reinstated for Urban Aid and the people from the BL group and the men who'd been involved at the Academy... (not all from the BL group) felt that they weren't getting a fair hearing from the committee, so what they did was get the chairman of the employment committee and give him a severe wigging, and told him in no uncertain terms that it's about time the Council got off their tails and did something for Armadale. And from that one of the Councillors came out and spoke to the ACE group and from that we eventually got £2,000.

A further development has been visible with respect to their families.

I think they are starting to involve their families in things as well, which is something I felt was sadly lacking throughout the whole thing. It tended to be them only, but just recently when we've been organising visits some of the wives have actually been coming along just to see what is going on, which is a good thing.

Women have taken the initiative in other areas too.

We have been looking at mechanisms for local women to set up businesses. There are two women who have been on a CP scheme which is due to come to an end soon. They want to set up a catering business so I have referred them to BASE, and told them that if they don't get much joy from them we can maybe look at a small company together and find out about a community business.

John has completed one and a half year's work with the unemployed – much of it not described in these pages. He has totally redefined his view of his role, which has vastly expanded.

Initially, when I first came into contact with the BL group my target was to make sure they got what they were after. I only saw that as a short term thing. What I thought, in my naivety, was that when I first met them I'd find out what their fears and needs were and be able to identify mechanisms within individual clubs, and, if they were interested in welfare rights, I'd pass them on to the welfare rights group. But it never worked like that.

As he deliberately moves away from frequent direct involvement with the group he continues to express his frustration about contacting the many unemployed in the Armadale area, who remain elusive despite door to door canvassing, leaflets, newspaper advertising and community surveys. He now reckons that the best advertisement for community work involvement in employment initiatives is, and will be, the men themselves – their new interests, their part in the developing business and a readiness to spread the word.

Points for Reflection

- Time scale
- Age of participants
- Variety of criteria of 'success'
- The value and possibility of establishing pre-redundancy links with local employers
- Contacting the unemployed

6 South Aston: Park Lane Garden Centre Julia Preece

This account contains a number of unusual features:

1 the adoption of an explicitly educational approach as part of an ambitious community education project, with the worker seeing herself primarily as a professional educator;
2 the positive steps taken to involve all sections of the multicultural neighbourhood;
3 the worker's intentional adoption of an interventionist style;
4 the local residence of the worker.

South Aston and the Derelict Site

South Aston is an island within a maze of motorways that isolate it from the rest of Birmingham. It is made up of a post-60s housing estate of tower blocks and row upon row of some 1,200 terraced 'town houses' (three-storey family blocks). Ninety per cent of this housing is council owned, (and most of the rest has been recently purchased from the council by its residents). Sandwiched between the estate's high rise flats are four shops, a community church, primary school and three acres of open ground.

Julia Preece moved there in 1978 as a probationary nursery school teacher in the local primary school. She described the area as:

> an average multi-racial, inner-city housing estate, with ordinary housing and social problems, more than average unemployment problems (Birmingham's worst: 31 per cent in March 1989), combined with a traditional mistrust and suspicion of education, teachers, and their own self-image of failure within the system.

On her arrival Julia was immediately struck by the unused potential of the waste ground adjoining the primary school, a site where an HP factory had recently been demolished. She was interested in developing play facilities for local children, and a recent study of the needs of the neighbourhood had identified play provision as an urgent priority. It happened that the minister of the local United Reform Church was trying to start a residents' association at this time, and at an inaugural meeting in September 1978 Julia Preece was elected secretary.

The South Aston Adventure Play Centre

Uninhibited by the 'facilitative' approach adopted by many trained community workers, Julia took the initiative and invited parents to attend a meeting in school time, using the nursery building, to discuss play provision and the old HP site. Thirty to forty people turned up, and somewhat to her surprise, everyone at the meeting agreed that the site should be used for a play area rather than public open space, which was what the City Council had scheduled it for. She had imagined that the adjoining main road, across which everyone going to the site (and primary school) had to walk, would be a major obstacle to the proposal. A South Aston Adventure Play Centre committee was formed and Julia organised a film show of 'Dinosaurs in the Playground' which demonstrated how children can design their own play areas. This inspired the committee to organise a play scheme for the following summer and to call a meeting with officers from the Council Planning Department. The planners turned out to be co-operative. The Council Estates Department owned the vacant site and had planned to clear it in any case. They now agreed that part of it could be used as a play area.

The project developed steadily from this point. From 1979 to 1980 parents built a hut on the site and a charity funded the first school liaison worker. In April 1980 Julia Preece was appointed as full time Manager of the Adventure Play Centre through an Innercity Partnership grant. In 1981 toilets and running water were added to the hut and another paid worker was appointed to the project, again funded by Innercity Partnership and local charity donations. In 1982 a YOP scheme built an office and in 1983 an urban farm was established and part of the site was landscaped for gardens by a locally managed Community Programme scheme. All these temporary workers were local residents, including their supervisor. Many of them had helped to build the first hut on the site. Julia describes her management of these developments as 'an interventionist interpretation of what kids wanted'. The children were constantly asked for their ideas about how to use the site and they were involved in its detailed design. However, strategic plans were generally proposed by Julia to the parents' committee, which would consider them and then present them to more open meetings. In 1985 Julia gave up the management of the Centre for another job, and her post was taken by Glenys Jones, a home-school liaison teacher. However Julia stayed on the committee as the Finance Officer, and therefore remained closely involved in its activities.

Developing the Idea of a Garden Centre

In January 1987 Julia returned to what had become the South Aston Community Project as a volunteer worker. During the previous year the committee had considered a suggestion from a local resident that a garden centre should be established on the site. It was thought that this might enhance the environment, meet a local need (most Birmingham garden centres were on the periphery of the city), and provide employment. When Julia returned she was happy to work on this idea, having considered such a project herself at a earlier stage in the development of the Play Centre.

Julia knew that the City Council would have to be won over since they owned the site: their initial response was to demand market research, feasibility studies and the support of other agencies. From January to November of 1988 the garden centre was the main focus of Julia's work. She rapidly established contact with numerous local agencies, but many were not suited to assist at this stage. For instance, the Small Business Advisory Service was unable to provide advice that recognised the non-profit maximising, community dimension to the project. In retrospect Julia realises that the garden centre might have been financially more viable if the principal 'shop' had been located on the edge of the city so that it could subsidise a smaller centre in South Aston. Birmingham Polytechnic analysed the project's market research findings, but the most valuable advice came from Birmingham Voluntary Services Council's Economic Initiatives Unit, and from Charles King, a man who used to run his own commercial garden centre. The Council's funding department, the Economic Development Unit, worked closely with these two contacts to ensure themselves that the scheme was based on sound economic research analysis.

The Broad Aims of the Garden Centre

It was intended that the garden centre would be a locally managed sub-structure within the wider community education/development scheme South Aston Community Project. As part of this wider project its aims were much broader than to be simply commercially viable. They were set out by Julia Preece:

1 Commercial viability – involving local parents in an advisory capacity on what sells, any plant knowledge, assisting with daily purchases and sales. People should pool skills and learn together.

2 Community development – residents should present ideas and help carry out practical jobs such as leafleting. Ideas so far have included a plant doctor service, gardens and window boxes, competitions, clean-up campaign, and garden clubs. With this would come community identity – labels are translated into Asian languages, photographs of people advertising goods are large blow-ups of committee members or project regulars.

3 Educational development – children of any age rarely visit garden centres. The centre would be adjacent to a children's play area, visited by school groups and controlled by people the children have known for years. Equally, South Aston can boast few shops, particularly of a non-grocery variety. Children would be stimulated to look, buy, ask questions and be involved in the shop's care and maintenance. School projects could include market research, information booklets and language development schemes.
Park Lane Garden Centre, as a member of Birmingham's school/industry Compact, operates from a 'teacher' insight and primary interest in client welfare rather than the ulterior motive of recruitment prospects. The centre will have a unique position – often relating to young people, throughout their school years, offering a rural-associated industry in the heart of the city as well as having a strong inside working knowledge of local schools and their needs.

4 YTS and Employment Training in horticulture, animal husbandry, community work, marketing and printing will bridge the gap between school, the community and the world of work in an area of Birmingham's poorest employment record.

A Directive Approach

In her work tapping the support of local development agencies, building up personal contacts and applying for funds, Julia Preece consciously pursued a directive style. In her own words:

> As professional fund raiser at this stage I played an almost exclusive part in securing agency advice, application refinements, academic analysis of the research etc.
>
> A more reflective educational and more traditional community work style would probably have required local resident leadership in areas where I clearly led from the front. But I believe the professional educator must also have enough vision to see the potential beyond the immediate.

Apart from the need to motivate people with long-term objectives that transcend immediate problems, Julia also felt that momentum had to be maintained by taking the initiative to raise funds quickly. She was aware that such an approach was problematic:

> A more controversial question is that of full participation at the expense of momentum or achieving objectives. Whilst client 'ownership' is important, this should be tempered by the practicalities of the moment. For instance, if fund raising is a major obstacle to parents starting their sewing club, then get a charity grant to fund it – they can always learn about fund raising later. Success is vital for motivation.
>
> Achieving one's objectives is not always possible without large cash injections and access to the financial system at a pace and level which does not wait for community educators or local residents. Every attempt should be made to involve people at all stages, but once the structural provision – a roof or sewing machine or garden centre – is available, it is then that consolidation of ownership is vital.
>
> Ideally, I should have at least involved a resident in work shadowing me. But two factors inhibited this. City Council timescales dictated delivery points which would have been hard to meet with any consistency by residents. The second issue was the language code required to make the proposal presentable for funding support. As a compromise, however, we were able to allocate a local mother, Jenny Godfrey, to a six month training course, leading to a small business proposal. This meant that the skills element of this package was at least in part made accessible within the community.

Although Jenny's business ideas were not realised, primarily because she became immersed in the daily administration of the garden centre, the training boosted her self confidence which was later reflected in her competence as Secretary of the Garden Centre Management Committee.

Julia Preece frequently 'stimulated an appetite' for community developments amongst local people, rather than just assisting them to achieve goals they had defined themselves. She appreciates that:

> How the project was arrived at can be challenged at length by community workers. It was the educational vision of the potential of a garden centre within the inner city-tapping into residents' interests – which was the driving force, not the campaigning activities of local people.

Achieving Multi-Ethnic Involvement

The directive approach was, to a large extent, adopted in order to motivate local people by retaining clear, long-term objectives and by winning funding at an early stage. A further reason for taking such a pro-active role was to involve Asians and Afro-Caribbeans in the garden centre and prevent it becoming dominated by whites. These three groups each make up about a third of the local population, but the whites are more assertive, have more influential contacts and, in general, as with most white communities, are racialist. If Julia Preece and Glenys Jones had not taken an active part in selecting the Committee it would have soon become entirely white:

> Again the professional 'intervention' was to ensure no one group of cultures or interests dominated proceedings. Although an open invitation was made to anyone to 'join' the Management Committee, additional invites were made to women and members of the black communities to come forward. The result was a start up committee of Asians, Irish, Afro-Caribbeans, plus the person whose idea it was in the first place. Since those early stages new recruits have been drawn from additional volunteers, including a teenager, and identified neighbourhood garden experts.

Thus although a local newsletter invited people to participate in the garden centre, the Committee was selected rather than elected. Apart from a co-opted council officer and Charles King, the professional horticulturalist, the Committee was entirely composed of local people. Glenys Jones and Julia Preece made a great effort to raise the awareness of garden centre staff and Committee members towards racism, and they were assisted by the City Council's high profile equal opportunities policy. This meant it was unacceptable for overtly racist comments to be made in Committee meetings, and no-one would express racist sentiments to Julia or Glenys. Over time attitudes did change, and Julia was very pleased when white Committee members themselves suggested that leaflets about the garden centre should be translated into Asian languages.

> One has to be constantly aware of the wider group needs – the cultural hopes and decisions of those communities represented on the committee. Ongoing effort was made to allow, in particular, the Asian members to achieve. Their translation skills have been used for publicity notices; a Caribbean member is also growing tropical vegetables for sale in the shop. A sense of unity of purpose is attempted by displaying large photographs of these members and other known community faces around the shop.

A Break-through: Prince Charles

By the summer of 1988 Julia Preece was still waiting for City Council approval for the garden project, although plans had been developed and feasibility studies conducted. A break-through came from her contact with Business in the Community: they managed to persuade Prince Charles to visit South Aston in September. Julia describes the effect this had on local people:

> The garden centre was used as a lever to invite Prince Charles and create a day of celebration for local people. What came out of this process was a sense of pride in themselves and a reflection on how individuals had contributed to the totality of South Aston. Confidence in seeing such achievements at all in an area like Aston will, in my philosophy, stimulate motivation for next time.

The presence of royalty had an even more magical effect on the City Council and funding bodies. Suddenly the Council approved the use of the site as a garden centre, and they allocated about £90,000 towards the capital cost. A further sum of about £15,000 was committed by private business – in particular Wimpeys and Barclays Bank – and by UK 2000 and the National Council for Voluntary Organisations.

With approximately £20,000 start up funding secured, the garden centre became viable and a Garden Centre Management Committee was established. In November 1988 Julia Preece was employed as Garden Manager.

Park Lane Garden Centre started trading in December 1988 and Jenny Godfrey became responsible for all garden centre administration. She responds to requests from local people as to what she should stock, while ideas for publicity, marketing and customer events come from the Committee.

In December 1988 an Employment Training scheme was started with the Council's Economic Development Unit acting as the managing agency. As well as horticultural training this provides experience in catering and a printing work shop. There are a total of seventeen ET places and the Training Agency funds a full time Training Officer who plays a major role in the Garden Centre's day to day affairs.

The Garden Centre was always intended to be self-financing (after capital costs). At present this has not been fully achieved, although some local manufacturers, in particular HP, buy all their office plants from the Centre. If other local firms could be persuaded to adopt a similar local purchasing policy it would ensure the economic success of the garden centre and greatly contribute to the local economy. However, as Julia bitterly remarked, in this respect local businesses do not always live up to the rhetoric of 'Business in the Community'. Enough funds have been raised to ensure the Centre's operation for the next twelve months, and an Urban Aid funded landscaping project, administered by the local Police Committee, will ensure a large scale order for plants in 1990. Beyond the Training Agency funded posts the Garden Centre employs two full time staff.

Julia Leaves the Garden Centre

Within approximately one year of becoming the main professional employed for the garden centre Julia Preece was offered another job outside Birmingham. She describes the consequences of her accepting this position:

> It tested the strength of the garden centre's structure, its local ownership and whether all the educational and community development aspects would remain, move forward or disappear.
>
> A number of things have happened. It was not possible to fully involve Committee management in staffing arrangements because my appointment is officially temporary and has immediate, albeit part time, implications for the shop's day to day needs. The 'handover' was rushed, undemocratic and not ideal. Nevertheless, the shop is now entirely in local hands. My job has been replaced by a shared responsibility between the project Chairman who is now acting as a paid 'officer' and greater responsibilities for the two other staff.

In retrospect Julia feels that the transition was complicated by not immediately appointing a new Manager. However, her post is for practical reasons only a 'secondment'. The Management Committee were anxious about being left on their own without professional support, and so she remains Finance Officer on the Committee and therefore retains a close involvement in the Centre.

Reflections on the Role of the Community Worker

Looking back on her work in South Aston, Julia Preece reflected on her role:

> I think I have operated principally from an educational vision. The community worker is more likely to think that targets are less important than the process. Whilst I support this in context, I think there is a more global need to change external structures.
>
> The following four issues are, I believe, essential foundations for the developmental work of community education – but which distinguish this role heavily from that of the traditional teacher:
>
> 1 *Live in or near the area of work* – If we take the earlier premise that community education is a long term process, scheme or topic, the 'live in' approach can be interpreted in context. For my particular role in South Aston I took this literally.
>
> So long as there is a continuity and trust in a relationship, then it is possible to operate a variety of styles. This trust has been built up because I am part of the neighbourhood. I share their lack of services, the broken walls, the graffiti and lack of greenery. We feel the same environment and we therefore know that I am responding as a resident as well as a professional.

2 *Create an acceptable identity* – Acceptability must be tackled by accepting others as they see themselves, culture, values and all. This in turn helps build an 'unthreatening image'. Human weakness is not necessarily a disadvantage if it provides an opportunity for someone else to shine or help.

3 Having assimilated the locality and its 'client' group(s) the community educator needs to *respond to locally expressed need* and start from where the 'student' is at. By starting from our client's point of comprehension (not ours)... the teaching or negotiations grow from a stronger foothold. Whilst the words 'client' or 'student' conjure up images of stereotyped relationships, I hope to show the community education relationship will at least end up as a partnership working together for shared goals.

But the educator, to be different from a community worker, must be pursuing some sort of interventionist approach according to the ethos of education. It is the **way** it is achieved which is different.

4 As professionals we must *evaluate* our own performance as well as the outcome. As participants in a changing political climate it is important to review current trends and needs. I have suggested that apart from an assessment of personal role strategies, the management of the group needs to be considered regularly in close consultation with the group, groups or individuals, with whom the worker should by now have spent some time. Whether this can be achieved in reality will of course depend on a number of variables. However, the principles must at least be on the agenda.

Points for Reflection

- The extent to which local residence allows the worker to pursue initiatives without imposing viewpoints from outside the neighbourhood
- The need for an interventionist approach to enable multi-ethnic involvement
- The importance of local authority funding and the limited contribution of private business.

7 Ferguslie Park: Flagstone Enterprises Neil Graham

The community business described here is one that has already received considerable attention. Neil Graham has written about it himself and others have used it as a test case from which to learn valuable lessons. We have chosen to include this account because:

1 Flagstone was one of the first community businesses in Scotland and as such, illustrates the difficulties experienced by pioneers;
2 the community worker plays a central and official role in the business;
3 the conflict between pursuing political and economic aims for the area was a major problem for the worker;
4 the difficulties in appointing and managing the Manager were significant.

Neil Graham returned to the Paisley neighbourhood where he had grown up, Ferguslie Park, near Glasgow, in 1978. He was appointed to follow up the work that had been done there as part of a Community Development Project (CDP) set up under Harold Wilson's Labour Government. He took over the Information and Action Centre as project leader for the Ferguslie League of Action Groups (FLAG) but, at that time, had no knowledge of community business.

> I didn't have a clue what it meant when I started in 1978. I had worked for an organisation called Crossroads Youth and Community Association in Glasgow, Gorbals and Govanhill – a redevelopment area. The groups I worked with were very much into political activity and challenging Council decisions, mainly about rehousing.
>
> I had come from a community action model of work, and that's what I wanted to translate into my work in Ferguslie. I felt that some of the CDPs in England had had a very high political profile, and were, in essence, an experiment to discover why, when we had a Labour government in power, there were still areas like Ferguslie where there were huge pockets of unemployment and deprivation. The CDPs in England quickly reported that it was the system which created these areas, but I found Ferguslie very reluctant to make these sorts of statements, and so I came very much with the idea of trying to introduce a political dimension that I felt had been missing during the days of the CDP here.

First Move: Origins in a Tenants' Association

Neil arrived at a time when the local Tenants' Association was discredited because of the actions of the Tenants' Association candidates who had been elected at the local elections in 1969. The CDP, which was begun in 1971, recognised the need for a broad based organisation, and produced the label of 'Action Groups' in order to introduce the concept of local activity without assuming that it should take place through tenants' organisations exclusively. However, the new FLAG was:

basically the tenants' organisation that really was two people, a guy who was a friend of the local councillor and a guy who had personal problems. I quickly realised that if anything was going to change in Ferguslie I was going to have to get rid of that guy and by June I had forced a special meeting of FLAG, and one of them was booted out as the Chairperson and the other as the Secretary.

This cleared the ground for a wider representation on the FLAG management committee .

Support: LEAP Advisor

Meanwhile, two events took place which were strongly to influence Neil's plans. Firstly, the Urban Aided Local Enterprise Advisory Project (LEAP), based at Paisley College of Technology, was set up with the remit of encouraging community enterprise in Govan, Glasgow, East Greenock and in Inverclyde. And, secondly, John Pearce came from England to promote community enterprise and work for LEAP.

John arrived in March 1978 and phoned me, out of the blue, saying, 'I've got this job to work in community enterprise'. From then on is the point when I began to get any sort of idea at all about local employment. I explained to John that I saw my priorities in this area as housing but that one of the other obvious immediate problems was unemployment, and though I wasn't terribly enthusiastic about some of the ideas I said, 'I'll help you, if I can'. He felt very isolated and at that point I felt very isolated because I had no sort of reference in this area in terms of contacts, and I knew John had worked in a very useful CDP, so we met a lot and talked.

Proposed Co-operative

This association was to prove fruitful over the years, and immediately led to John Pearce's introduction to FLAG.

John obviously had to go to FLAG meetings and get himself known, and the Chairman said he knew some guys who were interested in setting up a co-operative. I set up the meetings. John came along, did the business with them and me, and got to know them quite well.

There were some ten or eleven men interested in developing an enterprise.

John and I met with them regularly, and John arranged visits to Craigmillar in Edinburgh which was already operating either in a co-operative or a community business. We asked guys from Castlecliff in Edinburgh, which was a co-operative, to come through and talk to them. The FLAG guys had various skills, but generally of a labouring sort – joinery, and brickie skills, so they had an idea of a jobbing co-operative.

During the summer of 1978 John Pearce and Neil spent a lot of time with this group, arranging visits and encouraging them, but they were taken aback in September:

I woke up one morning and opened my Glasgow Herald and there on the front page was this Special Branch swoop on UDA arms sales. And it was the ten or eleven guys that John and I were working with! That shocked me, I must admit. I mean I got hauled in by the Special Branch, who asked me, 'What the .... are you doing with this shower?'

Disappointed, but not deterred, Neil was able to draw on the talents of two highly competent local people who were appointed as Chairpersons at the AGM of FLAG. A woman took on the role of Chairperson and John Bradley became Vice Chairperson. Neil had already been in contact with the woman through his advocacy work. John Bradley he knew less well.

But I quickly got to know John very well, a bright guy, an ideas man. He got to know John Pearce, took hold of some of the ideas that were floating around, and in November approached me and said he had this idea for a business, which was sandblasting. I said, 'Sandblasting?' He goes, 'Aye'. He was a sandblaster by trade, and he says, 'Look at Glasgow'. At that point everywhere you went in Glasgow, in every single street someone was sandblasting. He said, 'There's lots and lots of work to pick up, dead easy to organise, and not a lot of overheads once you get your basic equipment together. What do you think?'

Ideas for Business

Neil and John Pearce set up a sub-group of FLAG to look at employment initiatives. That group of six to eight met regularly, initially at weekly intervals. The group began with some confusion but after a number of meetings began to develop ideas and think about the structure of a community business.

At that point during 1979 people were coming to us with all sorts of ideas. You name it, someone probably came up with it. Eventually the sandblasting idea and the idea of some sort of environmental team were put up. Ferguslie was full of gap sites, so it was to do with cleaning up garden sites and creating small play areas.

Funding

They planned to get financial support from the STEP fund (for Special Temporary Employment Projects). The project was supported by the FLAG sub-group because it would provide work for about twelve people, and was about the biggest project that could be managed with the financial and manpower resources available.

For the sandblasting side of the business there was to be a five person squad, supported by MSC money through STEP funding. This they believed would ultimately become self-financing.

Applications for funding had to be written and, parallel with this, decisions made on the structure of the business. John Pearce drew up the applications and brought them back to the group for approval.

Choosing a Structure

Meanwhile the group tackled the problem of the appropriate business structure:

We were thinking about the structure we wanted – co-operative, community business, whatever. We decided on a community business, because we wanted a business that would always be controlled by a tenants' organisation.

The desire to maintain local control while at the same time satisfying business requirements had produced difficulties.

Once you set up a limited company that limited company is an independent entity, and we didn't want to set up a business that could become privately run or leave the sphere of the tenants' group. We had only Craigmillar Community Enterprises as an example to go on at that time and took a while to grasp the community business idea.

Business Advice

The group was offered advice by numerous well-wishers.

John Pearce had got people to give financial advice about the likely outcome of projects. They also talked about business plans. the MSC guy came and gave us lots of advice and the Scottish Action Resource Centre (SARC) which was meant to get businesses to offer resources to local communities, was also involved.

A blow to the plans fell in November 1979 when a moratorium was placed on all STEP projects, which seemed to bring an immediate halt to this source of funding. However, since the MSC were supportive of the sandblasting project and wished it to have a manager, the group kept up pressure on them to provide an early response to the application and continued to lobby the Regional Council for Urban Aid to provide a Manager, Secretary and running costs. Ruefully, Neil comments, 'As we are now aware Urban Aid takes about a year to approve!'

That was the lowest point in terms of the evolution of Flagstone, from about November 1979 to April/May 1980. Local interest began to wane.

Legal Advice

Nevertheless plans progressed and a community business was established in due course. Legal advice proved necessary, but a satisfactory relationship between lawyer and local group was difficult to attain.

We engaged the services of a local lawyer to do the Memorandum and Articles of Association. Again, this was breaking new ground for the community business. He would be turning up with a draft Memorandum and Articles and expecting to be able to go through them in a meeting with local people in the time he might have used with private business. What might have taken one meeting was taking four meetings to go through so everybody got it clear and were happy with it. Frankly, people weren't terribly interested, very dry stuff.

Waning Interest

Turnout for meetings dropped off, and Neil reports that he, John Pearce, the representative of the Scottish Action Resource Centre (SARC) and John Bradley, the Vice Chairman of FLAG and one or two others were the only ones to attend meetings regularly. It is obvious that, at this point, the possibility of control moving away from local people into the hands of professionals dramatically increased.

Control from Outside

They ran into further difficulties over funding and faced a difficult choice.

The Government was withdrawing a lot of funding from MSC and we were told that we could either have the twelve person environmental team or the five person sandblasting squad. This was quite an important decision and we decided for the five person sandblasting squad as we saw that as having a greater chance of being economically viable because environmentals just clean up and nobody was going to pay to do that in this area.

The wisdom of this decision was borne out by the success of both applications for funding. For the first time the Scottish Office approved an Urban Aid application for a community business in Scotland, and this led to the appointment of a Manager.

By July we had appointed a Manager under the Urban Aid contract and John as the sandblaster for the MSC project, and by September both projects were up and running.

The MSC had already exercised considerable control over what ideas were to be pursued and this continued.

The sandblasting squad had to be called a 'graffiti removal squad' because

MSC said you can't do commercial work. You have just got to do work for voluntary organisations and churches and public bodies. You are not allowed to make a profit.

A Leading Role for the Community Worker: Company Secretary

This led to a desperate search for work which involved Neil, who had, in the meantime taken on the role of Company Secretary, rather against his will. After the long period of delay and discouragement there was now pressure to progress quickly, which Neil responded to reluctantly.

> I was very much against it in terms of my beliefs about community work, but again I suppose it was expedient that I do it because I was around every day and I was able to handle correspondence. It took up an awful lot of my time, far more than I would have ever hoped to have devoted to it given what my commitment to the area was in terms of other issues.

He was only to escape from this burden with the appointment of a manager which relieved him of much of the obligation to find contracts.

Managers

Before the Board of Directors were able to find a manager with whom they were satisfied they had two misfortunes. The first concerned their arrangement to have a secondee from a company. The local radio station got wind of their intentions, and finding the Committee unwilling to give them information on a matter still under discussion, phoned through to company headquarters in Slough and spoke to their personnel director. The arrangement had been made at local factory level and was unknown to the director in Slough, who immediately 'put the kibosh' on the plan.

Selection

On the next occasion they advertised in the local and national newspapers and got about seventy responses. The Board of Directors, who succeeded the original sub-committee of FLAG, appointed another sub-committee to act as selectors.

> This consisted of three or four people, plus me, John and the guy from SARC as advisors. We went through it intuitively, trying to make up our mind on what people had written and how they had sounded in their applications. We invited eight people for interview, and shortened it to four after that. We seemed to be firing in the dark, though everybody who had interviewed had, at that point, a certain person in mind.
>
> SARC organised the personnel director of Coates Paton to come along for the secondary interviews, and after we interviewed each person in turn, that person spent an hour with him. He did a sort of circular chart with all sort of characteristics. So that took the whole day. The guy didn't tell us what he thought. He just gave us what he thought were strengths and weaknesses, and said, 'What do you think?' We said, 'Well, intuitively, we think this guy, and he says, 'Well, that's who I would have picked too'.

They had clarified the criteria for selection. These were that the appointee should:

have had some experience of running their own business first, have a degree of understanding of financial accounts, have some sort of empathy for the idea of community business and being accountable to local people, and, generally, a personality that would fit.

Friction in the Business

A manager was appointed in July 1979, but by September/October of that year the Board of Directors decided that a terrible mistake had been made. However, believing themselves to be a 'reasonable organisation', they persevered for some time.

> There were lots and lots of clashes between the workers, some of whom were key activists in FLAG, and the manager. Perhaps that was inevitable.

Neil attempted to reduce the friction to sustain the business, seeing this as an aspect of his role in the company.

> I was able to talk to John (Bradley) about it very easily. John and I got on extremely well and we were able to talk bluntly to each other. I would say, 'Right, I am going for a pint with you'. And we would go into the pub and I would say, 'John you're not playing the game here. You've got to concede that the Manager's right'. John would tell me some of the other things the Manager was up to, and I had observed myself, and I would agree with him on it.
>
> The trouble was that he (the Manager) apparently made mountains out of molehills and molehills into mountains. He would seem to crack up if one of the workers turned up ten minutes late but he wasn't chasing up work, he wasn't getting the squad together into a style of work that would enable them, after a year's MSC funding, to become a self-financing company. I wasn't happy with his reports or his financial accounting and so, by March 1981, (I was then acting as Company Secretary) I forced the Board into confronting him and laying down some rules that he would have to follow and show improvement in his performance.

Neil recognised a conflict between the need to drive the Directors into confronting the Manager, while himself being a 'detached company secretary' and a community worker. He was no longer able to influence the Board so directly through John Bradley, who was now only an Advisor of the Board, as its employee, and less crucial to its functioning. In the end, action was taken, largely as a result of drawing up plans in association with John Bradley (in his capacity as Advisor).

An Ultimatum to the Manager

> That March meeting took several crucial decisions about the operation of the Board: about the role of the manager, his hiring and firing of his workers, about the need to choose suitable work and finally, about the need to improve his performance within three months.

The next three months were no better. Among other things new premises were not a success, so the final decision to sack the Manager had to be taken.

> By this time the workers had locked him out of the new premises because they were dissatisfied with him but he felt that they were just being obtuse. There were personality clashes, no doubt, but he should have handled them a lot better than he did. He wasn't finding the work, John and I were, just through contacts.
>
> It was recognised that the Manager would have been in post for a full twelve months come July, and if we let him carry on beyond June and we had to take a decision to sack him later he could take it up to the industrial tribunal, which wouldn't be good for us or for community businesses generally.

> So we called him to a meeting in June and went over the decisions we had taken in March. He was most upset. I said in this Board meeting, 'I am afraid we are going to have to take a very serious decision. We either sack our Manager or we sack our ten employees from this area. The decision is ours'. Meanwhile, some of the workers' representatives on the Board were there and others were standing outside, because things had got to a pretty bad stage. I have never felt so bad in all my life.
>
> So the Chair, Jim, says, 'Right, who's going to put it to a vote. You have heard Neil (Company Secretary), you have heard the Manager. We've given the explanations. I am just going to put it to the vote. Do we want to sack the employees or the Manager?' It was unanimous that we sack the Manager.

The Board of Directors and Neil himself reproached themselves for having failed to select an appropriate person, and concluded that they and the Personnel Director of Coates Paton had been conned.

Assuming the Role of Manager: the Community Worker

The period following the dismissal of the Manager was also unhappy, since one of the workers exerted a malign influence on the others – volatile and violent he felt he should run the show. Neil and John agreed that quick action should be taken, and for the time being Neil acted as Manager.

> So my role at that point was 90 per cent Flagstone Manager and ten per cent anything else I could squeeze in. That was a very bad period from about July 1981 to about September/October.

To complicate matters still further some of the workers were arrested on a number of charges. At this time the police were on edge because of riots in Toxteth.

> So I got a phone call on the Saturday night saying that six Flagstone employees had been arrested. It was in the Herald on Monday morning and various funders (who were responsible for the grants) were on the phone, saying, 'What's going on down there? What are you playing at?' It was the last thing we needed!

The consequences were potentially serious since the police raided the premises, while keeping the six men in prison, but they failed to find any other incriminating evidence. However, Neil and the business were in trouble.

> I was getting all sorts of flack from everybody, particularly the funding agencies. My role during that period was to try and calm everybody down and say, 'Look, I think there's been a huge mistake'. The extent of the mistake was shown up by the fact that some twelve months later only two of those arrested were convicted of the minor offence of Breach of the Peace.

A New Manager Appointed

A selection committee of the Board of Directors chose another manager. This time Neil and John sat in as Advisors, but with some hesitation after the last debacle. On this occasion Neil felt that the decision should lie more closely with local people. A person was chosen who had worked as a manager for another company and after twenty-five years had suddenly been made redundant. A period of eighteen months unemployment had changed many of his previously held Tory attitudes, and this together with a good reference from the other company led to his appointment in September 1981.

From this point on, Neil's involvement lessened, though he remained Company Secretary and was the Manager's first point of contact with the Board. As he reflected on this part of Flagstone's experience, Neil concluded that the first Manager had been selected in too much of a hurry without sufficient thought about the sort of person they needed. He, John Bradley and John Pearce had believed that they could carry the newly appointed Manager, the newly hired sandblasting squad and the new business and its Board of Directors through the early days.

> But we didn't have time to teach people and they didn't have time to learn as they were going along. And suddenly major decisions were thrown in our faces, like sacking the manager.

A Role as Mediator

John Bradley, the man with both ideas and technical expertise, clashed with the new manager. Neil found that he had to explain the peculiarities of businesses with a strong community orientation:

> John was also active in FLAG, the tenants' organisation. John would often ask the Manager for time off to go to meetings with councillors about housing and poverty issues. And that used to get up the Manager's nose. I said to him, 'Part of the idea of Flagstone is that it's not your normal business where a guy works thirty-five or forty hours a week and that's all. We want people who work for us to have a greater understanding of the problems facing this area.' The Manager accepted this to a certain extent, and what we tried to do was arrange that John would get a set amount of time – five hours a week – so that he wasn't abusing it. It remained a stormy relationship and I think at least three times the Manager came to me and said he was resigning, and I would take him for a drink and spend an hour or two with him and get it sorted out eventually.

Putting the Business on a Sounder Footing

Further disagreeable decisions had to be made. Five young people were taken on to fulfil a contract with British Rail for basic cleaning. They were paid about £40 a week.

> Which was not bad, given what kids are getting these days. But one of them was cheeky to a BR official. He reported it up the line. End of contract. Five, six jobs down the drain, just like that, because of insolence.

The Manager was therefore starting in his job with only about two workers and not much work. He was using the golf course as the setting for contacting businessmen in building firms, and began to get jobs for the company.

Problems with Premises

Another problem lay in the premises, an old school, which had to be maintained while being constantly broken into.

> Break-ins were killing us, you know: calculators, kettles, all the things that make life a wee bit easier, plus the problem of the damage that was being done.

> So I called an emergency Board meeting in March of '82 and there we agreed that the Manager could hire and fire (which had been withdrawn from the last manager). We also agreed that he didn't have to employ folk from Ferguslie, because by that time some of the contracts required skilled stonemasons and we just couldn't find them there.

They pulled back into the old premises in the Flag Centre, and Neil moved out of his office so the Manager could move in.

A New Financial Crisis

Flagstone Enterprises began to pick up under the new management but soon found itself over-extended.

> At one point we were employing thirty-five people, and trying to fund that was unbelievable. We weren't getting the money in quickly enough to keep the current work going and to pay the current work force. The Manager, John Bradley and I had a crisis meeting and agreed we had better put the company into liquidation, otherwise we would find ourselves in trouble, because we knew we couldn't continue to finance it.

Neil nevertheless hoped to delay the decision during the time he was away with his family on holiday. When he returned he was delighted to learn that the Manager had chased up all the companies who were owing them money. A cheque for £9,500 from one of these companies was enough to save them from liquidation.

Delayed Payments

A basic problem for Flagstone lay in the fact that in the building industry payments are made every ten weeks, so the community business was having to fund a job for ten weeks before being able to draw on the contract money. This was more than the fledgling business could stand. Their difficulties were compounded by the fact that financial help was difficult to obtain.

Reluctant Funding

> We tried, over the years, to get financial help from the District Council, the Regional Council and the SDA, and in the form of overdraft facilities. But they were playing one off against the others so the District Council would say, 'Well, we're not taking a decision until we know what the Region and SDA are doing'. The SDA and the Region would say the same. Creative accountancy certainly helped us survive that period because banks were also refusing the overdraft facilities we were seeking.

The formation of Strathclyde Community Business with its own fund eased that problem .

> You can go to Strathclyde Community Business, get a decision within a month about major funding, and even quicker if the Director or the Chairman agree to it and subsequently get it agreed at a Board meeting. So that's been a major help over the last three or four years of Flagstone (up to 1988).

Other difficulties still beset them.

> The Manager was having to move workers from site to site, as we'd over-extended ourselves. The standard of workmanship fell and companies began to complain, saying they wouldn't stick to their contract as they were having to get other companies in to finish off our work.

There were also recurring clashes between John Bradley and the Manager, but these were not enough to destabilise the business.

> But we were never in the position of being self-financing. We were always in the position of relying on the Urban Aid grant for the Manager's and the Secretary's salary and for living costs. I had hoped that it would be viable by the end of the seven years' Urban Aid funding, which came to an end in July last year, but this has not proved possible.

In 1983 Neil decided that he no longer wanted to be so closely associated with community business, which for so much time had torn him away from other concerns of importance.

The Role of the Community Worker

For Neil, community business was not central to his conception of his role in Ferguslie although it played an important part.

> I saw community business as a means of keeping unemployment on the political agenda, and I saw the concept of community business as being like a tenants' association. I saw it as a place where people who had experience of this area, who knew the problems in this area, would get together and create employment that would be different from working for a private business. It would be, hopefully, more sensitive to the problems of local employees, and the business would in some way challenge existing business practices and structures. I saw it as a natural extension of tenants' associations which were active in terms of challenging housing issues. It was about employment, but it went out into the market place and won business from private business because there was no profit involved. There wasn't to be anybody walking away with £10,000 profits.

Even while he was heavily involved with Flagstone he was still going out to tenants' meetings at night and trying to follow up work that temporary workers were doing. While in some ways resenting the fact that the business took over his life during the big crises, he maintained his association with it because of his commitment to keeping unemployment on the political agenda and his association with John Pearce. Reports from Flagstone formed part of the FLAG tenants' meetings, and it was discussed by councils outside the area. Neil concluded that it reminded people that, 'unemployment in Ferguslie was unacceptable'.

The Move from Tenants' Association to Business

With hindsight Neil recognised that though people who were active in FLAG knew how committees worked and were used to getting agendas, and minutes, it was difficult to translate this knowledge into business understanding.

> I think businesses require managers to report what they are doing, to present a clear business plan that makes sense. I think there's a crucial difference. You have to know whether a business is doing well from one week or one month to the next. To do that I think you need experts. It wasn't until the second manager was appointed and he started to introduce those concepts that everything began to fall into place, certainly for me.

Neil stressed the need for understanding how a business works, first and foremost, 'because you can't take informed decisions unless you do know that'. He went on to conclude that through his own understanding he was able to help members of the Board of Directors to a greater understanding.

Naive Assumptions about Local Commitment

Neil and John Bradley put a great deal of effort into getting 'ordinary people' along to AGM's, and into providing annual reports that would catch the local imagination.

> But basically there was very little interest in the concept of community business in this estate, although there has been a fair number of people who have had jobs through it. I used to have this unrealistic expectation that the people would have some sort of extra commitment because it was a community business, and they were getting the chance of a job that they might not otherwise have got. But the workers used to mess us around regularly, you know.

That was one of the things the second manager brought along, a sort of new realism. He said, 'Look, we've got to get this business running first and foremost as a business. We will get the workers to negotiate with us in the normal practice of trade unions, and we will meet them, not as members of the local community but as trade unionists'. And that started to make a lot of sense to me, because up to then I had tried to bridge that responsibility and duty and tried to see the workers as members of this community getting a job through the community and contributing in some way to the community. But from their point of view they were getting a job, and if they could screw this job for as much as they could get out of it, then they would. Any perks that were going, they would grab them and they would abuse this company the same as they would abuse any other company. That was a bitter pill for me to swallow.

Neil's view that the workers were alienated, 'alienated in the sense that folk are alienated in most jobs', provided an objective way of viewing what was deeply disappointing. The fact that there were able and committed activists participating in FLAG who could transfer to other roles within Flagstone, he saw as encouraging, but this did not obscure the fact that most employees even in community businesses would bring with them the attitudes and values of the 'employee culture'.

Managing a Central Role in the Community Business: A Conflict of Principle

Neil would have preferred to point people in the right direction so that they acquired the necessary skills to enable the business to survive. This did not actually occur, and his role as Company Secretary was a constant source of anxiety.

It was expedient, as I had the basic numeracy and literacy skills that were necessary. I was also available and I had time. That was a key ingredient that made me end up doing it. At every AGM I would point out that I didn't want to do this because I think it's not the role of an outsider, it's the role of a local person. But at the end of the day nobody felt confident. That worried me, as the people I'd worked with in Crossroads had imbued me with a purist and idealist concept of the community worker – you don't take over what the people should be doing. That rankled with me and I was doing it all the time.

He felt himself forced into a central position not only because of his capacity to deal with the written aspects of the job but because of the need to be involved in meetings with councillors and members of the SDA (The Scottish Development Agency). He took along members of the company but found himself presenting the case.

It was my role to speak on behalf of the company, put forward a reasonable case. I had a lot of power because I had a lot of information about the company that local people often didn't have quick and ready access to. That put me into a difficult position as I had the confidence of the local people. They were perfectly happy to sit back and let me do it.

Neil regarded this as a regrettable dependency and put it down to the rush to get into business and the limitations that that had put on training.

The Activists and the Question of Expansion

Some six to eight local activists gave time and energy both to FLAG and to Flagstone. Neil had reservations about this. Firstly, he would like to have extended the committee membership and secondly, he was concerned that the original organisation – FLAG – was suffering as a consequence of the demands of the business. In recent years this has mushroomed to include four or five subsidiaries, as well as the overall holding company. This has led to the same few people going to a large number of board meetings.

Expansion has also led to the drawing in of advisors.

> You now have got folk from the District Council and from the Regional Council. You have got auditors and accountants. You have financial advisors turning up at every meeting, so your average board meeting will maybe be six to eight local people and at least six to eight outsiders.

Community Work Skills

Neil was not convinced that community workers should acquire specific business skills.

> One of the lessons I have learned is that there are people around in this world who are far better at doing accountancy and financial dealing than community workers, and they are the people we should use, without a doubt.

What he stressed was the need for basic community work skills:

> I think you need organisational skills first and foremost. I would hope you had political skills, because I think you would get caught up in all sorts of wheeling and dealing in terms of funding bodies, and I think you have got to hold on to some awareness of what the bottom line is for the area you work in.

A Warning to the Unaware

Finally, Neil recognised that community businesses had become 'flavour of the month' at one time. He was continually called on to give advice, but he observed:

> Various people would learn a wee bit about it and want to set up a community business just like that. And lo and behold, you would find community businesses springing up all over the shop, under-resourced, under-skilled, under-funded or using bad funding. It just gives the community business scheme a very bad name.

Points for Reflection

- Opportunities and opportunism
- Over-extending the key activists
- Local people's unrealistic expectations of community business
- Momentum of changes and Board of Directors' decision-making skills
- Role of worker as educator and facilitator
- Length of worker's involvement in key role

8 Shetland: Mossbank & Firth Community Co-operative Ltd
Tor Justad

The Mossbank and Firth Community Co-operative in the north of the Shetland mainland was formed to solve the geographic problems of retailing rather than the economic problem of unemployment. Although it was not funded by the Highlands and Islands Development Board, it was largely based on the HIDB's model of community co-operative, or Co Chomunn. Its creation must be understood in relation to the peculiar composition of the local inhabitants:

1 95 per cent of them were incomers from mainland Britain and had not known each other before coming to Shetland.
2 they were nearly all in well paid employment and many of them worked together.
3 most of them felt severely alienated from the local Shetland population and their efforts to form the co-operative were an attempt to combat their sense of powerlessness as well as build themselves into a community.
4 they were able to rely totally on their own finance.

The last point makes the project unique amongst those we have so far discussed and perhaps unique amongst all community enterprises in Scotland.

Background

Tor Justad was employed in 1978 as Area Community Worker, North Mainland. His work was essentially concerned with two contrasting parishes, the one, Delting, surrounding Sullom Voe terminal which had changed enormously due to the oil, and North Mavine which was a far more traditional crofting and fishing area. In the Mossbank and Firth area 250 houses were built (100 by British Petroleum and 150 by Shetland Islands Council) for the families of incoming oil workers, which greatly outnumbered the thirty original crofting houses. Tor Justad spent a lot of his time in this area for two years before the co-operative was first suggested, helping with the provision of a new village hall, developing links with a new school, getting play-areas built, working on housing issues, and so on.

The vast majority of the population in the Mossbank and Firth area were there to work in the oil industry. Although they were employed there was 'a certain feeling of alienation' which was connected to several factors:

> The people hadn't been used to living in remote rural areas. Along with that alienation there was also a certain amount of resentment because they had to get involved in raising the community's share of finance (approximately 10 per cent of the total of £140,000) with the balance being provided by Shetland Islands Council and the Scottish Education Department as this building was needed as a venue for social activities. Most of them had previously lived in areas where such facilities were either

provided on a commercial basis or as a direct provision by local authorities and therefore financed through the rates and other sources, but not by direct fund raising.

In addition they were incomers, they felt the chips were stacked against them. If you took the housing issues for example a local person would probably know, (if he didn't know the director of housing personally) he would know somebody in that department or he would know the clerk of works, and through an informal system people weren't waiting for years to get things done, or if they were they had accepted that that was the way it was going to be. Whereas the incomer, not knowing even where to phone, never mind who to speak to, felt very much out on a limb. They felt their employer, B.P., had let them down in that they had expected all sorts of facilities and clubs etc. to be provided which weren't there, and therefore they took it out in the direction of the local authority. This wasn't necessarily doing anything less than any other authority, plus the fact that their services were stretched to the limit, overwhelmed by the influx of people. The whole area had a sort of unfinished look, there were no street lights, there were no pavements, it was like a cowboy town, a boom town. It was the classic planner's error of plonking down 250 houses with none of the facilities that were needed, so that initially there was no school there at all. All the children had to commute to other schools in the area, there was no social meeting place of any kind apart from a church and the old run down village hall. There were no sports facilities; people had to travel six miles to the nearest health centre. People just felt they had been dumped in the middle of nowhere, there was a feeling of alienation and bitterness and resentment against the local community and their own company as well, who had promised them the earth to get them up there.

Very few people at Mossbank and Firth had known each other before arriving in Shetland, they came from 'every corner of Britain' and many had not previously worked in the oil industry.

It was like an overseas posting... I don't think many of them had thought it out when they first came. The younger kids were OK but the teenagers and adults who had been used to an urban lifestyle, discos and plenty of public transport and so on, they felt like fish out of water. There were a lot of casualties, a lot of divorce and a lot now of husbands still working up there but families have moved south and the husbands actually commute backwards and forwards, which is very unhealthy again for the total community because they are just there to work and they are not involved in the community. But certainly there is a fair proportion probably about forty to fifty per cent of the total who are planning to stay in Shetland.

The Residents' Association

The idea of forming some kind of community shop stemmed from the Mossbank and Firth Residents' Association.

This was basically looking at housing and environmental improvements in the whole area; and out of that stemmed the idea of some kind of improvement in shopping facilities, because there was only one shop in the immediate area and it was very unreliable in quality and delivery and freshness, didn't sell daily newspapers, didn't sell a lot of things like baby foods, etc. The newspaper thing was a big issue: when I first came you got your Sunday papers on a Wednesday. It was privately run and despite repeated requests from the community, even to the extent of people offering to work voluntarily in the shop to provide the service, the person who owned it was not interested. He also ran a pub in the same premises and because this was very profitable the shop was not important to him... The Residents' Association were also resentful about the shop keepers in Lerwick, twenty-five miles away. There was a genuine feeling that because people didn't have any choice shop keepers could charge what they wanted, and therefore they resented those prices. That was another negative feeling in one sense, in another it was quite a positive benefit to their commitment because they were determined to get even with the shopkeepers.

Exploring the Idea of a Co-operative Shop

A Steering Committee

The problem of the local shop was raised at the public meetings of the Mossbank and Firth Residents' Association in 1980. These were well attended and following considerable discussion a steering committee was formed to look at the idea of running a retail outlet. Fortnightly meetings followed to consider potential suppliers, sources of finance, legal structures and so on, and Tor Justad was co-opted onto this committee. The motivation to form some kind of store was primarily to provide a decent shopping service, but some people were looking ahead five or ten years to when the oil would run out and were thinking about employment for their children. The Mossbank residents looked to Tor Justad for guidance, but he was learning the subject of community enterprise himself:

> I did my training in community work in 1968 and at that time there was no community enterprise element in the training. I had worked as a purser in the merchant navy so I had some experience of private enterprise and business, but I had never run a business or had any training in business skills. I was relying very heavily initially on the field officers that were employed by the HIDB. One field officer used to cover the whole of Shetland, Orkney, Caithness and Sutherland which wasn't a very successful arrangement, but he would come in response to a public meeting or any specific request up to Shetland. So I would get some back-up from there.

Funding Problems

The field officer was specifically concerned with community co-operatives, Co Chomunn, which the HIDB had been pioneering since 1978. He informed the group about the HIDB's model co-operative and its legal structure, and also about the finance that was available. However, apart from some initial support and information no financial help from the HIDB was ever received.

> The Highland Board will not support a community co-op where there is a similar service being provided in the local area, and the council also had a rule that they wouldn't support a shop where there was a similar shop operating within three miles of it. So that ruled them out of any funding from what would have been the main sources of funding in any other situation. The private shop was the block, because he was there and trading. It wouldn't have mattered if he had sold one packet of cigarettes a week, so long as he was there and was a grocery store. Generally local authorities in fact don't support retail outlets very much anyway, but in Shetland they do. They have a specific scheme to retain rural shops and they will support schemes usually by taking them over; their own property company takes them over and leases them back to a tenant at full commercial rate.

Lack of Support for the Worker

There was qualified support from Tor Justad's employing department, Leisure and Recreation since economic development was not seen as a priority within the department and there was some hostility from the department responsible for economic development, the Research and Development Department towards Tor for his involvement in this field, which was regarded as crossing departmental boundaries.

> I was never told I couldn't work with economic development but it was never heavily encouraged, and towards the latter part of my stay in Shetland it was actively discouraged in a kind of roundabout way – saying that I wasn't spending enough time on other things which were more of a priority in terms of the management's

> views. Although I had backing from the local community and local councillors in the work I was doing it wasn't seen as a priority in the department. Therefore what I actually ended up doing was working double time. I was so involved and keen to see these projects develop that you were having to spend out-of-work time to do that, because of all the other things, so you couldn't give management an excuse to say you weren't doing the things that they regarded as priorities, which is really very sad. I think at that stage it is better to pack it in.

Tor's relationship with the Research and Development Department was always problematical although he tried to seek support from officials, but often had to turn to councillors to seek their direct involvement in support of the co-operative. The Research and Development Department did not see co-operatives in any different light from private enterprise and offered them no special concessions and therefore tended to support the existing status quo of the trading shopkeeper.

As far as his own Leisure and Recreation Department is concerned Tor had to cope with the lack of priority for community enterprise while at the same time trying to offer the community co-operative adequate support and back-up.

> In addition there was the inter-departmental pigeon-holing that goes on which says that economic development is the responsibility of X department and social development is the responsibility of Y department and never the twain shall meet.

Furthermore, few officials in the local authority perceived unemployment as a major problem and there were few specific measures to deal with it in outlying areas, although there was support of prepared initiatives brought to the Research and Development Department for funding, but little targetting of resources to specific rural areas.

> I think because the majority are doing OK, and actually their standard of living has increased, there is a tendency to forget about the minority who are doing actually worse than they were before oil developments.

The steering committee looked for funding elsewhere, beyond the local authority and HIDB, but in every case either their investigations or the community worker's information showed that they would not be eligible.

Setting Up the Co-op

Eventually the steering committee resigned themselves to getting no external funding. In 1982 they decided to raise their own capital by selling £25 shares to Mossbank and Firth residents. 100 shares were sold initially to a population of about 800, raising £2,500 which was all they had to buy their initial stock. This exceptional form of financing for a community enterprise must be seen in relation to the fact that oil related workers were employed in relatively well paid jobs, many earning about £16,000 p.a. For them £25 or £50 (some bought two shares) was not a great sacrifice, whereas for many in deprived areas it would be close to a week's income.

Leasing Premises

Raising their own capital did not, however, allow the Mossbank residents to progress rapidly. Their next problem was finding suitable premises. The local authority ruled out a new building and there did not seem to be any suitable existing buildings. Rather than being daunted the group's determination grew stronger with every setback, and they approached the oil company who were persuaded to release a chalet that had been built for two families, and by knocking out the central wall it became quite a reasonable sized shop. The oil company did not want to be involved in leasing property so they handed it over to the local authority to manage.

> The local authority then put it out for leasing, the co-op's tender was below a tender from another local shopkeeper who already owned two shops in the area, but due to a lot of political lobbying by me and by members of the co-op, the local authority agreed to lease it to the co-op, although they had the lower tender. But the legal department of the council advised that this was illegal and the matter would have to be referred to the Secretary of State for Scotland.

The Secretary of State said the council would have to take the highest tender, and although the local councillors did everything they could to find a way around this ruling, it ended up with the steering committee having to meet the highest offer that had been made. The only concession the council could make was to defer first payment of the higher rent for six months. This legal wrangle took up at least eighteen months, and it was only in 1983 that the Community Co-operative could start trading.

Appointing a Senior Sales Assistant

Once they got the premises the co-op was soon established, providing a comprehensive range of general groceries and most of the things that had not been available at the original shop. However fancy goods and hardware were not stocked. It was being managed and directed by the voluntary committee (now the Management Committee) and for the first three months the only way they could operate profitably was to rely entirely on voluntary staff. After about three months they employed some part-time staff and shortly after that their first senior sales assistant was appointed. The post was advertised both nationally and locally and an interviewing committee was set up, but the man chosen was not a success. Within a few months the Management Committee had come to feel that he lacked the necessary retail and management experience, and furthermore he had not established a good working relationship with them. In the first months of trading the volunteers had built up substantial expertise, and the senior sales assistant had a difficult task of combining this with his own overall management. Getting rid of the senior sales assistant was not easy, particularly since he was a local, but he eventually left by mutual agreement.

After a short space the second senior sales assistant was appointed, who remained there until late 1987. He kept the place ticking over and assured the Management Committee that things were running smoothly, but in fact an unacceptable level of credit was building up.

> Although the committee didn't have the skills to know it, he wasn't doing a good job for them either. I was unhappy. It sounds like being wise after the event, but I never was happy. I didn't have the expertise to be able to translate that concern into actually demanding the full accounts, but I knew he wasn't presenting regular accounts to the management committee... Most community co-operatives certainly try to get someone with business experience onto the management committee... Some experienced people can be totally inappropriate and retired bank managers are not always the best members of management committees. The fact that somebody has been in business does not mean they are any good at running a community co-operative. We had a very conscientious and very hard working treasurer. She was OK at keeping the books and making all the right entries, and she was aware there was a cash flow problem, but she was obviously getting reassurances from the manager, who was being paid to do the job, that everything was OK. Was it my role to push for an explanation of the accounts, or just to try and

convey that need to the other committee members and hope that they would put the pressure on to get these accounts?

This classic community worker's dilemma between a facilitative or interventionist role will be discussed in the next section. The manager left Mossbank Co-operative in the late 1987, again by mutual agreement, although it was made clear that since he had not heeded several warnings his departure was inevitable. He has not been replaced and, like many Co Chomunn, the Co-operative found that a good supervisor is entirely adequate for the running of a retail outlet. Such a person, recruited locally, is currently employed.

A Problem of Capital

Tor Justad's opinions on how the co-op should be managed differed from local people's views in several other respects. He was always very keen to diversify:

because apart from anything else I could see that as a route to getting funding from the council and from the Board, and they could have used that as a roundabout way of getting funding for the total enterprise. They did look quite closely into setting up a small brewery at some stage because there is no beer brewed on Shetland at all. It would be a small operation just supplying initially two or three local pubs, but it might have expanded. But it is a strange community because although they were all incomers they were actually extremely inward looking in many ways and very much concerned with their own front door steps. All they primarily wanted was cheap provisions and daily newspapers. That always remained the focus, to provide cheap and reliable goods. There is nothing wrong with that, but because there were always teething problems and it never got out of the woods in terms of having a settled management committee with a settled manager with no financial problems, it never ever escapes from that. I suspect, wearing a financial cap, that had a lot to do with being under capitalised initially, so that they were always catching up or trying to.

Another difference Tor had with the management committee was over the original shop, which the previous shopkeeper eventually gave up. The co-op took it over against Tor's advice, partly because they felt it would be a loss to the community who had used it for so long and partly because they were worried a competitor might take it over. The shop has been a constant drain on funds ever since the co-op leased it.

Self versus Community Interest

Tor was very keen that the co-op should do van deliveries, mainly as a service for older people without cars (the majority of whom would have been indigenous Shetlanders) and as a way of publicising the co-op. This was never comprehensively developed which reflects the underlying motives behind the formation of the co-operative. It was established for instrumental motives, the mutual self-interest of most local inhabitants, and ideals of a community enterprise never played as full a part in its development as it could have done.

There was a crisis meeting where they couldn't raise enough members for the management committee, and the most vocal people were people who were saying that they had put £25 in and had got nothing back. If you went to somewhere like Barra or any of the other community co-ops in Shetland the idea that you would get anything back from your £25 would be laughed out of court. That is seen as a genuine investment in the community not something you get a return on. But there has always been a committed core of about one dozen people which have managed to keep it on its feet. Membership has changed considerably over the years, with some coming in and some going out. Two of the Chairmen have been quite active Labour Party people with a commitment to co-ops as an ideal. I think as people got into it more they did have a motivation which included the wider community benefit... all the conversion work was done voluntarily, and through the years there has been

> quite a bit of altruism mixed in with the desire to get their own fresh bread and vegetables etc. But at the end of the day it always had to come back to arguments about the price of mustard, or six eggs, the parochial detail of prices and how useless the manager is and this sort of thing.

Recent developments in the co-op since Tor Justad left Shetland in August 1987 have been the provision of a dry cleaning agency and a banking service. A branch of the Royal Bank of Scotland was established and opened two days a week from summer 1987 to summer 1988. The cash flow problems and threats by suppliers to stop delivering, due to the incompetent manager, have led to the management committee approaching the HIDB again for funding. Now that the other shop in the locality is part of the same business they could be eligible both for HIDB and council support, and they are hoping to get a grant that matches the money raised through shares. ACEHI (the Association of Community Enterprises in the Highlands and Islands) are acting on their behalf. The co-operative currently employs three full-time, two part-time and four casual staff.

The Role of the Community Worker

Tor Justad was at an advantage working in Mossbank because he was another incomer himself and therefore seen as 'one of us.' Rather than being viewed as a meddling local authority official he:

> became a sort of friend of the family and the group: it was very much a partnership working together.

An Enabling Approach

He was also lucky in having a particularly determined group to work with who needed very little support to maintain their motivation, despite three years struggle to get the co-op established. At first they looked to him for guidance and he felt that he had 'to keep one step ahead of the group' in teaching himself about community enterprises. If not, an enormous amount of time could be wasted if he was not able to be used as a resource.

However Tor was very conscious of the dangers of being seen as the expert.

> In certain instances when you go to a meeting you want something productive to come out of the meeting so you want to go along with the latest bit of information or handouts, but that doesn't mean that you are going to a meeting every time reporting what you have done, and they just sit back and wait for all the answers. I wasn't in any sense trying to take the initiative away and that is one of the points I make continuously here and I have always made, officials can kill a project stone dead by taking too much of the initiative and in fact if you start getting worried about pace I think we all do this, the tendency is then to jump in and start madly phoning around and writing letters to get the thing moving faster, at the end of the day that is of no help to the group because they haven't been involved in that process and the initiative is taken out of their hands. They will become dependent on your participation.

Tor was co-opted onto the original steering committee to set up the co-operative, and when the first management committee was elected he was co-opted onto that as well. This was his only formal role in the co-op, never acting as secretary and only once as chair of the committee (to resolve a bitter clash between committee members). His policy was never to try and impose his will against the majority, even though he had considerable influence in the early years, and later on the group became more confident in their own decisions.

As we have already noted, this democratic approach had certain drawbacks, most seriously in respect to the failings of the manager. Because Tor Justad decided not to intervene when he had misgivings about the way the manager presented the accounts, and because his suggestions for other committee members to investigate the accounts were not taken up, the co-operative got into severe financial trouble.

Tor Justad feels that in rural areas there is no need for community workers to act as animateurs in the organisation of local activities and local events. The important role for the community worker is in providing a link between the community and the powers that be. Links may be made with national and local agencies, and with specialists able to give advice and support in fields such as community enterprise where no local expertise may be available.

Community workers should also use the contacts they make in their everyday work as a platform for community economic development, an area in which they have a strong interest and commitment, Tor would hope.

> Community workers have a crucial role to play because they have got those skills in bringing folk together and getting them to work together as a group, which can then transfer into economic activity where some of the same basic skills are needed with the gradual addition of additional expertise.

Group Development

Tor discussed the community worker's role in terms of two elements: community and/or group development, and business input. He was clear that the former is essential for a community worker involved in employment initiatives. They must commit themselves to a long term development lasting years rather than months, and during that time they must be prepared to devote a considerable part of their working hours: 'it is not something you can dip into.' Whatever the role of specialist community enterprise agencies they cannot substitute for the community worker's development role.

> Community workers in Central Region would probably like to refer groups to us (CESU – Community Enterprise Support Unit) and not get involved, but it makes our job twice as hard, because we are trying to fulfil both roles, both doing the development process side of it and providing the business input as well. Where you have examples of a community with an active and involved community worker, they don't have to be expert but even the fact that they are meeting regularly with a group, and doing all the sorts of things that community workers will do with any group, is a basis to build on. Whereas if that is not happening at all, and we are expected just to move in and work with a group, there is no way we can work intensively with all of them.

Business Input

On the second aspect of the community worker's role, business input, Tor was rather ambiguous. He acknowledged that he found it necessary to learn the fundamentals of business management for himself in order to help set up the Mossbank and Firth Community Co-op, and that the limitations of a community worker without technical business training were evident from the way the second manager got away with unacceptable levels of credit. He thinks that community workers should have some idea of business management and legal structures, and be able to assess the economic viability of projects, but he also feels that they should not 'try to learn everything there is to know about business' and become experts in that area. Presumably the far more comprehensive structure of community business agencies that now exists across Scotland, in contrast to the early '80s when Tor was developing the Mossbank and Firth Community Co-operative, makes it less necessary for community workers to have technical business knowledge.

What Tor felt was an essential skill for community workers was the ability to refer groups to the appropriate specialist agencies and appropriate sources of finance. A lot of time needs to be spent visiting and liaising with the diverse community enterprise/economic development agencies in order to know which people can best help one's client group. Furthermore, often alternatives have to be sought to the main stream accountants, solicitors and other professionals, since they do not have the necessary understanding of community enterprise objectives.

Points for Reflection

- A community enterprise based on the HIDB's community enterprise model
- Lack of departmental support for the worker
- Ensuring accountability to the management committee
- Conflict between self and community interests
- Intervention to prevent problems
- The use of main stream advisors

9 The Town End Farm Estate – Sunderland North Community Business Centre Alma Caldwell, Dave Irwin

This account is interesting in that it demonstrates the range of initiatives engaged in by two community workers in the space of an eighteen month period. The initiatives reflect something of a continuum of community and employment development which embraces four discrete areas and which called for different approaches and strategies on the part of the two workers. The four areas were:-

1 enabling an individual to re-establish links with the community and to develop his potential for future employment and for the training of others;
2 assisting and supporting two skilled and motivated women identify and pursue their objective to set up a workers' co-operative;
3 enabling and supporting local people develop the educational knowledge base and the practical skills required to consider and subsequently move into self employment initiatives;
4 recognising and responding to the employment needs of the wider group of unemployed people in the local area for whom self employment, or, workers' co-operatives routes were neither attractive nor realistic options, but, for whom the need to be in work remained a pressing concern.

Background to the Project

Alma, the first of the two community workers, had previously been engaged in Voluntary Community and Youth Work Projects, funded by MSC prior to qualifying as a youth and community worker in 1984. Her first post was concerned with developing a homeless project for young people in Newcastle. After two and a half years with that project, she decided to move on and was attracted by the developmental aspect to the post of Project Manager of a new initiative sponsored by a voluntary organisation. This had formerly been an Unemployed Workers Centre and now was designated a Community Education Centre called Turning Point. It was set up as a limited company and registered charity, grant aided through the Education Department.

> The role of the Project Manager was to develop a derelict three storey block of flats into community use with a brief to develop employment initiatives in the area. I didn't know that ground at all but the development side of the exercise interested me. I didn't have business skills and I didn't feel it was realistic to expect a community of long term unemployed to all become 'budding entrepreneurs' so to speak.

I started in November 1986 and my post was for three years. When I got here the building work was supposed to have been completed and ready for me to develop the activities within it. But, because of difficult union negotiations in relation to the MSC labour force, this had not happened. The building work didn't actually finish until February 1988. But, that gave me an ideal opportunity to really find out what people wanted to see happening in the area. The original plans had been drawn nearly two years earlier and of course, the original group of people who were interested had long since disappeared and given up hope as time had gone on. So, I more or less had to start from scratch. I would go and talk to people on the estate, visit groups, go to meetings and generally find out what was going on in the area, trying to do an assessment of the needs of local people; and working with people to change the building plans as we went along.

The following year (October 1987) another post was being applied for through Urban Programme – all the capital had come from Urban Programme. It was for a Training Officer, as, at that time, most of the space in the building had been designated as training workshops. However, through discussions with the management committee and the co-ordinator of Turning Point, I said that I really thought that I would like to find someone who had skills on the business side, perhaps in co-ops and small business because I didn't have those skills. So they changed the designation of the post from Training Officer to Employment Development Worker. We were fortunate enough to find Dave who was a Community Worker, but who also had background knowledge and experience of setting up co-ops, which was ideal for us because it combined the community work element and the business element together. Dave started in 1987 and his post was for four years. So from that point onwards, we worked together to contact local people and find out what kind of small business and training ideas could come forward from the community.

Alma and Dave have been successful in developing within the building, now called the Sunderland North Community Business Centre, a range of leisure, recreational and educational activities which are organised and managed by local residents. These include a youth facility, cafe, gym, computer facilities, a creche, meeting rooms and training and start-up work spaces. However, the following account reflects only the employment development dimension of their roles as community workers attached to the Sunderland North Community Business Centre project.

Rehabilitative Work: Project One

There was a room vacant in the building which we had originally designated as a print workshop. Although the plans had been open to the public and local people had seen them, no-one actually came forward and expressed any interest in a print workshop and I didn't have any real interest in it either . . . so it was just left. As it happens, the caretaker for this building, who is a woman who lives immediately across the road, has a husband whose hobby is electronics in her home He has been long term unemployed and on invalidity benefit for a number of years. He suffers from stress and a nervous problem which doesn't allow him to work due to claustrophobia. At the time he was really isolated in the home surrounded by his television sets which I think wasn't healthy for either him or his wife. It was through his wife that I contacted him and encouraged him to set up a workshop here. It took him a long time to come to that decision but now he is fully integrated. He came across in the evenings when it was quiet and it was empty and set it up and worked on his own. And then because other building users were around in the evenings, he made contact with people, and slowly that brought him back into the community. He repairs television sets and radios and household goods really cheaply at cost price to local people.

He now teaches people voluntary on a one to one basis and that really works well. He gets no financial assistance at all and we don't have a materials budget for the workshop. None of the training workshops we have here bring in an income, other than if there is a television repair, for example, or a radio repair, where there is a very small charge which is donated to the centre to help with heat and light.

The long term possibilities are that if he felt he could cope, then we would look at a business idea with him. But that might be a long term process and he may never get to that ever. However, he might be able to train other people who would be keen to do it. So, something could come of it in the long-term.

The Joinery Co-operative: Project Two

There were two women who worked in the area offering training to other women in joinery skills. Their background was in teaching joinery at a training project organised by the Women's Skills Centre which promoted training courses in non-traditional skills for women. However, the money ran out and the project was closed down, which put the two women out of work. As they were still around offering training on a freelance basis to other groups and projects in the area, we had discussions with them about what they wanted to do themselves and talked about the business idea. Out of that we decided to give them the opportunity to have a go at setting up a business here in this building.

The decision to opt for starting up in business was the result of a combination of factors pressing on the women:

From a practical point of view, one of the main motivational factors behind them doing it was the fact that the joinery teaching work and other odd joinery jobs which they had been doing were building up to such an extent that it was almost becoming a full time job; consequently, they were worried, that somebody was going to 'shop' them to the DSS. So for them it was a question of 'Do we carry on doing this knowing that it is almost becoming a proper job, or, do we make a commitment to trying to do it full time?' A lot of people find themselves in that frame of mind and they were feeling like this at this time. In fact they were quite frightened because they had a number of freelance training courses going on and they were also doing bits of work in people's homes – joinery for relatives and friends and so they had to make a decision.

The Role of the Community Development Worker and the Limits to Economic Development Work

My role hasn't been a typical one because these women are both very highly motivated people. They haven't needed a lot of real personal support that a lot of local people had in trying to start up a business. They already had a good business idea and had years of practice doing it in the informal economy. So for them it wasn't such a gamble. It was a natural progression. They didn't have anything to lose by it; for example, they could go on the Enterprise Allowance and give it a year. That is £40 a week and in their case could be better than being on the dole. It was a handholding exercise more than anything else. Passing them on to the right people.

We negotiated space for them here, and from the start I was involved with them in general discussions – a sort of animation process really. We spoke of how the business could develop: about the different formats, and the different types of business structure which might be suitable for them. They decided that they would form a partnership because they wanted to make a start right away. Again because they had all this work going on and they were worried in case somebody shopped them. But they were also very interested in the co-operative idea because they had been working in voluntary projects which had been workers' co-operatives. However, becoming a workers' co-operative takes longer. We got them going on Enterprise Allowance pretty quickly as a partnership and then we had some informal discussions with a local development agency because of its expertise in co-operatives who continued to work with them.

The Financial Role of the Development Agency

The development agency have a budget for development work which works out something like £500/£600 per new group, and is funded by the Local Authority. That money is sewn up in Sunderland by the development agency, which is why we can't get any! So it was a process of trying to get the group/the agency access to that fund because we couldn't help them here without funds. For example, they needed to have promotional and publicity material, and we just couldn't pay for it. The group also needed money to go and visit other similar kinds of businesses; to do feasibility work – we couldn't offer that whereas the development agency has cash to do that. There is also the Registration Fee which amounts to £200 to register a company as a co-op – they have that – so it was trying to get as much as possible for the group.

The development agency has since been doing most of the development work. The group have been keeping in touch with me and I have been sitting in on the development meetings: really playing the devil's advocate between the group and the development agency. They were very keen to get involved here for political reasons. They were a project funded to work throughout the borough of Sunderland and viewed this as an ideal opportunity to ensure their continued funding as they had been criticised in some quarters for not doing so. So they were very helpful. My role with the group has been trying to capitalise on that by screwing as much out of them as possible.

The women started as a partnership for about six months and then converted their rules through the development agency to register as a workers' co-operative.

Developing the Business

The group are now at the stage where they have got quite a lot of work – mainly on the training side. The actual building of furniture in people's homes and joinery work has taken a bit of a 'back seat'. They have made contact with another regional development agency who have got a marketing guy who has been doing some kind of audit with them to look at where exactly they are making their money. They are conscious that their Enterprise Allowance runs out in six months so they need to have a sound balance sheet if they are going to continue. He's working with them looking at the books; looking at the actual work and just trying to see what is their most profitable areas. They produce really high quality interior furnishings and it may be that their time would be more productively spent doing that and selling it to the right market rather than carrying on with the training work.

The Food Co-op: Project Three

Assessing the Centre's Resources and the Needs of the Area

We recognised if we were to get involved in employment development, that the building here doesn't lend itself to manufacturing, and that it would have to be something in the service sector.

We carried out a simple 'needs-survey', knocked on the doors of about 10 per cent of people on the estate asking questions like 'What services do you need and want?'. We were getting ideas like a 'Supermarket', a 'Cobblers', a 'Launderette'. We were also asking people what their gripes were about living in the area. It was things like 'poor transport', 'too isolated', but the main one was 'the shops'. The prices in the shops are ridiculous because it is so isolated. It costs a pound to get into town and back which is about a five mile bus journey. It costs 50p to go to the nearest supermarket which is in Southwick. So the shops have a captive supply of customers. They can charge what they like and the prices are extortionate. It's crazy. Really we've got the highest unemployed population in the Borough and the prices in the shops are the highest. The shops will charge what the market will stand and people are not likely to hop on a bus and go to Southwick for a loaf of bread; it's just not economical; so they might pay an extra 20p/30p on a loaf.

From my work with developing the local Credit Union, I got round to discussing the findings of the survey with this group and started looking at ways in which we could tackle the situation. Was there anything we could do, practically? I think there were four people in the group at that time who were interested and concerned enough to do something about it.

The Food Co-op – the Role of the Community Development Worker

I've been involved in trying to set up co-operatives in the past and I thought a food co-operative would be a good way to organise cheap food onto the estate because it was quite obvious that there wasn't enough cash in the area to sustain a supermarket – that's why there isn't one. I had the idea of a food co-operative which I sold to the group. There were three men and one woman in the group, all long term unemployed, some for as long as seven or eight years.

We started up as a membership scheme and local people joined. We canvassed in the church, the old people's home, community projects, neighbours and friends and there were about sixty-seven people on the list. They paid a pound a year to join. The group went round the 'cash and carrys' and the trading estates and every week they would produce a list of 'orders' with the minimum quantities which they would need to order to make buying feasible.

We used to distribute the food at a set time every week. The people would pay for their orders on a Wednesday and get their food on a Friday morning. Sometimes they would deliver the orders. It was all paid for, so there wasn't any problem. We would bag it up according to the weight ready to be collected. At the start, we didn't have the money for scales and things like that and I think we raised something like £150 for the project to buy weights and a set of scales.

Factors Affecting the Development of the Food Co-operative

A combination of factors subsequently shaped how the food co-operative group was to develop.

1 The Social Factors

We decided that we should try to provide the small quantities of food that people wanted. If you've got a limited amount of money, if you are living on your own you often can't afford to buy two pounds of sugar. Half a pound of sugar is going to last you a long time. We were selling smaller quantities than the shops. We would also sell loose food because we didn't want to compete directly with the shops. I have got to make that clear, otherwise we would have been in the business of employment displacement not of employment creation. It would be putting the shop out of business. So we didn't want to compete directly, but, we saw there was a market. We were selling things like powdered milk, pulses, flour, sugar, cereal, coffee, tea bags in small quantities that single people could buy. Much smaller quantities than people could buy in the shops.

We would go in to the cash and carry and say, 'We want so many pounds of something, what will you give us it for' and we would get discounts. For example seventy small orders for coffee brings an awful lot of buying power so we were getting great discounts in some of those trading estates. We would sell it and people would get a refund with their order because we had been able to get a better deal. Sometimes it was powdered milk. Last Christmas it was flour for baking cakes. People were getting change back with their order because we were getting a better deal by shopping around. That worked really well. There was a lot of time involved. Bagging up the foodstuffs, measuring it out, going and collecting it, etc. But the group were quite committed to the idea because they were getting cheap food as well. There was also a sense that they were doing something for the area, which was needed.

2 The Educational Factors

At the beginning the co-op didn't even have the confidence to go in to the cash and carry. It was a whole new process to find out how food actually got in to the shops. They didn't actually realise people went out and bought it in.

It was simple and anybody could do it. We went in the car and filled it up and brought it back. And they said: 'Is this all it is; is this all the shop keeper does?' So, it totally demystified the whole process of business and the workings of a business to such an extent that their confidence grew.

3 The Economic Factors

We were getting a lot of orders in, so we thought: 'Hang on; there is quite a lot of money here. There might be a chance to create some jobs here as a registered workers' co-operative.' So we started to do a business plan, a feasibility study and started to write up everything we were doing, or the group did rather, I didn't do anything practical.

It was a training exercise for them to establish skills, the business skills they were going to need if they were going to make it a going concern at a later stage.

So anyway, that happened for a while. We identified three empty shops on one of the shopping precincts in the area that could be a likely base for the co-op and we also identified this place (the Centre) as a likely base for it as well.

4 The Political Factors

We put the idea to our Solicitor, who is also our Ward Councillor and leader of the Council, because we were not very sure about how we stood having people trading in the building, because of our lease. We mentioned the idea of this food co-op who had been working together really well and who were now looking at premises. He drew our attention to the potential conflict of interests bearing in mind the fact that we were LA funded and they could not be be seen indirectly to subsidise competition with existing traders. To pursue the idea could have an adverse affect on our funding.

What we were arguing was that there were two quite distinct goods on offer and two distinct sets of people who would want to buy. We were delivering small quantities of loose food to elderly and housebound people.

However, the group then had to look at an alternative and decided that they could go mobile. There is nothing the local authority can do about mobile shops. You get a hawker's licence and away you go; a transit van and you are off.

We decided we could help them establish the mobile shop idea and that was when they decided to form a workers' co-op. We contacted the development agency we talked about earlier who had cash funds to help the group develop.

Enter the Economic Development Agency

Obviously they needed various bits of money and also help to look at loans for transport. But their experience of working with the development agency was a very negative one. In fact it was an absolute disaster, which destroyed the group. They went from being four very committed, very energetic people in the space of about five months to being – well they got to the point where they just said, 'Sod it!'

They were really frustrated. It was a cat and mouse game. The development agency would come out and work with them on their business plan one week and the next week would say 'That's a load of rubbish, you've done that wrong. That's no good. Go away and do something else'. So they would go away and do something else and then they would come back and they would say: 'That's very good, now you need to do this'. So they would go away and work on it all week and come back and be told, 'What have you been working on that for, you should have been doing this.'

I suspected the organisation did what they did because obviously their time was limited and their financial resources are limited. If they are going to commit a worker to work with a group they have to be certain that the group is committed and that the group has a good business idea and that they are not chucking money down the toilet. So initially they try to make the process of forming a co-op seem as horrendous, as tiresome, as boring as possible so that they can sort the groups out. We have to do it to a certain extent. You don't want to go out giving people false hopes. You tell it like it is and often you err to be cautious and paint it a bit black and I think that went on for a while. I told the group this: 'The worker is just trying to sort you out to put you off to test your commitment.'

The development agency is based at the other side of town and it was very difficult for the group to go downtown to make the meetings because they have got kids. They had to arrange child care to get down and then they had to go by public transport which is an hour's journey or vice versa if the worker were to come out here. The group got so fed up in the end, so frustrated. They just gave up on the whole thing.

The End of the Food Co-op

I was quite firmly identified with the group throughout that time and offered support. Obviously I made contact with the worker (at the development agency) to say that things were not going very well. That wasn't received very well either. We did meet and they didn't get a very satisfactory response. The worker's stance was: 'I'm a very busy person. I've got lots of other groups to work with. What do you expect. We're snowed under here, we're working with thirty groups and there are only six of us', or whatever it was, which was all very legitimate. But I think it was a communication problem. The group needed to manage their lives around this development worker and I don't think the development worker consulted them enough.

Consequently there was a big 'clear the air' meeting which I felt wasn't right for me to attend and I just stepped back from it and the group told her in no uncertain terms what had been happening. By then it was coming up to Christmas so they decided on a cooling off period to reassess. The group had a business plan two or three inches thick at this stage and the only thing they were waiting for was access to funds to get them started to buy initial stock, to buy a mobile shop, etcetera. Over the Christmas period they just decided that it was just too much hassle. It just wasn't worth the bother so it stopped. I can't say I blamed them.

The constraints on the role of the Local Development Worker were also evident at this stage.

We couldn't help either. The group was at a point where they required money and we didn't have it. We did try and negotiate with the Local Authority and say look this is what we are doing, this is what we have achieved so far can we have some development money to help these groups move on to the next stage.

We were told the development agency have it all at the moment. There is no money available. Community Business is not recognised as a valid means of economic development. The Borough's EDU has no understanding of the concept and relates entirely to the commercial sector.

There was no political support. Not just because of the group's background but because they were in the service sector and there isn't any grants to help this sector any more. It is usually grants for manufacturing that are available. The fact that the group had done a study and proved that it was feasible to create jobs, four jobs in all; that they could pay the basic union rates for the work and make a healthy profit and the fact that they had premises lined up at the industrial estate down at Southwick and it was all set ready to go, was neither here nor there. Because they were not in manufacturing, they just couldn't attract funding from anywhere.

The Phoenix

So it just blew up. They were so disillusioned. But it wasn't a total failure – it was only a failure in the sense that this particular venture didn't come about.

However, because the four people had been through that process of doing a feasibility study, actually thinking about alternative forms of employment and confidence building, they didn't want to waste that. So they each individually looked at other forms of employment. One of the blokes now has a base in here and has been trading successfully as a freelance photographer for six months and is doing well. He did an excellent business plan and he went to Barclays or Nat West and they gave him a loan for a couple of thousand pounds for his initial equipment. He wouldn't have been doing that if he hadn't been part of the food co-op. Another guy has started a building firm with his brother using the experience that he has had. They didn't have a lot of capital to start with. They got their initial funding from the private sector. They are going out to the countryside in Weardale and Northumberland buying cottages which have been derelict for years, renovating them and selling them at ridiculous prices to people who are wanting to move to the countryside. The woman is now providing child care for local community groups and she is thinking of doing that as a small business. So, because of that process they have gone on to other things. That is quite common. You often find that. Ideas spring from other ideas and out of people's experience and confidence. So it wasn't a shock that they could do that, because we knew what they were capable of doing.

Widening the Scope of Employment Development

We got the building sorted out. Then we got some employment initiatives going. Then it was a case of, right, there are over 10,000 people out there, most of them are not going to be interested in co-operatives or, community business or, self employment. They just want a job. What are we going to do for them? What can we do for them? What can we help them do for themselves? It has been a linear progression.

That progression manifested itself in three separate initiatives – Training, an Unemployment Forum and a Job Shop

Training

We are working at the moment with The Wearside Opportunity and the Tyne and Wear Development Corporation. TWDC gave us a small grant to do a feasibility study to establish who the new investors were going to be and who the current employers are and to talk about developing links directly with the local community here in terms of offering real job opportunities. The Wearside Opportunity are helping build an extension to the rear of this building to establish training workshops for local people to establish the skills that the new employers particularly require and a private ET Agency will come in to offer the training facility. The training that is going to be offered is directly targetted to the big new investors that are presently negotiating with Wearside Opportunity to move in to this area. What the Wearside Opportunity will be saying to them is one of the conditions of moving in to the area is that they will consider the local long term employed and target a particular percentage of their vacancies towards Town End Farm. That is one of the initiatives that we are working on at the moment.

Enterprise Forum

To establish those links and to keep those links with employers open, we are about to set up a Community Enterprise Forum which would be made up of the representatives from the public sector, the private sector and local people including our organisation, who would meet on a monthly basis and all sit round the same table and look at the employment strategy for this area. This particular estate is surrounded by enterprise zones, development zones, industrial development sites. I think there are about four surrounding this area. So, it's about saying to those employers, 'We are stuck in the middle here. How about giving us opportunities at the jobs that are coming in to the area and getting involved in looking at training schemes for local people.' This Forum is going to start in January, 1990.

However, both Alma and Dave believe that the new employers are not necessarily aware of the needs of the long term unemployed, the young unemployed and women workers and so aim to see that these local employers become better informed.

We are hoping that through this Enterprise Forum that we will be in the right place at the right time to motivate, educate and hopefully create opportunities for local people.

Job Shop

The other thing that we are trying to establish is a local Community Job Shop, supported by the Employment Services and hopefully to be run and managed by local people with advice sessions from Employment Services who will go along twice a week to the area, bringing vacancies with them from their job board. But, through our contact with local employers we are also hoping that they will target a percentage of their vacancies directly into the Community Job Shop which will again give local people a chance at a job. At the moment they have less access to the job market than most people because they are on an outlying estate. Unless they travel to the town centre Job Centre, or Southwick Job Centre (which is four miles away) and camp on the doorstep, any jobs that they could perhaps qualify for in very low skill manual trades, have gone within ten minutes of them being put up on the board, which means they missed the chance. Also the bad reputation of the area has worked against local people even reaching the stage of interviews for jobs. We need to break down that bad image. The new investors haven't got this pre-conceived idea of the area because they come in from other parts of the country, so it is an ideal opportunity.

Community Education and Employment Development

I think among our Community Education colleagues there is a feeling that the Community Worker shouldn't be involved in this field. It is working with the private sector. It is business. It is a dirty word.

Certainly we both felt that Community Workers have been tinkering with unemployment for about ten years and have been working with unemployed people around recreational and educational activities. But you can educate people as much as you like and give them as much leisure activities as you like; what people want – more than anything – is a job and if we are in a position to be able to do that we should get stuck in and get involved in it... Industrial estates are coming. Enterprise zones are coming, come what may. All we are trying to do now is get the best deal possible for local people. We don't think there is anything wrong with that.

Originally the work met with scepticism. But, I think people are beginning to recognise you can get results. Certainly, we have put it on the agenda and other community workers in the town now have picked up on our lead and are trying to copy it. In fact, it is not just in Sunderland, in other parts of the North East people have seen the model we have applied here; the model of grass roots community development. The sort of traditional community work approach of confidence building and small group activity. We are providing a range of employment opportunities and also making links to the private and to the public sector. We are acting as a broker, if you like, as a lever trying to initiate new strategies to bring jobs into the area.

Skills for Enterprise

I think you use all your community work skills and community development and group work methods to motivate local people and to get them involved, to see that they do have value and to heighten their own self esteem. You use the same skills to get people to that stage – it is just we emphasise the economic side of community development.

Communication Skills

However, I think the most important skills for this kind of work are communication skills on two levels. On the level of working with groups of older people, you must be able to communicate often very complex ideas about business structure and finance so it appears simple or relatively easy for people who have not got that background to be able to understand. That is absolutely essential. If you can't do that, if you can't get an idea across you may as well just pack in to be honest. So you need to be a good communicator on that level.

At another level, there is a huge credibility gap between the voluntary sector and the private sector. We are working with the public sector and the private sector. But, to be able to do that effectively, their preconceived ideas about the voluntary sector being bad managers, time wasters, trendy leftists, do gooders, who haven't got a clue of how to manage a budget etcetera – all that needs to be challenged. In our dealings with the private sector if we want credibility with them, we have got to be able to talk their language, as well as communicate our ideas to them so that they can understand what we are doing.

Presentation of the Right Image

Presentation of the right image is also important. Often if we negotiate with somebody, they come here and they are 'gob smacked' with this building in terms of the decor and equipment. It is probably one of the best in the North East: they come out and expect to see a traditional community centre. They have this vision of what a community centre is like and they come out here and they see this, and it has an impact straight away. We back that up with the fact that we have achieved this through sound management and through being able to communicate our ideas effectively with funders. So you need to project your image as well. (In business terms – a marketing strategy!)

Marketing

Marketing the work is an important skill to attract funding and support. This calls for a pro-active approach on the part of the two workers.

It is a conscious decision to do it first of all. You must have vision. We ring people up and say we hear that you have got money going. What is it for and how do we apply for it? If you believe in what you are doing, if you think it is a good idea, why not tell people. 'Look, we are doing this, it is really worth while. Why not give us some money and help us to do it better.'

Let's face it the writing is on the wall for Urban Programme money which is going to disappear or is going to be negligible. A lot of authorities don't have the resources to fund projects to the standard that they should. The voluntary sector has contracted in this area at such a rate that if community workers are serious about putting their ideas into practice, they have to go to private sources. Money is money. It doesn't matter where it comes from, whether it comes from Urban Aid with strings, or whether it comes from Barclays Bank with strings. It is what you can do with that cash rather than who you are getting it from that is important.

Seizing Opportunities

Alma and Dave extended their network of contacts by seizing potential opportunities:

By attending meetings and meeting people. You go along to a buffet not with the sole intention of just getting a free meal but because you know that other people are going to be there. You check the list of potential people who are going to be there. You identify certain people and you bend an ear. If they can't help you, they will mention someone else who can help you and you do exactly the same again.

Success

This facility has been available and equipped for local people to use only since March this last year, so, we are in the very early stages of stimulating local people to get involved in employment and economic initiatives. Measuring success is therefore difficult.

That takes time. The individuals we work with tend to be the long term adult unemployed who perhaps have a skill that is now outdated. They perhaps worked in the shipyards or heavy engineering and were redundant and they haven't got the confidence to walk down to the Enterprise Centre in town and say 'Look I want to start a business. How do I go about it?' We are building people up to that stage. We are going through the process with them. We are saying: 'Look, this is the range of options open to you.' We are not prioritising them; it's their decision. It's whatever they want to do. We are just saying: 'Look if you are interested, we can help you.' Often we say: 'Look there is space here.Charges are minimal and include heat/light and power. There is access to a telephone and photocopier'. There is little risk to 'get involved' and we bring people to the stage where they can then go down to the Enterprise Centre and say: 'Look I want to start a business.' If we can motivate and encourage them to expand and develop their skills, that is one measure of success.

We also measure success in terms of:- credibility with public and private sector bodies, who now actively support our work

- the motivation of those who are involved in the building and its developments; whether voluntary or paid
- the enthusiasm and commitment of local people to make the building work and the pride and respect they have for it
- levels of vandalism, graffiti and theft within the building which has been nil to date
- local people are involved in the day-to-day management of the building. As workers we do not need to be here to supervise all its opening hours
- the individuals who express improvements in their personal mental and physical health since becoming involved in the building.

However, both Alma and Dave were conscious of the work still needing to be done in the locality.

First of all in the estate there are probably still people who would deny that they even knew we existed so we go from that element of the estate to those who are heavily involved and are very active within the building itself. So, I think we still have to get out there and activate a lot of people if we can, and, if they want to be involved.

We are hoping that the new development ie the Community Job Shop, the Training Centre extension and the Community Enterprise Forum will enable us to reach more of the community in terms of providing real job opportunities.

Points for Reflection

- The limited knowledge of economic enterprise held by one of the workers at the outset of the initiative
- The complementary nature of the skills and expertise of the two workers
- The grass roots nature of much of their economic development approach
- The Food Co-op's negative experience of the local development agency and the parallels with the Renton group's account
- Possible problems in handing over the group's development to other agencies
- The constraints on the two workers in developing enterprise initiatives
- The broad strategic response of the workers to local unemployment
- The workers' own professional and educational development as a result of their involvement with the enterprise initiative.

10 Renton: Renton Regeneration David Mitchell

There are three features which make Renton Regeneration, Dumbartonshire, distinctive in relation to the other community enterprises described in this report:

1 David Mitchell, the community development worker in Renton, had already had direct practical experience of a community business;
2 he took on the role of company secretary, which gave him a more direct responsibility in the business than any of the other community workers described except Neil Graham in Ferguslie Park, and Julia Preece in South Aston;
3 Renton Regeneration's relationship with Strathclyde Community Business was not entirely beneficial, and what was regarded as a financially viable project was blocked.

However, other aspects of Renton Regeneration's development give it certain typical characteristics of many community businesses:

1 the community business developed out of a pre-existing Community Programme;
2 there was a group of very capable, committed local activists behind the project;
3 SCB was used as a one-door funding agency, and
4 the community business has become a holding company for several wholly owned subsidiaries.

Background

David Mitchell came to Renton in 1985, employed as a community development worker by the Strathclyde Region Social Work Department. Unlike any of the other local authority community workers interviewed in this study, David arrived in the area with practical experience of a community business. For a year he had previously worked in Ferguslie Park, Paisley, and had been company secretary of Flagstone Enterprises Ltd. He described his remit in Renton as being the broad community development objective: 'to identify needs and try and assist people in meeting them'. However, his team's philosophy was to concentrate on three particular issues: housing, employment and poverty.

Renton is a de-industrialised village of 2,600 people on the road between Alexandria and Dumbarton. David recounted its history:

> At the turn of the century, dyeworks, turkey dye came from here. 'That was the dye that founded the British Empire', was what somebody told me recently! You know, the robes and regalia and that sort of stuff, well turkey dye was used to dye that. Anyway that was the major industry, it was dyeworks, and they were all along the Leven side there, but that's died a death, maybe before 1930. And this place used to be about two or three times the size in terms of population, and so is seriously depopulated.

Even with large employers like Polaroid and Westclox nearby, the male unemployment rate is around 32 per cent if temporary MSC jobs are ignored. Renton folk are rarely employed in the local industries.

Occasionally you get a lot of women involved in short term work, especially in Polaroid. When they are doing special production runs, maybe short runs, new cameras for instance, you'll get maybe thirty or forty local women involved in that, but it is only short term employment, maximum of a year, and then they are off again. Polaroid like publicity. 'We're taking on 200 people this week', and you never hear when they pay them off a year later.

Renton Action Group and a Community Programme

When David Mitchell came to Renton the principal community organisation, Renton Housing Action Group (RHAG), had already applied to the MSC to sponsor a Community Programme, initially intended to provide a grafitti removal squad. In fact it later developed over 18 months to encompass a wide variety of other things: council house insulation, a lunch club for the elderly and disabled, environmental improvements, a local history project and a community newsletter. The last two involved computers in the form of word processors. At its peak the Community Programme employed 100 people, which absorbed most of the male unemployed of Renton. David therefore arrived at a point where local community activists had already taken an initiative in generating employment.

How Renton Regeneration Developed From Community Programme to Community Business

The RHAG activists were well aware of the limitations of a Community Programme even before it was established, and so they were very receptive when David Mitchell suggested the idea of a community business.

It really came out of an informal discussion. We were in the MSC premises and just happened to be talking to some of the main people involved. Basically all I did was inform them that there was the idea of community business, and explain what it was and the concept of it, and that it was attempting longer-term employment at a proper wage rather than a low wage. I think I mentioned it as a possibility, to contact SCB and gave the group a couple of names to contact. Now luckily for them they'd previously had contact with Colin Roxburgh who had been involved in the pre-SCB days, I think it must have been. So they already had some contacts and credibility with a member in SCB.

They took it up. I was in touch with people in SCB and arranged the initial meetings with them. I seek their (SCB's) advice, they (local activists) seek their own, and a sub-committee was set up of RHAG to look at the idea of community business and adapting a bulk buy scheme for food co-ops.

This development was around August 1986, when the first workers on the Community Programme were about to be laid off, having completed a year. Initially everyone involved in the community business sub-committee had been involved in the Community Programme; about half had been managing the CP and half working in it. Numbers at the meetings rose from around ten to twenty or more when it was learnt that jobs might be created through the project, but it was never felt necessary to publicise the meetings widely because in such a small, close-knit community it was assumed anyone interested would have already known of them.

> The idea initially was that anyone who could be identified coming through the Community Programme who you thought might be suited to work as an employee of a community business could be recruited. Like a screening.

Renton Regeneration

SCB considered the various articles for community businesses and set up a constitution; Renton Regeneration was incorporated in March 1987. The new directors of the company immediately negotiated funding through SCB and qualified for European Social Fund money for a vocational training programme. As activists in Renton Housing Action Group they had previously been successful in winning an Urban Aid grant (£11,000) to refurbish a building to be used as RHAG offices. Once the community business had been formed RHAG's intentions altered, and the building (Red Row) was refurbished to become office workspace rented out by the community business. The original Urban Aid funds had to be spent within a month of the incorporation of Renton Regeneration, which gave great urgency to its first activities; and having completed Red Row the work force went on to convert domestic garages that had been burnt out. These were leased to RHAG by the District Council who wanted them off their hands. In the summer of 1987 the community business refurbished Heatwise's offices in Dumbarton. This contract was won through one of Renton Regeneration's directors who was on the board of Heatwise. Since this spate of refurbishment work no more has been undertaken to date.

A Feasibility Study: Mushroom Production

The burnt out garages were given to RHAG on a twenty-five year lease.

> ... We were trying to think of something to use them for when one of the Community Programme workers came up with mushroom production. The idea was initially treated with disdain, but they got a feasibility study done by an Agricultural Consultant who gave them information and said it was viable to do it and costed it out for them. He gave them a feasibility in terms of, not the market, but in terms of production and using their units .... and it was feasible so they costed it up, and investigated the technical details of how to do it. Then they did a small bit of market research by going round contacting the main sort of fruit and veg merchants in the area and locality, and said 'Look, if we can produce local mushrooms, would you buy?' or 'How much would you buy and how often would you buy?' and stuff like that.
>
> Quite big concerns like Caulfields which is a big concern in the area were interested. So basically by contacting three or four different fruit and veg merchants we came back with the fact that those three and four alone in fact even three out of the four would absorb their production totally. In fact I think one of them could have done it – that was the big one – so they then realised there was no problem with the market. It wasn't as if they would have only one person that they could supply to, which would mean if suddenly they decided to cut them off then that would be that ....

They worked it all out and it was a very profitable thing to do.

Rejection by SCB

> Taking the capital out of consideration it was very profitable. They knew they were probably going to get capital to do the buildings up anyway so we were not worried about the capital aspect. Even then the return on the investment was pretty good. Certainly if you leave out the capital element it would break even in its first year and it would make a £15,000 profit in its second year – that's employing two people. Strathclyde Community Business knocked it back on the basis that there wasn't enough employment.

> I thought it was worthwhile because the profitability element could have been used to promote further employment.
>
> It seemed like a good excuse or a poor rebuttal on their part...
>
> The group themselves pushed it and said 'What was the score?' I think basically the problem was because it is mushroom production – I mean it seems quite a silly notion. I mean initially the attitude to it from people here was that it was laughed at, and then when they looked at it more closely they saw the real viability of it and that it isn't a silly idea at all and even when I got to SCB's Board they saw the point. But they have got a monitoring board for new proposals. The capital grant was coming from them to refurbish the buildings so they had a veto on what we did. They said it was inappropriate.
>
> Any mushrooms you buy in the supermarket will almost certainly be from Ireland, the Republic of Ireland and Northern Ireland so that's why these people, the traders, were very interested because the possibility of local mushrooms would be a lot fresher.
>
> Yes. I think it is a huge market. If you think three local traders here could have sucked up their production, no problem, totally absorbed it, then it's a big market.

Other Funding

> The group have not yet completely ruled out the idea, and have found a possible way of by-passing Strathclyde Community Business: we have identified other premises which maybe don't need capital grant and we could get a capital grant from elsewhere and we can use the premises to do that. There is a particularly enormous building we have identified with and it's looking as if we will get money from the Heritage Trust or some Council that is involved with listed buildings anyway ...and the District Council will help too if we can get that from them. Either the area within the building itself, or the basement area which is enormous, could be used.

From Refurbishment to Running Work Spaces

The initial proposal for the community business had been a refurbishing squad who might get building work through the District Council, but as yet Renton Regeneration has not won any more contracts beyond the original work done in 1987. Instead of mushroom production, SCB suggested workspace units:

> so we followed that path and are at the stage of consolidating that. I mean we are virtually there in terms of renting premises out, and again we've expanded beyond that idea to retail premises, so we have now got four shops along there from the kid's clothes shop. These are self employed people. They have support in terms of the Community Business has put up money for fixtures and fittings, to paint the shop, shelves and stuff.

Renton Regeneration either remains in ownership of the furnishings in the shop, or, preferably, the person renting the shop repays the community business over a given time. Apart from initial capital costs Renton Regeneration also provides support through bookkeeping services; there is a self-interested motivation in this, for it allows the community business to monitor the finances of its debtors while ostensibly providing a service. The shops and workspace units are each given assistance according to their individual needs: some frequently use the secretarial staff of Renton Regeneration while others operate almost entirely independently.

At the moment Red Row Office workspace contains a hairdresser, two young women doing catering, the offices of the Heatwise Community

Programme and the local history project Community Programme, the local authority's trading standards and social work offices, and the Renton Regeneration office. The Backstreet workspaces currently have garage services and a self-employed roofer/roof insulater, but a couple of plumbers are also likely to rent space. The shops consist of a domestic appliance repair shop, a child's clothing shop and a double sized unit that will probably be re-opened as a food co-op.

Bulk Buy Food Co-operative

One of the first ideas considered by the RHAG community business sub committee in 1986 had been a bulk buy food co-op. This was actually started in January 1987 on a voluntary basis before Renton Regeneration was officially constituted.

> ... it was mainly committed individuals from the workforce who made up that group who probably in their self-interest invested interest in it .... because they hoped to get employed in it.

The co-op was a non profit making organisation officially distinct from the community business, but in fact it operated under the auspices of Renton Regeneration. However it suffered several setbacks, the main ones being security problems (a lot of stock went missing unaccountably) and its dependence on one particular individual who found paid employment. After he left the co-op closed, but Renton Regeneration still owns a thousand pounds worth of equipment in freezers, slicers, and so on, which makes the re-opening of a food co-op all the more viable.

Renton Regeneration as a Holding Company, Valley Enterprise as a Subsidiary

Once Renton Regeneration had been established as a company with articles/memorandum a problem immediately arose in tendering for District Council renovation work. The community business could not officially trade commercially, since it was charitable, and so to fill in the council forms to offer a tender they would have had to lie about their constitution. It was necessary to establish a wholly owned trading subsidiary, even before they had any business to trade in, and so in the spring of 1988 Valley Enterprise was constituted. At the moment

> ... the Council's prepared to give them work but they have been caught out in terms of not being ready. They have got a workforce but they haven't equipment and they don't want to commit without getting some idea of what kind of work they are going to get. But I think we will resolve that ... the District Councillor involved, I think he is a Housing Convenor, and he is also the local councillor as well as one of the three original community activists in RHAG ... so he is well in tune with what is happening and will support us.

Lack of Local Skills

Valley Enterprise has already submitted tenders for building work, but of the work force they have lined up only one person is from Renton. This is due to the lack of trained workers in the village and the fact that the few people who are experienced in building trades are already working 'on the black' (in the hidden economy). Even in this precarious form of employment they feel themselves to be better off than in a community business. There is a long term intention to train up local people for building work, and the need for a skills audit in the village has been recognised.

A Taxi Service

Another project which the community business might soon get off the ground is a taxi firm. A feasibility study showed that this had grant potential as a consequence of the deregulation of the bus services, and Renton Regeneration is currently applying for start-up funding from SCB for three cars.

Active Participation by Locals

When Dave Mitchell started work in Renton there were three people at the centre of the Renton Housing Action Group, all of whom had been instrumental in establishing the Community Programme. Only one of these people remains active in the community business today, which reflects a constant changeover in the group of activists participating in the community business at any one time. In the early days of the RHAG community business sub-committee meetings numbered twenty or more without any recruitment necessary, for villagers were expecting jobs to be created. The early setbacks with SCB and the Council did not deter these activists but rather spurred them on:

> No funnily enough at that time ...they wanted a fight. The people involved in the early days are tremendously good when it comes to fighting for resources: will fight for anything and win. They are really, really able.

A Legacy of Political Activity

Dave thought this might be a legacy of the political activity which earned Renton a place in the literature of Red Clydeside.

> Renton is famed for its militancy if you like. For a long period the local council has had communist councillors, so it's got a tradition of left wing politics, and certainly there's a lot of people involved in the local labour party. They've got this tradition of political involvement. So I assume it's been passed down.
>
> I mean the notion of, the thing that motivated a lot of people with the community business, was the community control aspect. They felt that their village should belong to them as much as possible, so that's what's peculiar about this. That's got quite negative aspects. I would say most participants are skilled. There's still a lot of people out there in this village who are unskilled; can't read and can't write. There's a lot of that. It's just that the ones who are good are very good, and that's what makes the difference.

Apathy over Management

Although the activists of Renton thrived on campaigning, they were not keen on management.

> The problem with them is that when it gets to a sort of plateau, where you've fought your fight and have now got your resources and it's there and the sustaining period comes in, they're not so good at that and it's not so much that they're not so good at it, they're not so interested. The adrenalin isn't there.
>
> They don't like the managing aspect. I mean that's not true of all of them. There is still some of them there, but certainly just now is a kind of crisis period in terms of people's motivation because there hasn't been a great deal of progress made other than consolidation. People don't see the value of consolidation as much as all the growing. I would say that the majority of the time is spent not so much about motivating them to do things; it is more like trying to stop them and get them walking before they run off with themselves. That's more the role: to dampen it

down a bit, and controlling it and focussing it, more than actually having to motivate people.

Turnover in the Board

Largely because of their lack of interest in management many of the original board of directors left.

> ... people have kind of fallen away, the fighters, and maybe the people who have sustained us. Usually the people with vested interests have come in ... Either looking for jobs or looking for jobs for relations, which is difficult because, the peculiar thing is, it is very difficult for someone not to be involved or a relation in this village. It's so close and everybody is related to somebody else in some way.

Some of the directors left because they found employment for themselves, such as the man running the food co-op, while others became despondent about the way the community business had come to be primarily concerned with renting out work spaces.

> They would have preferred the mushroom idea and reluctantly went along (with SCB's work space plans). Recently there have been noises from the board that basically we shouldn't go into this. Now that's fair enough as far as it goes, but it is not merely a question of creating a community business. (Work spaces) help create employment in some respects, but it's self employment and they don't really see that as the avenue to follow. OK it's another way of employing people, but they would prefer to have an actual Community Business which employed people.

> A Director is resigning on the basis of 'I don't want to be here to be a Factor. I want to be here to be creating Community Business.' I couldn't argue with him, you know. He is involved in the church so that's what he's doing. He is giving more time to that.

As far as Dave Mitchell is concerned, the departure of certain other directors is not to be regretted, for they were do-gooders, scandalmongers and shit-stirrers. Notwithstanding this latter group, the lack of consistency on the board of directors has been a major problem for Renton Regeneration. Apart from the one original community activist who has played an important role since RHAG days, the only other long-term members of the board are from outwith the village: the Regional Councillor, a further education lecturer and David Mitchell himself. Dave feels that perhaps too much is being expected of the directors, and either the board will become increasingly specialist and professional and distant from the village, or the directors will have to be paid in some form, in which case they would become more accountable.

Extending Membership

At the moment there is a tendency for the community business to be seen as only representing a limited group of individuals within the village, according to David Mitchell. To combat this a newsletter is being produced with the front page devoted to community business activities and the rest full of information on anything else going on in the locality. It is intended to communicate what Renton Regeneration is about, to encourage people to get involved again and to attract new members. It is hoped that the closure of the community programme in August (resulting from a decision not to collude with the new MSC benefit-plus regulations) will give a new boost to the community business. The skilled workers on the programme are likely to take an interest in Renton Regeneration, which could be particularly valuable for the newsletter:

> They are doing stuff that involves using word processors and research, stuff like that, so they're pretty skilled individuals. The signs are they are also involved in newsletter production to a large extent. I would imagine that they will be quite keen to investigate business ideas to keep themselves employed. They are all local people too.

The Community Worker's Role

When discussing his role in Renton Regeneration David Mitchell continually emphasises how competent the initial participants in the community business were. This was partly due to their involvement in the community programme and partly to their years of experience as community activists; he did not feel there was a need to develop any generic skills prior to establishing the enterprise.

> I found that the thing that struck me most was how these people were sophisticated: not the way the (community worker) course depicted them, as poor, deprived people, unskilled etc.

Since they were so able, and had such enthusiasm to campaign, Dave played a fairly minimal facilitative role once he had informed them of the concept of a community business and put them in touch with SCB.

Advice on the Constitution

> But if I feel that my experience could benefit them then I will chip in. There had to be inputs in terms of meetings to discuss the main articles of the constitution. I put a lot into that meeting, because I had had experience of how (a community business constitution) could work, like the example of what to do if board members don't turn up and can't be made to resign... The constitution is a pretty intimidating document. It's all in legalese.

Dave went through the model constitution explaining the different options open to the group, but adding fairly direct advice on the basis of his experience as company secretary of Flagstone Enterprises. As a result the main articles of the constitution were resolved in one meeting rather than three or four, which might have been necessary if he had played a less directive role.

Company Secretary

At meetings of the board of directors Dave tries to play a background role in decision making, only contributing his views when he feels his particular expertise makes them valuable. On one occasion he found he had the decisive vote on a contentious issue of temporarily loaning people £1,000 to start on the Enterprise Allowance Scheme. He would not be persuaded to cast his vote (although he was privately clear about his support for the proposal), and instead the decision was left to the next meeting when more directors were present. But this largely passive role in meetings belies Dave's considerable influence as company secretary of Renton Regeneration. His experience in this role with Flagstone meant that early on in the development of Renton Regeneration he was persuaded to take on the post. He was not at all happy that this key position, of instructing the administrative worker, furnishing information and signing documents, should be taken by an outsider to the community. However, once he had set the precedent of fulfilling the role competently everyone else was very happy to let him continue in it. Worse still, the other directors would pass on to him administrative duties and decisions which they might have taken on themselves. Consequently the role of company secretary became far more arduous and responsible than it might otherwise have been, and so the local activists were all the more averse to taking it on themselves. Recently Dave has threatened to resign, but 'People are scared of the responsibility: fear of the unknown.'

Skills and Attributes Needed by the Community Worker

David Mitchell is quite clear that his community worker training did not prepare him for work in community employment initiatives.

> I hadn't a clue. It was totally new ground for me. I had never been involved in employment issues in any capacity, so I floundered, and I think the community business manager, if it hadn't been for a very good community activist, would have run roughshod over everybody including myself. But that wouldn't happen now, I have learned a lot. So I felt very ineffective, and I don't think my training prepared me for it at all. There wasn't anything on it, not on my course anyway.

Nevertheless his training was valuable in providing group work skills which, he feels, are essential for working with local people in almost any subject area. What he lacked was any understanding of the process involved in setting up a community business: 'I don't know whether that can be taught or whether that just comes in time.'

The sort of areas Dave feels could be covered in a training course, which community workers should be acquainted with, are assessing economic feasibility (market research, operating costs, overheads), looking at different models of constitutions, and knowing the various sources for funds and how to fill in the application forms. Something else that is of great value to a community worker involved in employment initiatives is personal contact and credibility with the business world. In this they have a double handicap, being in a profession that is conventionally antipathetic towards the private sector and being in locations that are often no-go areas for business.

> I know this from personal experience of Flagstone. When I was a company secretary, there was a building merchant's company who the community business were trying to get credit from. Now my stepfather happened to be the credit controller for this firm, and he phoned me up and told me that he normally looked at the directors' list and if they were not from Ferguslie Park, they get money... He phoned me and I said they are solvent and you won't have a problem, and they got the credit, but if it hadn't been for that contact they would have been written off because they are based in Ferguslie Park.

A community worker's experience, contacts, and credibility with the private sector are all extremely useful in helping to establish a community business, according to David Mitchell. However it is usually the community business manager who has the greatest link with the private sector, coming from that sphere himself. These contacts have to be exploited to the full, even to the extent of allowing the manager Friday afternoons to play golf with his business friends, as was done in Flagstone Enterprises.

At a wider level Dave thinks private sector involvement in community businesses is essential if they are to survive. They have to be dissuaded of their perception of community enterprises as amateurish, and they have to be encouraged to second their able staff to assist community businesses (not just their surplus personnel).

Questioning the Community Worker's Response to Unemployment

David Mitchell is not convinced that facilitating community businesses is the best way for community workers to tackle unemployment in deprived areas.

Problems in Sustaining the Business

> I'm now beginning to wonder about it in terms of time commitment. If you do it right and there aren't problems your business manager should mop up the majority of the stuff, but if you get problems then the involvement becomes greater. Certainly if everything works all right then ideally you only have big commitments at the start. If you get key people appointed, like a business manager and directors, and they are relatively sound, then you can withdraw at that point. It would be quite logical for you to do so. I've found that the problems are after that. The problems arise in sustaining it, and I wonder if it's worthwhile.

Contacting Local Employers

An alternative approach to unemployment which Dave has considered is to campaign for greater recruitment of local people by the neighbouring employers. This could be done on at least two levels: to investigate the companies' employment policies and attack any discrimination against local folk, in the style of the famous American campaigner Saul Alinsky, and to link up companies' personnel needs with training schemes for local people. Dave thinks that welfare rights work should be left to others (e.g. social workers) because it tends to be very individualised case work, not really community development, although he has been involved in benefits campaigning.

The practical ideas Dave has about a community worker's role *vis à vis* unemployment are reflected in his criteria of success for a community business: 'to sustain as many jobs as possible for as long as possible for local people.' Second to this objective comes education, and Dave feels that more could be developed in Renton to this end. Unfortunately local activists have little motivation to attend the SCB courses on business management, particularly since there is no proper accreditation.

Dave concluded our interview with a rather negative summary of the community worker's role in community businesses, based on lengthy experience:

> So I just wonder about it. If it works out OK fair enough, but if there's problems then they always end up on your lap, at the most inopportune time. If you can be very ruthless about it, get in there, do the initial work, get them set up, get a business manager, director, then go, then fair enough, it's worthwhile, but in my experience it never works like that.

Points for Reflection

- The quality of the participants
- The use and effects of a Community Programme
- Problematic relationship with support agencies: compare with preceding account of the Town End Estate food co-op
- The use of capital/equipment
- Dependence on a small number of activists

11 Little Hulton Community Enterprise Project Ltd
Karen Minnitt, Cliff Southcombe

The Little Hulton Community Enterprise illustrates the kind of community economic development that can be achieved in less than two years when community workers pursue a project pro-actively. This account highlights four features of the Little Hulton enterprise:

1 the diverse local economic development that can be established within two years;
2 the involvement of local activists in a project initiated by the professional workers;
3 the community enterprise structure of a non-trading holding company linked to largely autonomous smaller enterprises; and
4 the partnership between a community enterprise development worker and a community worker during the early stages of the project.

Background

Little Hulton is a massive post-war overspill council housing estate, seven miles from the centre of Salford, Greater Manchester. It was built around the core of a former mining village and is divided into five separate estates, the residents of which maintain relatively distinct identities. The population of 20,000 includes three large disadvantaged groups: the unemployed (registered unemployment stood at about 20 per cent in 1986 which was probably an underestimate, being primarily male unemployed); single parents (the illegitimacy rate in 1986 was 46 per cent, which gives some indication of lone parenthood), and the disabled (over 2,500 registered disabled in November 1989). The ground level housing in Little Hulton has led Salford Council to relocate disabled people there from the high-rise flats elsewhere in the city. To some extent these three groups overlap, but the figures above show why Little Hulton ranks with inner city areas of Salford as one of the most economically marginal and socially disadvantaged estates in the city.

The Little Hulton Community Enterprise Project was initiated by two professional workers: Cliff Southcombe and Karen Minnitt. Cliff Southcombe was employed as a development worker in January 1985 in the newly formed Salford Community Enterprise Development Agency. Although this soon changed its objectives to promoting small business start-ups, and came to be known as 'Start-Up', Cliff Southcombe retained his original job description. He had previously worked for four years as the Co-ordinator of 'Community Routes', a community transport scheme in Hattersley that grew into a large community enterprise (*see* MacFarlane, 1989 for an analysis). This gave him considerable experience in local economic development: assessing the viability of diverse business ideas; understanding the advantages and disadvantages of a community development approach, and finding the most appropriate constitutional structure for community enterprises. Before working in Hattersley Cliff had trained as a Youth and Community Worker and had also completed the first year of a Business Studies degree course.

In his new job with the Salford Community Enterprise Development Agency, Cliff Southcombe went around the council housing estates looking for a suitable site for a community enterprise. He found some estates much easier to work on than others because there had previously been 'some element of community development or community organisation on the estate'. Unfortunately these areas were the exceptions: the local Labour council was fairly conservative and had not funded much community work in the past.

The Mobile Community Shop

In 1985, following a meeting at which he spoke to the Salford District Labour Party, Cliff Southcombe was invited to Little Hulton by one of the three local councillors. He was eager to initiate some kind of community enterprise, and together they organised local meetings about the potential for community economic development. Out of these meetings arose a 'Local Economy' workshop, attended by about twenty people who were recruited by the councillor. During the day the local economy was analysed and measured, a skills register was drawn up and ideas for retaining money within the locality were considered. The councillor proposed starting a mobile community shop and within a few weeks a Steering Committee of interested people was set up (primarily professionals and councillors), a van was secured and volunteers were recruited. The community shop began operating in October 1985, but very soon a combination of inter-estate rivalry, the involvement of the 'worst kids', too hasty a start-up, and, above all, poor local leadership and bad management led to its demise. After a few months it was taken over by a local MSC project. Although the community shop was unsuccessful, it left Cliff Southcombe with a fair understanding of the economic potential for Little Hulton, and a clearer view of the local social relationships.

> The important thing was that, at the end of nine months, by being on the estate I had a fairly good idea of the estate and who was doing what, and what the divisions were, and where the talent was.

The Initial Idea for the Project

Karen Minnitt got a job as a community development worker in Little Hulton in October 1985, employed by the Salford Council for Voluntary Service (CVS). She had completed social work training the previous year and had been doing voluntary work in the area, in particular setting up a Welfare Rights Drop-in Advice Centre. Karen had lived on a local council estate since 1981 and her prior experiences of life as a single parent reliant on state benefits meant that she had first hand experience of some of the problems faced by residents in Little Hulton.

During her first few months in post, Karen began to compile a directory of local voluntary groups and statutory organisations which was later published as the 'Little Hulton Information Guide'. During this period of local investigation she became aware that the problem of unemployment in Little Hulton was being dealt with through the provision of around 200 short term MSC

Community Programmes' places. These were administered by a large voluntary sector agency which was neither locally based nor locally accountable. The agency initiated new schemes within the district with little or no public consultation and began to snap up available buildings that were sought for use by local informal groups of residents. Karen was concerned that these short term schemes were potentially subject to a sudden withdrawal of funding with consequent collapse of services to the local community. They were outside of local control, had an increasingly poor reputation, lacked any long term commitment to the area and, because of MSC rules, tended to discriminate against women. There appeared to be a need for a project which overcame these shortcomings.

In the spring of 1986 there was a CVS staff meeting about the churches' role in Urban Priority Areas, arising out of the *Faith in the City* report. This meeting prompted Karen Minnitt to make contact with the local clergy in Little Hulton, and in May she met Bill Taylor, the Area Dean. He was enthusiastic about *Faith in the City* and mentioned that Salford Education Department had just handed back to the Parochial Church Council a school building in the centre of Little Hulton. Karen immediately saw the potential for such a building and arranged a further meeting to introduce the Dean to Cliff Southcombe and to discuss the future of the school. Cliff suggested converting the building into a multi-purpose community facility with workspaces, an idea which Bill Taylor liked and which he implied his congregation would support.

Soon after this initial meeting it was learnt that other uses for the school were being suggested (including a lucrative offer from the 'empire-building' MSC agency), and so Karen and Cliff felt a 'directive' approach was demanded if the opportunity was not to be lost. Within a few weeks the Parish Treasurer was consulted on costs, an architect was commissioned to examine the potential of the building (funded by Start-Up), an application for funds was submitted to the Voluntary Projects Programme of the MSC and the Parochial Church Council (PCC) was approached for their support.

By September 1986 the three instigators considered they should involve more people in the project. Because of worries from within the PCC that control of the school building could be threatened by any new 'community' project, there was a decision (which may appear undemocratic) that the number of places on the proposed Steering Committee would be strictly controlled so that the PCC reps outnumbered the community reps by one. Thus, a Steering Committee was effectively handpicked: the Dean selected five members of the Parochial Church Council; Cliff invited various professionals with whom he had previously worked (a businessman from the Action Resource Centre, a solicitor, a community architect and a representative from the Greater Manchester Co-op Development Agency), and Karen invited four local activists.

In his previous work Cliff had learnt how essential it is to co-ordinate the contributions of outside professionals to community schemes and he therefore drew up contracts between the professionals and the Steering Committee. Karen aimed to select people who would be responsive to the idea of a community co-operative, who were assertive, who knew the needs of their community and were not enmeshed in inter-estate rivalry, and who were generally respected by others in Little Hulton. They were all socialist and each had a history of local voluntary involvement, in organisations such as residents' associations, welfare rights groups, trade union branches and the local Labour Party. They all happened to be women, since these were the people Karen had been working most closely with; this gave some balance to the Committee since four out of five of the PCC members were men. None of the local activists had been involved in the Community Shop experiment.

The first Steering Committee meeting was held in September 1986. Cliff presented the idea of a community enterprise to the Committee and a list of potential initiatives for development was circulated. Following discussion the members decided to prioritise three ventures which they considered would be particularly valuable in Little Hulton: a clothes recycling business printing facilities and a café. The Committee agreed to set up a community co-operative for the following reasons: to allow participation amongst workers, volunteers, users, community groups and local residents; to allow individual groups to retain their autonomy; to establish a holding company for the purpose of building up assets under community ownership and control; and to maintain accountability to the local community.

Cliff and Karen were authorised to make further applications for funding, while the Dean was encouraged to approach the mayor for support. In subsequent monthly meetings Committee members suggested further ideas for development in response to expressed local needs. Most of the ideas considered are listed below (those marked with an asterisk have been developed since 1986):

Ring and Ride for housebound persons	Workshops for start-up businesses
Lone parent information and support centre	Small office spaces
* Computer services	* Clothes re-cycling
Draughtproofing	* Sewing, knitting and other crafts
Community cafe	* General information and advice
* Printing services	* Credit Union
Creche facilities	Estate security service
	Theatre and media project
	* Launderette

A division of tasks quickly emerged with Karen and Cliff fundraising, Karen and the women activists starting a clothes recycling business in a modest way, and Cliff, the solicitor and the PCC members concentrating on drawing up a draft constitution. Rather than involve the whole Committee in joint activities, members were encouraged to pursue those tasks that they were interested in.

The Community Workers' Approach

Cliff and Karen employed a rather directive method to establish the Steering Committee for the Enterprise Project but they offer differing explanations for this course of action.

Cliff does not subscribe to the conventional community work principal of prioritising local involvement and control. From his experience with Community Routes in Hattersley, Cliff had concluded that when a community worker 'comes in and simply applies strict community work models it simply doesn't work: it doesn't work with the people and it doesn't work with the enterprises'.

Karen, however, regards local participation and control as principal goals for the Enterprise Project. She viewed the selective creation of a Steering Committee as a necessary compromise to allow the Project to begin functioning, and believes that without this initial closely circumscribed structure lack of trust between the 'church' and the 'community' participants would have prevented it's conception. Substitutions on the Steering Committee began to occur fairly soon after it's formation and no complaints were received from local people who felt excluded. Elections held later allowed open access to the

Council of Management for any member of the Project.

Cliff's concerns about the conventional community work approach can be reduced to three main points:

1 The most fundamental problem is that conventional community workers do not recognise why local people get involved in community enterprises.

> The work of a community development worker is to develop groups, and the purpose of the groups is about people's development and their ability to make choices and control their own lives . . . one of the principles of the community worker is that local people will eventually run and control the enterprises, and my job as a community worker is to eventually step back and release the reins. I have great problems with that: it assumes that people aren't going to move on.

Cliff's experience suggests that most competent people involved in community enterprises do move on, in fact that is often one of the main motives for their involvement: to use the project as a stepping stone to provide the skills and experience to get out of the estate. 'These enterprises have a death factor, in so much as all the people with ability move off the estate at the first opportunity'. The benefits of community enterprise for individuals are not necessarily the same as the benefits of community development that are claimed for communities.

Karen commented that:

> This has not been the experience in Little Hulton to date, but it may occur later. Most of the active participants in this Project are women, many of whom have dependent children, and they cannot easily gain paid work elsewhere because of child care problems, benefit earnings restrictions and lack of well paid employment locally. Some of the volunteers have become paid workers within the Project (albeit on a part-time basis) and those who have gained alternative employment have so far remained living in the estates and generally retained close links. In the main, I believe that most of the Project's volunteers and workers regard the benefit to the community as being of equal or greater importance than their own personal ambitions.

2 the business needs of the enterprise are often in conflict with the principles of community work, particularly in relation to meeting deadlines and making executive decisions; and

3 the ideal community worker 'works herself out of a job' and hands over control to the community, yet it is often the professional input from someone outside the estate that is the catalyst for a successful enterprise.

Steering Committee meetings were run in a formal manner right from the beginning of the Project. This was not problematic because the Chair, elected at the first meeting, was already skilled in the role and encouraged dialogue between the various sections of the Committee. Virtually all the participants were experienced in formal 'business' meetings from their membership of other groups, eg trade unions, PCC, Labour Party branches and so on.

This formality at the committee level contrasted with the informality of the first trading operation which developed along fairly conventional community development lines. 'Off the Rails', a clothes re-cycling scheme, was initiated by Karen with women Steering Committee members and volunteers who had been recruited by word of mouth and through the local paper. Meeting once weekly, and forming no defined management structure for the first year, the volunteers gained experience in pricing and labelling, selecting and displaying clothes, financial control and book-keeping, presentation and sales work, public relations, publicity and advertising. After several months of operation, one of the volunteers began work on a feasibility study to re-open the local derelict launderette, an idea which had been raised at the formal Committee meeting by one of the 'community' reps. Thus 'Bubbles', the launderette project, effectively grew out of 'Off the Rails'. The volunteers retained close weekly contact through the clothing scheme, and this supported them through the frustrating period of waiting for funds to materialise to re-equip the launderette. After one year, the volunteers, all of whom were women, had built-up the confidence to make the leap from a once weekly clothes sale to a full time service running a shop. Karen summarised how local participation and control worked in this project:

> They had moved the clothing scheme along at their own pace and in their own way. Once shop premises were acquired, they decided to formalise their structure and created a Committee which gave power to the Secretary who became a Voluntary Co-ordinator. The shop functioned without a paid worker for a year and offered an increasingly professional service. Eventually, it generated sufficient income to employ a Co-ordinator, who brought extra skills with her.

Most of the initiatives that were eventually developed into viable businesses were included on the list of suggested projects which Cliff and Karen had presented to the Steering Committee at it's first meeting. These largely matched the Committee's views of the needs of Little Hulton and also Karen's analysis of the problems. Cliff had added some more imaginative ideas to the list, eg a Credit Union, a theatre, a media project and an estate security service, but only the Credit Union has been developed to date. This contrasts with Cliff's experience in Hattersley where ideas were successfully 'imported'. He explained his misgivings about brainstorming local activists for business ideas:

> People will come up with things which they've been exposed to or which are obvious to them or which reflect the local trade and industry. We deliberately did a list away from that because we think that community enterprise can be much more imaginative. One of the things we learnt at Community Routes is that a lot of the ideas come from outside: if we'd just used the community work process of getting indigenous ideas we'd have been stuck with painting and decorating. The ideas of a taxi for the disabled, a transport scheme, inflatables: they all came from elsewhere. One of the problems is to raise people's expectations . . . to try and get people to think a bit more energetically. So we drew up a list of starter ideas . . .

The collaboration between Cliff and Karen during the initiation of this project proved effective despite their differing goals. Cliff visited the project about once a week and was mainly involved with the creation of a suitable legal structure and the recruitment of outside 'professionals'. Karen worked full time in the area and was able to provide regular direct support and trouble-shooting expertise, with the primary aim of community development placed before the secondary aim of creating viable trading operations.

Training

From the start members of the Steering Committee recognised their need for training in order to make an effective contribution to the project. Cliff distributed a questionnaire for members to indicate what they considered priorities for training, and a number of training sessions were held on Saturday mornings.

Co-opted professionals on the Committee were asked to give basic introductions to their area of expertise, thus the lawyer guided the group through constitutions and the businessman explained business plans.

Because of the recent collapse (with heavy debts) of a Salford based MSC Community Programme agency, the men from the PCC (who were largely owner occupiers) were particularly concerned not to take on any financial commitments (either personally or for the project) without first being clear of their liabilities. They therefore identified 'legal implications' as the first priority for training, and Cliff met this demand with a workshop in January 1987 which took them through the issues of ownership and control of enterprises and the various models of community enterprises currently known. Although the Committee were presented with various options as to the most suitable structure for the enterprise, they adopted the model advocated by Cliff which was essentially recreating the structure of Community Routes.

The Constitution

At the first AGM in 1987 the community co-operative was legally established as a Company Limited by Guarantee. The structure adopted was designed to be highly flexible. The holding company, Little Hulton Community Enterprise Project, owns all the assets of the various associated 'satellite' projects, since these are regarded as part of the community's wealth. Since the holding company is not trading it can claim charitable status which greatly broadens its eligibility for funding. The holding company provides support services to the affiliated businesses and employs a Co-ordinator to assist in the maintenance and development of the Project. The business ventures within the community enterprise are largely autonomous trading organisations which are not allowed to hold any assets. Their constitutions vary to suit the particular circumstances of the business. Cliff described how, within a community co-operative, there are different ways of setting up enterprises, all of which are legitimate:

> The first one is the top-down one. Someone in my position has a well thought out idea that's been used before and you set it up and recruit people for it. At the other end of the spectrum a group of people come to you and say, 'We've got a good idea, can you give us some help in doing it?' We say, 'Yes, we'll give you the support and we'll fund raise for the assets.' Those are the two extremes, and in between those are various permutations.

Membership of the Community Co-operative is open to anyone who lives locally, anyone working in either the autonomous businesses or the holding company itself, registered volunteers, recognised user groups (even if outwith the community), plus anyone else the Committee wishes to co-opt as a member. It thus involves the workers in the community enterprise in a direct way, unlike the Scottish Community Business model which only allows membership to be bought by local people.

Funding

Cliff and Karen felt it was essential to win substantial funding within a few months of the first Steering Committee meeting in order to convince the Committee that the project was feasible and to prevent the group breaking up. Initially they therefore took the responsibility to raise money themselves, but later on they clearly had the greatest expertise and therefore the Committee still deferred to them to complete funding applications.

Apart from applying to the MSC for Voluntary Project Programme funds, Karen and Cliff applied to over a dozen charitable trusts and statutory bodies in the first few months. Their applications were based on a provisional first year budget which included the employment of two full time project workers, capital costs for office space, volunteers' expenses and running costs totalling £62,000.

The first breakthrough came with a grant from the Royal Institute of British

Architects to pay an architect to re-design the school building. This boosted confidence and allowed professional plans to be included in future applications for funds. By May 1987 Karen and Cliff had secured a £5,000 grant from the Tudor Trust with a further £5,000 to follow in 1988, a training grant of £2,000 from Start-Up and funding for a community development worker to work for six months full time on the project. The person appointed was David Eatock who had previously worked in CVS; when his contract came to an end funding was found to keep him employed part time for a further six months. The Project then ran without a Co-ordinator for the next fifteen months until funding was acquired for one year. The new Co-ordinator, Julia Morgan, had been both a volunteer and part-time paid worker within different parts of the project since 1987.

The search for funding has never been entirely straightforward. The original application to the MSC met a favourable response and the Steering Committee were led to believe that funding would be forthcoming right up until the Voluntary Projects Programme was dissolved in August 1987. An Urban Aid application took two years to be processed, but it was worth waiting for, bringing £14,800 for office and training equipment, launderette machinery, kitchen renovation, printing materials and clothes re-cycling machinery.

Later grants were sought for specific businesses, rather than to provide core funding for the community co-operative. Karen worked closely with Julia Morgan, then a volunteer from 'Off the Rails', on fund raising for the re-equipping of 'Bubbles' launderette. Brian Barker (Action Resource Centre) was also involved in fund raising for 'Bubbles'. The following bodies were among those which contributed either to the Community Enterprise Project as a whole, or to the individual enterprises within it: British Telecom, the Clothworkers' Foundation, the Glynwed Trust, the Granada Telethon Trust, Norweb, Salford City Council Urban Programme, Shell, Start Up and the Tudor Trust.

Local Involvement in the Community Enterprise

Within three years of the first Steering Committee meeting a wide variety of businesses and activities were established, and representation of local people in the management of the Community Cooperative had changed. Originally local representation on the Committee was made up from the 'appointed' PCC members and community activists, few of whom had regular involvement with the daily activities of the Project. Over time, a broad range of local residents have become involved in the different ventures within the Enterprise Project, and through election many 'active' people, both part-time workers and volunteers, have gained a place on the Council of Management. The Project has over sixty members and a Council of Management of twenty directors.

Karen described how, apart from creating several part-time jobs, the Project has harnessed voluntary participation in many forms.

> For example, when 'Off the Rails' (the clothes re-cycling scheme) moved into shop premises on the local precinct, the property was rapidly adapted and decorated by volunteers. Local firms donated materials, such as a window, a door and quantities of wood, and these were utilised by unemployed volunteers. When a Playshed was latter added to the shop, the bricking was undertaken by the Chair of the Council of Management, the concreting was carried out by the husband of the shop's Voluntary Co-ordinator, the woodwork was jointly undertaken by a PCC rep and an unemployed volunteer. Finally, the children of the volunteers painted the internal walls with their own cartoon characters.

The transfer of 'Off the Rails' from the school building (now known as the Church Hall) in 1988, represented a significant change of direction for the project. It had become clear that the PCC members of the Committee had hoped that the Enterprise Project would generate enough income to solve the church's financial problems (by providing rent from the building), but they did not wish to hand over sole use of a large part of the premises to the Enterprise Project for workspace. The decision was taken to concentrate new developments in other locations in the short term, with the registered office and printing project remaining in the Church Hall. Karen described the current accessibility of the Project to local people:

> 'Off the Rails' and 'Bubbles' (the community launderette), both situated on the local precinct, have become the public face of the Enterprise Project and function as informal community centres. Many local residents call in daily just for a chat and new contacts are made, new relationships formed, which bind individuals together in a mutually supportive network.

Businesses and Activities

'Off the Rails' Community Clothes Shop and Information Centre

The clothes re-cycling project 'Off the Rails' began its life in the St Paul's Peel Church Hall in April 1987. It opened once weekly, selling donated good quality secondhand clothing at economical prices. Demand for the service gradually built up so it was decided to move the project into shop premises to make it more accessible. 'Off the Rails' is staffed by volunteers and a part-time paid Co-ordinator; the clothes are donated both locally and from as far away as Wensleydale in Yorkshire. Income from 'Off the Rails' pays for the rent, rates and running costs of the shop and the Co-ordinator's wages. It also pays a regular sum to the LHCEP to support the work of the Project Co-ordinator. Further, 'Off the Rails' pays for the costs of running an Information Centre which is based within the shop.

The shop is now open five days a week. Income from 'Off the Rails' has supported other community activities including a 'Women's Health Day' and the Little Hulton Carnival, as well as the LHCEP, and surplus clothing has been distributed to many local groups for fundraising activities.

Information Centre

On the same premises as 'Off the Rails' is an Information Centre that offers a weekly welfare rights 'drop in' session backed up by specialist advice from the Social Services Welfare Rights Officer. On alternate Thursdays a Little Hulton Councillor runs a surgery at the shop. Once a month there is an opportunity for individuals interested in setting up a business to take advice from Start Up. The shop also provides office space for the organisation of the annual voluntary sector 'Little Hulton Carnival', and the annual Enterprise Project Summer Playscheme is also run from here.

'Bubbles' Community Launderette

The 'Bubbles' launderette opened in April 1988. The previous launderette had shut down over a year before, leaving the machinery in such a serious state of disrepair it was not viable for any ordinary business person to consider reopening it. However, the Little Hulton Community Enterprise Project saw the possibility of bringing this much needed service back into existence, while also creating jobs. A volunteer with 'Off the Rails' undertook a detailed feasibility study which involved visits to other community launderettes. Funding applications followed and within a few months the Project managed to attract grants of £17,500 to provide new machinery.

The machinery bought remains in the ownership of the LHCEP and is leased to 'Bubbles'. Bubbles is registered as a Common Ownership Collectively Run Company (workers' co-op), and employs one full time worker who is assisted by three part-timers.

Streetgate Printing

In July 1987 a print service was started which included the production of a free monthly Little Hulton newsletter (circulation 2000), and printing of leaflets, posters, newsletters and letterheads for local community groups and businesses. This has included printing a quarterly newsletter for CRY-SIS, a charitable organisation whose National Co-ordinator is resident in Little Hulton.

The LHCEP has an off-set litho, photocopier, headliner, and other machinery and office equipment provided by Salford CVS who obtained a grant from the Trustees Savings Bank Foundation. Recently, a second litho machine has been purchased. All of this equipment has enabled the print service to develop, assisting many local community groups.

Credit Union

In January 1988 a public meeting was held at St Paul's to launch the idea of developing a Credit Union in the Little Hulton area. The meeting was addressed by Joseph Yewdall, Chair of the National Federation of Credit Unions, who subsequently visited Little Hulton monthly for a year to undertake training of the committee members. The Credit Union has developed alongside the welfare rights service to enable people to gain control over their finances, reduce the activities of 'loan sharks' in the area and encourage people to work together for their mutual financial and social benefit. The Credit Union currently has forty members and became registered in October 1989.

Future Planned Development

Negotiations are currently taking place (as at December 1989) to obtain a derelict house located at the centre of one of Little Hulton's most deprived council estates. This centre will be operated as a multi-use building incorporating community, training and employment projects. Initially the centre will be run by Little Hulton Community Enterprise Project who will develop it towards being a self financing independent company limited by guarantee. It is planned that the centre will be used by established groups for specific purposes rather than as a drop in centre. Uses being considered include: childcare provision, meeting rooms, adult education, office space for support agencies, training for women in new technology and researching employment initiatives.

It is also planned to set up a landscaping project as a subsidiary of the LHCEP. 'Greensleeves' will be operated by one person initially and not only engage in landscaping/gardening, but also handle recycling waste products and environmental education.

A further plan is to start a van service which will service all subsidiary projects in the Community Enterprise, in particular 'Greensleeves' (transporting workers and equipment), Off the Rails (for clothes collection and perhaps a furniture collection), and Bubbles (for a laundry collection and delivery service).

Points for Reflection

- A project initiated in a directive manner, subsequently developed using a more facilitative approach
- Compare the need for pro-active approach with Ruchill Community Business
- Structure of largely autonomous businesses
- A business idea identified and developed by experienced community workers

12 Ruchill: Greater Ruchill Community Business Ltd Caroline Coleman

Greater Ruchill Community Business provides an example of:

1 how an active community group and dynamic community worker can establish a successful community business in six months;
2 the central role of an experienced community enterprise agency in achieving this;
3 the drawbacks of establishing the business so quickly from a community development point of view;
4 the problems of business management that can arise once the business is trading.

Caroline Coleman went to Ruchill, in the north west of Glasgow, in 1983, to work on an Urban Aid funded community medicine project, called the Ruchill Community Project. Although she had worked in many different areas such as community care and welfare rights advice, she had no experience of community development work and had no formal qualifications. Her immediate impression of Ruchill was that:

> there were absolutely no facilities at all, no place for the youth to meet. There was bad housing, pre-war housing not modernised, a lot of poverty and a lot of people not aware of what their benefit entitlement was: that was a task for the workers. There were a lot of single parents and elderly, and also people not having the confidence to approach authority or being able to send a letter.

The only community group was the Community Council which, at that time, was not very active.

> They met once a month and looked at things like traffic, and maybe somebody had a broken bathroom or something like that, simple things, no organisation, no campaign facilities, badly organised, possibly for the lack of direction.

Initially Caroline Coleman was entirely involved in advice work, but the project provided a catalyst for community development, first, through the need to train the entirely local management committee of the Project how to manage, and second, by establishing the Ruchill House Improvement Campaign. The management committee were elected by Ruchill inhabitants and although they had no experience as managers they turned out to have great enthusiasm for learning. Crossroads, a youth and community development organisation, provided their training.

Local Awareness of Community Businesses and a Crucial AGM

The management committee and Caroline Coleman became aware of the possibilities of a community business when they set up a food co-operative in 1984/85. The local activists wanted this to be a workers' co-op and they sought funding from a number of different sources, being successful with the MSC, Urban Aid and the Health Department.

> We then approached Strathclyde Community Business for a start-off grant. It was the co-op's idea. I was working with the group and we looked at a number of possibilities. Certainly I had given them all sorts of bumf and literature, but they themselves decided to contact SCB. I always feel that there is no point in having experts coming in to tell a group what is on offer unless they are ready for the change. Unfortunately we did not fit in with their philosophy of a business because we were not profit making: the aim of the co-op was to provide cheap fruit and vegetables. So although we had the lease of a shop we did not want to go down the avenue of a business. That was the first experience that I had with Strathclyde Community Business and the structure of community business, and the first experience that the volunteers of the co-op had. Strathclyde Community Business did provide training for the co-op in terms of book-keeping and management, however, and it was very useful.

In October 1986 the Community Council had it's AGM and Caroline suggested that they invite two speakers from SCB, an idea that was supported by co-op members who were on the Community Council. Not only did representatives from SCB attend the meeting but also the Area Manager of the District Council Housing Department, and after the main business there was a long discussion about employment initiatives.

It was resolved to form a steering group to look at the possibility of establishing a community business and this was welcomed by the Housing Area Manager. He told the Community Council that Glasgow District were intending to arrange a contract for security guards in the Ruchill area, and that in Possil Park, 200 yards from Ruchill, such a contract had gone to Possil Community Business. Glasgow District were pleased with this arrangement, which they found very cost effective, and it was suggested that if Ruchill could form a community business within six months they would get the security contract. If not, Possil would get it.

Forming a Community Business

This was a great incentive to act fast, and things progressed rapidly after the AGM:

> We met immediately after that meeting, the very next week, because they were aware that if they could get their act together they would get it. They weren't elected. There was a steering group formed at the Community Council meeting by just asking who was interested. There were 6 or so people agreed that they were interested in the possibility of setting up a community business. Myself and a colleague who works here within the Community Education Department agreed to convene that meeting. It was held here and the first meeting was really just a general chat, about the AGM, about the speakers who had come out, about what we thought, where do we go from here. So we decided then to get back in touch with Strathclyde Community Business. That task was given to the chairperson of the co-op because she had previous contact with them, and they came out the next week, the development officer of SCB, to talk to the Steering Group. Almost immediately it was decided: yes, this was what we were going to look at.

The group then had to tackle how they would go about establishing a community business, what its aims and objectives should be and how a board of directors should be formally elected.

Caroline Coleman had no business experience at all, so she was keen to leave the specialist training to the SCB development officer (a division of roles discussed later). What she felt would be a valuable contribution to setting up the business was to publicise it as widely as possible and to carry out a skills survey of the neighbourhood (an idea suggested by the group). The survey combined both objectives for it involved going from door to door enquiring about the skills people had and the kind of training they would like to do, so all households in the area came to hear about the proposed community business. Organising volunteers to carry out the survey turned out to be a nightmare, particularly since the group failed to get any funding for it, but although the co-ordination might have been better the main objectives were achieved.

To meet the aims of a community business it was imperative that local participation should be maximised, and so one of the objectives of the survey was: 'to try and involve as many new people as possible, and not people who had been involved in other community groups.' SCB insisted that to be a real community business at least a dozen local people would have to be involved on the Steering Group. At the time only six people were meeting regularly, so beyond the publicity involved in the skills survey, posters were put up, adverts placed in the local community newspapers and individuals sought from existing community groups. Much of Caroline's time was taken up in encouraging wider participation which led to the Steering Group's expansion to twelve members.

While the publicity and survey were under way the Steering Group members embarked on a wide range of courses in committee procedures, SWOT analysis, business skills, accountancy, marketing, advertising and so on. This intensive training was organised on a weekly basis by Glen Buchanan, training officer of SCB, once more general topics had been explained such as the basic steps to be taken in forming a community business, how grants are applied for and how a board of directors is formed. SCB secured funding from Urban Aid of £36,000 p.a. for five years, extendable to seven years, by which time the business was to be self-financing. this money was to cover the salaries of a manager and a bookkeeper/administrator, as well as all running costs (which were substantially reduced by a cheap lease for offices from the council). Because of the urgency in setting up a community business the training had to be fairly directive: there was no time for the group to explore the issues long enough to recognize which skills they needed to learn for themselves.

Conflict Between Community Work Practice and Business Practice in Rapid Development

The need to meet the council's deadline meant that establishing the community business and training to be able to act as directors demanded an enormous commitment from the Steering Group. It also necessitated an ability to learn fast and act under pressure, and the consequence was that some people dropped out.

> People have moved on and people dropped out. A core group of people were given responsibilities and specific tasks because of trying to meet the deadline; I think perhaps the less able folk on the Board dropped out because we had to look at other community businesses, draw up a contract for security, look at forming a community business and all that that entails with the liability of what a board of directors is, formulate the aims and objectives of a community business, make an application for money: it had to be done very quick. This had advantages and disadvantages. It had advantages in that a small number of people were very intensively trained and some blossomed out of it, but along the way we lost some people. I think it is possibly necessary in terms of forming a community business, but may be bad community work practice... You have to be aware of this conflict. As a business, particularly at

the beginning, you might have to make decisions very quickly, and some people on the board might not understand them. Whereas as a community worker I would always want to be clear that people always knew what they were voting on: a slower process.

Despite some of the original participants lacking confidence to take on the responsibilities involved in setting up the business, Caroline felt that the remainder of the Steering Group worked well together.

They mostly knew each other. The ones who had done community development they understood committee procedures, but some people who had never been involved before stayed with the group. I think they have developed an awful lot because they learned a lot of new skills, which are different from other community group skills, and also they are very aware of the company and that they are liable. Most people found it very interesting, very challenging, and enjoyed the training sessions and the input from other professional workers: the process of addressing each particular part of setting up a community business, the objectives and strategy for them. Each training session was separate: they had notification of what it was going to be, it was very structured. I saw them become a very strong group.

The Ruchill activists succeeded in meeting the deadline, and in April 1987 a formal constitution was adopted for Greater Ruchill Community Business. Glasgow District Council then turned out to be late, and it was six weeks before the contract for security patrols was secured. There were twenty jobs to be created in the security business, and when they were advertised 1,500 people applied. This mass of applicants was reduced to forty by excluding everyone from outwith Ruchill, and the Board of Directors (ex-Steering Group) then tried to encourage some women to apply. Very few expressed interest because of the assumption that security guards have to confront intruders, whereas in fact they only have to report them. The one woman who was appointed declined the job when she realised there were no other women, which was a disappointment to Caroline Coleman.

Management Problems

As soon as the community business had been established the post of manager was advertised in the national press, but the salary that could be afforded –£13,500 – was not expected to attract someone with extraordinary business experience. A sub-group of the Board of Directors were trained by SCB on how to establish what they were looking for in a manager, how to interpret application forms, and how to interview. Caroline Coleman was away when they appointed the manager, but by the time she returned, six weeks later, they were already dissatisfied with him. Like many other unsuccessful community enterprise managers, his business background seemed to be at the expense of any community development skills. The Board knew this, but they had not expected his unwillingness to share future planning with them, nor his poor negotiation skills with district and regional councillors.

There was no community worker around to assist him either, which might have been helpful, but I was away for six weeks. He was also told he would get support. SCB, in fact myself, advised them to look at a model of training for him and call in a consultant to assess him. They were really adamant he was going, and that is what happened. I supported it because they are local folk and that is what they wanted. I don't really think it was good practice... I am not so convinced that with some sort of training and negotiation he may have been the right person. He mostly patronised them and they were not prepared to put up with that. It is a difficult job – community business manager. So that left them without a manager, they gave him a handout

> when he left and they couldn't afford anyone else. Also, a publicity manager was appointed in my absence and he started two businesses on the recommendation of the previous manager and there was no funding for that.

The publicity manager turned out to be a source of contention within the Board, for although he was very good at his public relations work, meeting a lot of politicians and building up the business's image, he was unable to generate his own income. This had been the naive assumption of the Board when they agreed to his appointment. When it was clear that the business could not afford to pay for someone to be exclusively concerned with public relations, most of the Board wanted to terminate his contract. However, two directors argued for his retention, largely because they were friendly with him, and this became an acrimonious issue dividing the Board into two camps. In the meantime the publicity manager was made acting manager, in the absence of a new manager, and for six or seven months the Board took on much of the management work themselves, with the invaluable help of the administrator. She ran the office, Caroline negotiated with politicians and the Board managed the workforce. Caroline thinks that the Board had perhaps become over confident in the six months prior to establishing the community business, and the problems of management once it was trading came as quite a shock. Nevertheless the business did not lose money as a result of poor management during this period, and the directors learnt a great deal from the experience.

A new manager was appointed in May 1988, selected in the same way as his predecessor but with the proviso that whoever was chosen would have had some kind of experience in charity or community work. With his appointment the publicity manager's contract was terminated since there were not the funds for both posts.

Diversifying the Business

The Board of Directors always intended that Ruchill Community Business should diversify beyond security contracts, but the management problems side-tracked them. Several consultants were asked for suggestions and the directors went to Lewisham in London to see its self-built houses project. This idea was explored in detail but was abandoned because there were no factory units in the area.

> George Innes, a volunteer business man who lived in London, was back up on holiday and they roped him into doing some work for them. He planned a number of factories and approached businesses on their behalf with a number of different ideas, but they couldn't get space for anything they looked at, whether viable or not, there was no space anyway.

A knitting project was considered and rejected, but more promising was French polishing. Although contacts were made with Arnotts and Frasers and others who might have given them work, this idea never materialised, and to date the only other business besides security is a painting and decorating firm. It is called G20 Decor, and employs two people.

> G20 is the post code: we don't want to call it community business because they think it will detract if they are tendering. Community business has not yet reached a stage where it has got credibility... But it is going badly, because of the business, badly because of the fighting on the Board. They had a lot of very good ideas that were not pursued, but they will be pursued. I suppose in a way it will also have strengthened the local folks' ability within themselves, because yet again they have come over another hurdle.

Caroline is optimistic about the future, with hope that the community business might get the contract to build a planned extension on the Ruchill Community Centre. She hopes the manager would be able to negotiate an advance with the Region to buy the necessary machinery and tools and then pay this back later. There is also a plan to develop training for young people of a more substantial nature than the YTS. This would be based on market research on the mismatch between jobs and skills, and would be organised in conjunction with the job centre and local colleges.

Broadening Participation

Ever since the community business was first being developed, Caroline Coleman saw one of her principal roles as a community worker being to widen local people's involvement in the project. Membership of the community business was initially priced at 50p and 100 people paid to join it, but in keeping with the conventional image of the business, most of these people were men. Caroline is hoping that the Board will make an active attempt to involve more women:

> An AGM is due quite soon, I was suggesting that perhaps at the AGM they should not just promote community business but perhaps alongside have a Well Women Clinic and that might attract women in, that is the kind of things I could set up. I have discussed this with the new manager and he seems to think that is the kind of approach they would accept.
>
> The Community Business AGM would be from 7.00 to whatever, coffee and tea will be available, and we would have posters and a video and make it like a whole day of it. Make it an attractive day and have creche facilities so we can attract parents, and it is local for people to come in. Obviously folk are not going to come in all day for that, but they might come in and then come back.

However, Caroline is careful not to be seen to be trying to dictate the profile that the community business should have: this should be left to the manager and the Board of Directors. 'I see the role of the community worker to encourage other people around here to perhaps join the Board of Directors.'

Recently it was decided to make membership of the community business free in order to expand numbers beyond 100.

The Community Worker's Role

When the idea of a community business was first explored Caroline Coleman felt insecure in her role. She saw her skills being in community group work and, in particular, developing groups, which was quite different from business ventures. 'I don't have that kind of background.' This is generally one of the main reasons for community workers to be averse to getting involved in community enterprises. Caroline concentrated on the skills survey and trying to maximise local participation in the project, leaving the technical business matters to the SCB outreach workers. However, she attended all the Steering Group meetings (later to become Board of Director meetings) as a non-voting adviser, and

> there was concern by some people on the Board about where did my role stop: being community worker or business adviser. The number of different consultants that I had met or recommended – I would go to the manager, and say this may or may not be a good scheme – because I would be in touch with other people just by the very nature of their work. So there were some people who thought I shouldn't discuss business at all. That was around the time of all the difficulties.

I think just confusion about the role of community worker and whether or not it is useful for me to continue supporting the group. I have drawn up a paper for them and they are going to discuss it next week in fact.

This paper is a statement of how Caroline sees her role in the community business, and she feels that the Board of Directors know her well enough now to be able to formulate what her role should be. She thinks that community workers should be accountable to the local people they are working with: 'community work is by mutual consent.'

Caroline is sure that there is an important role for community workers in a community enterprise, even when a community enterprise agency has its specialists assisting with the project.

I think it is a joint area of work, I think community workers have skills and knowledge of local areas of the local economy, SCB workers have expertise in developing feasibility skills or business expertise. I think it is very important for a community worker to establish a relationship with development workers working alongside community business. I don't think a community worker, unless they have had a community business background, should really try to give any advice at all on business.

She thinks that training to give an initial understanding of sources of funding, grant applications, feasibility studies, constitutions, accounting and so on is valuable for community workers. But it should not be the community worker's intention to be a key adviser on these issues: she should be sufficiently aware of what is involved in business management to know her limitations. Community workers should not overstretch themselves for they:

are not a jack of all trades and I am worried about them being here, there, and doing everything, I think it is taking away from the professionalism of community work.

Caroline sees the value for community workers of basic training in business skills as primarily giving them confidence in the area, so that they can do their own professional work better. If they feel more knowledgeable, and therefore more secure about the context in which they are working, community workers will be more competent in their group work and community development roles. This is particularly important with community enterprises for personal antagonisms are far more forceful than in other community activities simply 'because there is employment at the end of the day.' Reflecting on a bad period early on in the history of the community business, when people were not turning up for meetings and certain directors were being very negative, Caroline thought the community worker must:

get people to look at something of the issue and not try to dwell on personalities: try and be prepared for that. Community business was new to me: if it was a different group I might have pre-empted some of the things that may or may not have happened, because your colleague or someone else has worked on it, or seen it before, or seen the practice, or you have a theory of it. Community business is new.

Points for Reflection

- The advantages and disadvantages of pressure to develop quickly
- Compare with Little Hulton, where there were similar pressures for urgent development
- Women in community business and the role of the community worker with regard to them
- The qualities needed in a manager
- The role of the community worker once trading begins

13 Sunderland Common Ownership Enterprise Resource Centre (SCOERC)

John Blackburn

This case study has a number of points of particular interest:

1 the development from a fairly narrowly defined initial enterprise to a range of activities that had not been contemplated by its originators;
2 the educational implications of involvement in housing co-operatives;
3 the value of an existing (union) organisation in creating a disciplined approach to the development of a co-operative;
4 the development from Housing Co-operative to Workers' Co-operatives and the creation of an Economic Development Zone.

This is the account of the development of an enterprise through the eyes of John Blackburn who joined the project in 1976. John's background prior to becoming involved with the project had been that of councillor for an inner-city ward of Sunderland and of experience of personnel management in industry. The former provided an important knowledge base of the workings of the local authority and, equally important, an understanding of the sets of issues facing the residents of the inner areas in which the enterprises were located.

John's colleague, Kevin, a trained community worker, with whom he has worked from 1986, had previously been a Welfare Rights worker in the East End of Sunderland and had been actively involved in campaigning as well as providing support and information for claimants. As a result of this work, he was also knowledgeable about the plight of local people and had a wide network of local contacts and associations which were to prove important elements in the success of the initiatives described below.

Background: Stage 1 Banks of the Wear Housing Association and Sunderlandia Workers' Co-operative

In the mid 1970s John became involved with a fledgling Housing Association (later to be known as the Banks of the Wear Housing Association). The formation of an Association had been encouraged by a workers' co-operative of jobbing builders, Sunderlandia Ltd, who were interested in carrying out improvements to the terraced cottages that were a feature of Sunderland building. Sunderlandia hoped that the Housing Association would wish to undertake their improvement in collaboration with the co-operative.

> Having in 1974 been a councillor for an inner city area and represented an area that contained quite a number of unimproved properties, I was naturally interested in seeing those properties improved, otherwise they would have been demolished.

Ideologically too the proposal was an attractive one.

> ... you had that nice relationship where you had a democratically controlled housing association having work undertaken to their properties by a democratically controlled workers' building co-operative.

At the time, however, the Registrar of Friendly Societies considered the proposal to be too incestuous, and it fell through.

In 1976 Banks of the Wear Housing Association Ltd became registered with the Registrar of Friendly Societies and the Housing Corporation, from whom the Association was to obtain its money, directed the Association to the Hendon area of Sunderland.

> At that time there were two alternatives for the area, clearance or a Housing Action Area scheduled for improvements. The local authority, having heard that a Sunderland based Housing Association had been set up which the Housing Corporation was prepared to support, declared the Hendon area a Housing Action Area.

According to John, the decision of the local authority to support the Housing Action move was finely balanced.

> They did their sums and found that the properties could be improved within the costs limits laid down by the Department of the Environment at the time. It was a rather fancy equation. If the cost of the improvements exceeded a certain amount then they were demolished. If not, then they could be improved.
>
> The Banks of the Wear Housing Association were then able to buy properties which after improvement would provide eight homes in one particular street. And I am very pleased to say that the first property was improved by Sunderlandia Ltd. So for me it was completing the circle.

Stage 2: Setting up the St Vincent Housing Co-operative and the Banks of the Wear Co-operative Housing Services Ltd

> The next stage in the initiative began when some residents in neighbouring areas in Hendon became interested in the development and wanted to set up their own housing co-operatives, or, democratically controlled organisations.

This expression of interest by local people not immediately involved in the initial housing project also gave rise to the first of a series of growth and extension points in the development of the primary initiative.

> Instead of Banks of the Wear extending itself, both in terms of the ownership of a number of properties and of its geographical base, it was decided at the time that a new Association be set up, the St Vincent Housing Co-operative. This new housing co-operative represented a name change from that of the Banks of the Wear. A second, and completely new organisation was then set up trading on the name and goodwill of the initial project, the Banks of the Wear Co-operative Housing Services Ltd, the purposes of this new organisation being to provide architectural, financial, housing management advice and support to other groups who wanted to set up housing co-operatives.

From the development of the St Vincent street co-operative housing venture, the new Banks of the Wear Co-operative Housing Services Ltd organisation was able to help other interested local community groups.

> What we had then were two or three embryonic housing co-operatives. We helped one group draw up a Housing Action Area report for submission to the local authority which did not succeed, unfortunately; they decided nevertheless to proceed with the formation of a housing co-operative and they now have a number of properties in

their ownership. Then another group, the Peel Street housing co-operative was set up and groups in other areas were formed in subsequent years.

Today in this part of Sunderland there are four adjacent housing co-operatives who between them own something like 120 homes and flats – all modelled on the first St Vincent Street housing co-operative.

These co-operatives are virtually independent now of Banks of the Wear except for complex finance advice.

Furthermore, the general success of the initiative is such that *Banks of the Wear Co-operative Housing Services Ltd* provide housing advice and architectural advice to housing co-operatives throughout the Region.

Today the number of homes owned by the different housing co-operatives in the Region is approximately 600 and the annual turnover of the *Banks of the Wear Co-operative Housing Services Ltd* is in excess of £1 million pounds.

The Housing Co-operative Development Process

The social and economic base from which John initially worked with local residents presented a number of parallels which community workers encounter in other types of work with disadvantaged communities.

This area of Sunderland was regarded as very much the 'downtown' area of Sunderland, where dependence on the statutory services of the police, social work and the fire brigade to come and rescue people from desperate situations was quite high.

The nature of the housing too presented its own range of problems for both the residents and for the development workers.

The majority of the prospective housing co-operators were tenants of private landlords. Many of the tenants had different landlords and there was not one landlord who owned a portfolio of properties among the housing located in the Hendon area. Moreover, the tenants, themselves, had different problems: high rents, poor maintenance, over-crowding, lack of services, and harassment. There was never one issue around which the tenants might naturally gell.

At the outset, a number of tenants were highly sceptical of the prospect of improvement to their housing conditions. This scepticism was grounded in their everyday experience and in the fact that each street had its share of derelict and boarded-up premises, a number of which had had compulsory improvement orders served on them by the local authority or had a demolition order.

Trying to explain to tenants who had lived with that eyesore for a number of years that their homes could be improved and that 'money was there' for improvements wasn't easy to get across. At the end of the day it was the realisation among the tenants that, 'Well nothing can be lost through this' that marked the start of their involvement.

At that time I was working with a nucleus of about half a dozen tenants, although the tenants' involvement used to fluctuate.

The Educational Process

For John there was a major educational task in promoting understanding of an unfamiliar form of public management of housing. Housing co-operatives operate on different principles from those readily available to scrutiny – not only differing from private sector housing for which the profit motive plays a major part, but also from local authority housing. Local people might have some grasp of how to influence local authority council housing management. They might realise that they must seek the support of their elected representatives. They might hope for the representative's support in articulating their housing needs at a full housing committee meeting. They would, however, be unlikely to have any real sense of participation in decision making. By contrast, in housing co-operatives the emphasis is on the democratic participation of the members.

> The common denominator for this type of work, apart from the energy and commitment, is the realisation that what one is trying to introduce to people, not impose, but to introduce with people is a form of public management over housing which is significantly different from that which has prevailed so far.
>
> What we are talking about with housing co-operatives is participatory democracy.

This is an alien concept and experience for many individuals living in run down areas and conscious only of their inability to affect events. John consequently saw his role as enabling local people to grasp the implications of this new form of co-operative housing ownership.

Group Support and Training

The nature and amount of support and training required by the different housing co-operative groups depended very much on the base level from which the development process sprang. In the case of the first housing co-operative project, the St Vincent Street Housing Co-operative, the process was somewhat protracted in the early stages.

> With the St Vincent Street group it was a much slower process. It was having to explain the procedures that would have to be adopted in relation to forming a co-operative body; that one could not just meet in a pub and talk about things and things would happen. It does not happen like that. It is necessary to form an incorporated body and that there are certain responsibilities associated with that. Were they willing to undertake that responsibility and were they willing to see it through? And so it became either – or. At that point, in the very early stages there were only about half a dozen people

The group's response was,

> We'll give it a bit of a try, and you will help us, won't you?
>
> Yes, but I was not prepared to always deliver the agendas. There has got to be a bit of effort from the group.
>
> I would take them through the agendas and explain things because most of the items were related to development work anyway at that stage, rather than the housing management.

The subject of housing management was in fact to come up later for the group as the initiative developed.

Later on, the process of development work with other fledgling housing co-operatives in the Hendon area followed a similar pattern. In the early stages, it was a case of bonding the group together, helping them to understand agendas and work through meetings and take on a degree of personal responsibility.

> The process in *Hendon* was being available; talking things through even if the problems were trivial, and engendering a sense of confidence in the group members,

preparing agendas that were not complex and written in language that was easily understandable and not 'highfalutin', and having minutes written in a form that was easily understood, endeavouring to encourage people to come to meetings. Sometimes these meetings were in a pub. In fact more often than not, they were in a pub so that there was a social aspect to it afterwards. And, people living in the street who had never spoken to each other, not even people living closely, they began to speak to each other in the pub. Amongst the women particularly there was a great cross fertilisation of ideas and the realisation of common problems.

The development process in Southwick, another district of Sunderland called for a different set of skills on the part of John the worker.

In *Southwick,* it was a very different matter altogether because the community was disciplined and the discipline came from the men with their attendance at lodge meetings of the National Union of Mineworkers. I fully remember attending my first meeting over there. I arrived a minute late. They were all there. The three officers were there behind the table. I was reprimanded for being late, was told where to sit and to speak when I was asked to speak. That was discipline!

They had already prepared an agenda and the secretary was fully prepared to take the minutes, although he later needed some help over the minutes because the subject matter was obviously different from what he had been used to.

The motives of the mining community in considering the housing co-operative option were mixed.

The local people in Southwick were attracted by the work of the St Vincent Street co-operative, but more so they were dissatisfied with the Coal Board who had refused to improve their homes unless the miners started paying a full rent. So there was an economic attraction, you have to realise some miners over there, not many but some, only paid water rates and lived rent and rates free.

With the housing co-operative being formed, the true rent as determined by the rent officer would be phased over three years. So they would be much better off with the housing co-operatives than with the National Coal Board. So there was a bit of a mercenary appeal.

The money to purchase the homes from the Coal Board came through the Housing Corporation, but, not without a fight. This was partly because of the success of the housing co-operatives in Hendon in demonstrating that the housing co-operative sector could develop schemes and give value for money. Even so, a small group, including two workers, a miner, a paid regional officer of the Corporation and a representative of the local authority, were required to travel to London to press their case with the Board of the Housing Corporation. In the event the miner had to wait outside and the Board met with the other representatives. The group won their case to purchase the Southwick properties.

However, much of the power base providing the strength to press forward with the proposed initiative came from the mining community itself.

The situation in Southwick was such that people had been waiting for years to have their homes improved and when initial approval came through from the lodge of the National Union of Mineworkers, public meetings were held in the large hall of the College in Southwick. About three hundred people came down, so there was no problem about community interest.

My role at these meetings was to stand near the door! People wanted to know, not so much about how they would manage a housing co-operative, but when the work would start and what sort of improvements could be undertaken. So it was one of explaining that they could not have gold taps. That if they wanted a coloured bathroom suite, then they would have to pay the difference between that and a white one (because the Housing Corporation using public money would not give permission for coloured suites to be installed).

Again at that point, it was the women who were quite vociferous, not just the miners.

Coping with the Development

John went on to point out some of the biggest difficulties identified by himself in the development of the housing co-operative initiative, especially in the Hendon areas.

The biggest problem with a housing development is the period from having identified a property that could be purchased and actually getting that property improved and completed.

You're talking about a year, sometimes longer. That's an awful long time for people to wait who have been living in poor conditions, but who want to continue to stay in the area. Because at that time, they also had an opportunity to move to living in a new flat or a new house elsewhere. People got very impatient at the time.

John attempted to deal with the tenants' objections and feelings by seeking to explain the difficulties and by trying to help the tenants reach an understanding of the situation and of the different role of the architect and the building contractors. Part of the task was the educational one of helping people understand that where the architect was dis-satisfied with the builders' work and when that in turn resulted in delays, this was necessary to prevent more serious problems occurring in the housing at a later stage. An additional set-back to the initial projects was the moratorium placed by the government on projects in hand which effectively 'froze' the work for a period of some three to four months. That too was difficult for local people to bear, and again called forth particular sets of skills and sensitivity on John's part.

Optimal Size of the Housing Co-operative

What we are talking about with housing co-operatives is participatory democracy, and housing co-operatives, if they are to be effective, have to be fairly small. They have to be of a size in which people can feel comfortable. They have to be of a size where people can say

'I live where I belong and I belong where I live.' We're talking about fifty homes in Hendon. Over in Southwick where streets of property were purchased from the National Coal Board with the approval of the local lodge of the NUM, then you are talking in terms of 150 homes. But, you already had a community there so the approach was very different from this area of Hendon where there had been no feeling of community whatsoever.

The question of optimum size was also clearly recognised by the tenants themselves. Certainly this was true of Hendon:

It got to the stage where the housing co-operative said 'No more properties! No more properties. We have reached our maximum size.', at least as far as they were concerned. 'We are able to manage and maintain our properties satisfactorily. There is no wasted energy in the sense that properties remain vacant for a long time.'

The size of the enterprise was such that there was no sense of dealing with a bureaucracy.

In comparison with what we have been living under with a private landlord or the local authority, this is heaps better.

From Development to Management

In the early stages much of John's development work centred more on helping the groups become established and familiarising groups with the procedures involved in meetings and in gaining an understanding of the concept of both co-operative housing and the philosophical base of participatory democracy on which it rested. With the completion of the houses, however, the emphasis for both the group members and, therefore, that of the worker, switched to housing management.

In the early stages of the initiative, the allocation of housing was not an issue for the respective co-operatives. This was because there were more vacant properties or half-vacant properties available at that time, so that people could chose which property they would move into. Later, as the housing co-operatives became more successful, a waiting list for the houses began to build up and it became necessary for members of the housing co-operative to decide who should be living in their co-operative. They did that by visiting the applicants in their homes and finding out themselves the housing conditions in which the prospective new tenants were living; asking them to attend co-operative meetings to determine the level of commitment which they had to the co-operative and looking at what they could offer.

Initially, it was the same nucleus of members who were involved in these activities and in the training and support which underpinned the work. Later, as other co-operatives reached a similar stage of development, different people became involved and the responsibilities undertaken were spread over quite a number of people.

Not only was there the task of selecting new tenants, the groups were confronted with the problems of how to collect rents. This latter problem was resolved by the housing co-operatives having their tenants take a paying-in rent book to the local bank each week or fortnight and then having the bank send off a statement to the co-operative, so that it was possible to determine who had paid their rent.

The understanding and reconciliation of the bank statement with the rent book can be taught in a relatively short period of time or given the opportunity, people were willing to grasp what had to be done and take responsibility for doing it. I found people were willing to take on responsibility.

Also these were people who had been virtually denied responsibility in anything that was important to them, both in their home and in their neighbourhood.

Obviously there were some problems. Sometimes things got a bit sticky -when there was a delay on the rent payment, or, people were not undertaking what they had offered to undertake. Then the easy response of individuals was 'Well, I'm going to resign. I've had enough?'. So when that happened, there was a need for the worker to talk it through with the individual or the group.

'You can't do that. You've got to think of the effect it would have on your co-operative.' I think the strength of the housing co-operatives now is that the people will fight to defend them.

Today members of the co-operative management have quite a lot of responsibility. When you think about the amount of money which they have coming through for the maintenance and management of their properties, we are talking about five figure sums.

Specialisation and the Division of Labour

If the success and expansion of the housing co-operatives had extended the roles and responsibilities of some of its key members into the area of the management of housing and resources the same development also served to highlight and separate out in important ways their relationship to the *Banks of the Wear Co-operative Housing Services Ltd*. As the co-operatives developed,

> all the problems associated with the housing management were investigated. The housing co-operative struck up a contractual arrangement with the Services organisation and said 'We will be responsible for this and we want you to be responsible for that, and in return we will pay you so much out of the allowances which we receive from the Housing Corporation'.

So the work became costed by accountants from the *Banks of the Wear Co-operation Housing Services Ltd* who are brought in to check the books every month, then a charge is made by the Banks of the Wear Co-operative Housing Services Ltd for the work done.

By that time the Banks of the Wear Co-operative Housing Services Ltd were able to employ more people who became more specialist. We had started off with the workers being very generalist and then as people were taken on some people became more focussed on particular areas of activity.

No local residents moved out of the co-operative housing sector into the Services sector as employees.

From Housing to Work

As a result of their involvement with the housing co-operative initiatives, people began to exercise skills which were associated with enterprise and furthermore to recognise these personal changes in themselves and their outlook on life.

> They were taking responsibility. They were negotiating with people in power and authority; they were going to the Housing Corporation or meeting council officials or Banks of the Wear professional workers. They were delegating responsibilities and ensuring that some of these responsibilities were being undertaken. They were sussing out the strengths and weaknesses of people. They were evaluating performance. These are the skills of enterprise. And it wasn't long after people were living in their improved homes to say, 'I've got a decent home and a roof for myself and my family and that is very important. Now I want to earn some money.' 'I've acquired all these skills – I am confident in talking with people on the phone; I can do some financial analysis for work because of what I have been doing in the housing co-operative. How about looking at the skills that I used to have and those that I have learned and create some work opportunities for myself and my family?'.
>
> That came from the previous chair of the St Vincent Housing Co-operative.
>
> 'Well, look, I've learned an awful lot'. 'I'm amazed at how much I've learned', or 'I never knew I could do that' is a common cry of people in the co-operative sectors. The growth of personal confidence in people is absolutely enormous.

However, there were also a few who had worked on the 'Black' doing a whole range of jobs but not enough to make a living, who were also arriving at a similar viewpoint of the need to think of alternative routes into employment.

Pursuing Economic Development

From the success of the Banks of the Wear came the realisation that the only way to create some wealth was not to be dependent on the private or the public sector. The private employment sector in this area had fled to the green fields sites of the Borough or had disappeared altogether: in the public sector, public work undertaken by local authorities had also been severely constrained as a result of Government action.

The only way to create some wealth was to use one's ingenuity, skills and talent.

In the late 1970's there was a limited amount of worker involvement in the development of workers' co-operatives through the Banks of the Wear Co-operative Housing Services Ltd, which had been helped along by a small grant by the Calouste Gulbenkian Foundation and the Building and Social Housing Foundation.

But Banks of the Wear did not have the remit to help people set up workers' co-operatives. It only had the remit to promote, develop and support a housing co-operative activity. So it became necessary to try and establish a Co-operative Development Agency which would help people form workers' co-operatives. From these origins, and from the realisation that within Sunderland at that time – the early '80's – there was no co-operative development agency, an Urban Programme application was submitted by myself to the local authority. As a result of that application, we received £14,000 to employ one worker and we were able to set up a co-operative development agency called the Sunderland Common Ownership Enterprise Resource Centre (SCOERC) which means exactly what it says, although its a bit of a mouthful.

The enterprise resource centre was established in October 1983 and in recognition of its close links with the housing co-operative movement in Sunderland, SCOERC based its office and its one full-time worker in the same block of property as the Hendon Housing Co-operatives and the Banks of the Wear Co-operative Housing Services Ltd.

The agency was principally established to help people in the housing co-operative sector develop their work opportunities and create work opportunities for themselves and their friends, as well as to try to provide some form of co-operative development service in Sunderland. An impossible task.

Recognising that the task was clearly beyond the scope of one worker SCOERC made early efforts both to increase its existing level of funding and also to seek support from the EEC Social Fund for establishing a 'Co-operative Development Zone' for the North Hendon/East End area of Sunderland, the latter being set up in June 1986.

From that we were able to submit an innovatory project to the European Social Fund for the setting up of a Co-operative Development Zone in the East End North Hendon area, an area of Sunderland recognised by the local authority as an urban programme area of greatest need.

It was also necessary to try and engender work activities from the bottom-up rather than rely on the traditional top-down approach which had failed in inner city areas like Hendon and the East End.

Today I am pleased to say that there are now five workers' co-operatives which have their origins in the housing co-operative sector and within this area of Sunderland there are now fifteen workers' co-operatives and a credit union.

In fact during the twelve month period 1986-87 SCOERC were able to help eleven workers' co-operatives become established. The majority of those assisted into self employment in this way had been unemployed for as long as six to seven years.

However, the context of this development presented a number of ideological and moral dilemmas to the workers quite apart from the economic and educational issues.

In an area such as the East End and North Hendon which is the site of this co-operative development zone, where unemployment is extremely high, where people have had a life of make-do government training schemes and make-work schemes, the problem is: should we as an agency be looking at the problem of full-time employment for some, or, wealth creation for many? That is the debate that we workers have had to address and are still addressing.

In the interim, however, they responded by undertaking development work with individuals who approached the agency for particular support and guidance in setting up their own workers' co-operatives or focussing on local community entrepreneurs operating on the fringes of the Black Economy.

The Economic Co-operative Development Process

We undertake development work by trying to help people develop their idea into a viable business proposition; help them to draw up a business plan; help them get funding and help them find premises.

The Roofing Workers' Co-operative

The roofing co-operative emerged from a housing co-operative in Ashington, Northumberland. Initially, they wanted to clean and re-seal asbestos roofs on farms. They did one or two farm buildings which were successful. Unfortunately, the work did not come forward as rapidly as expected. Originally, there were four in the Roofing co-operative, now there are two, but are seeking to expand again.

They realised that they had to get into conventional roofing work in order to survive and went on a government training course. They succeeded in that and now they are recommended by the Grants section of the local authority as competent roofers.

John's role in assisting the roofing workers' co-operative,

was helping them look at the idea again. Helping them undertake some new market research; helping them think about contacting a new range of prospective customers – the usual thing that is associated with business plan preparation. In this case, the development took about eight months. That included their registration as a company limited by guarantee. The more enterprising the people are, then the quicker things move along. With some prospective co-operatives however the process can take twelve to fifteen months. If people are looking at you all the time to make contact then it takes a longer time for the process to develop. However, you then realise that these people are not going to be enterprising enough to run a business. The roofing co-operative started in 1984.

As part of the economic development process with new groups, John and his fellow development workers encouraged the groups to look objectively at the sorts of business ideas that they were proposing to implement. This involved not just the discussion of the nature of the business and how that would be financed, but also involved a certain number of practical tasks.

The sorts of tasks were to go and look at the competitors and see who they are and what they are doing, the type of work they are undertaking and where they are based. With some businesses it was 'Well go and and park outside the factory gates and see who goes in and out. See who the customers are.'

Or, contact such and such a person and see if they would buy your service etc.

So we set tasks for the group and would say, 'Before we meet again, I want you to undertake these things,' and then if they haven't done it, then there is some pretty straight talking.

The Jobbing Builders Workers' Co-operative

The founder members were involved with the Council of Voluntary Services as part of a Community Programme, they felt there was a market for their work and approached us to see if we would help them. They wanted to use the contacts which they had with the likes of Age Concern and Help the Aged: the co-op was formed on the belief that they could undertake work for the clients of these organisations and for the housing co-operatives.

They too were able to tap into the feasibility grant; prepare business plans, then approach various organisations for funds. None of them had capital or collateral themselves. It was all loans. The co-operative company came about because they had heard about workers' co-operatives and the 'co-operative option' through the success of the housing co-operatives, and, through a bit of the promotional work which we had been undertaking.

They went for the co-operative because in some cases they did not have the capital to set up their own private business and so the banks would not look at them.

And, there was the realisation that whilst they could enjoy the fruit of success, they would also have to bear all the responsibilities and problems; they were also working with friends. They lived in the same street or in the same area and recognised that their friends had complementary skills to themselves. So instead of one person being 'the boss', or, having the worries of a partnership, they said lets see if we can form a co-operative company.

As a part of this promotional activity SCOERC has published a quarterly newspaper entitled 'Jobs for a Change' which is distributed to all the households and business premises in the Co-operative Development Zone. Its main purpose is to stimulate people into exploring alternatives to ways of living and working.

Looking more generally at the development process John went on to identify several issues.

We are fortunate in Sunderland in the sense that the Urban Areas Act applies to Sunderland and provides up to £1,000 to allow people to undertake feasibility work. The cost of travel, postage, market research, visits to similar organisations elsewhere in the country are all borne by the feasibility money. We have had to wrap our minds around each different project – there is a bit of re-orientation necessary amongst the development workers. Sometimes it gets difficult if at one part of the morning you are talking with a group of fishermen and then later on you are meeting or galvanising a group of roofers or builders. Then it gets a bit difficult.

Its not very difficult these days really to help people draw up a business plan. What is extremely difficult is ensuring that the business will survive in the market place, and in providing the time-consuming; energy sapping, demanding work of after-care.

The Housing Co-operatives as Potential Markets for Workers' Co-operative Services

As with other workers' co-operatives which grew up within the Sunderland housing co-operative sector, there was a desire to make use of that relationship by looking to the housing co-operatives to provide a source of work. At the outset, that appeared to be a reasonable and mutually beneficial expectation since a number of the workers' co-operatives were concerned with building and construction work and much of the activities taking place within the housing co-operatives sector at the time were to do with building construction and house maintenance. Certainly, the roofing workers' co-operative and the jobbing builders' co-operative could benefit from a share in some of the construction work and maintenance work undertaken on the housing co-operative properties. However, the general relationship between the housing co-operatives sector and that of the workers' co-operatives has had its share of frustrations and difficulties. The ideologically attractive concept of democratically controlled housing co-operatives having work undertaken to their properties by democratically controlled builders co-operatives was not realised in practice for a variety of reasons.

> We look at work in a way that is not profit maximisation but involves a different relationship between the customer and the provider. That is not being achieved however, because the housing co-operatives are looking to the cheapest provider of the service. One would like to see that change and we're forever trying to push that line. But there is a certain degree of pressure on the members of the housing co-operatives to accept the lowest tenders above a certain amount. But whilst the job could be done cheap, to do the job properly may be more expensive, but, in the long term it would save money.
>
> What is also required is for the housing co-operative members to understand that work has to be charged at a level that allows a profit element – for slack times in the business. So there has to be an education process in that area.

Even if they are sympathetic to the concept of workers' co-operatives, there is a responsibility on the part of the housing co-operatives sector to operate within its own financial limits. It certainly has no responsibility to subsidise other co-operative ventures in the commercial sector. This in effect, has placed the workers' co-operatives in the position of having to compete commercially in the market place for work within the housing co-operative sector. There is also on the part of the housing co-operatives, a reasonable expectation that the quality of any work undertaken, and the after completion service would be of a satisfactory level – irrespective of who had been contracted to carry out the work.

However, as John remarked

> Perhaps their experience of the workers' co-operatives may have been bad.

For their part, the workers' co-operatives have had to understand that the services provided by themselves to the housing co-operatives had to be at least comparable to that offered by their competitors, not only in terms of price, but also in terms of the finished product.

> The workers' co-operative too have got to understand that they can't leave properties or front gardens in a mess. 'You only get one chance' when it comes to business. So there is also a process of education there.

Workers' Co-operatives and After Care

The on-going support and after care of workers' co-operatives in the area placed continuing demands on the time and energies of the development workers.

> It is not very difficult these days really to help people draw up a business plan, or, to try and get some money for a business. What is extremely difficult is ensuring that the business will survive in the market place. A lot of after care work is necessary.
>
> We keep tabs on the workers' co-operatives; either they come in and tell us, or, because we know what's going on anyway. Some demand more attention than others. Sometimes it is problems associated with personnel in the co-operative, people leaving. Sometimes it is the difficulties of the market place.
>
> In many respects their problems are no different from that of any small business. Something like 48 per cent of all new small businesses in Sunderland fail within the first three years. So there is no need to feel ashamed about the failure of a business. The market place is extremely harsh.
>
> Also the climate for co-operatives is not all that conducive. If co-operatives are to be successful in the long term then we have to look at a co-operative economy. We have to look at a trading relationship which is very different from that of profit maximisation.

Given that the market place is extremely harsh, members of the workers' co-operatives were encouraged to draw positive lessons from any business setbacks and difficulties and also to celebrate their successes. In spite of such adverse conditions, however, only two of the workers' co-operatives with which SCOERC has worked, since being set up in late 1983, have ceased trading.

Continuity of Funding

In 1983 SCOERC received financial support from Sunderland Borough Council via the Urban Programme. That grant was subsequently matched by European Social Fund money in 1984. The Urban Programme expired in March 1989. This joint funding provided for the employment of two workers and accounted for 40 per cent of the SCOERC annual budget. In 1985, European Social Funding was approved for the North Hendon/East End Co-operative Development Zone project for a three year period with matching Urban Programme monies being made available till March 1989. This source of joint funding provided the other 60 per cent of the agency revenue income and covered the costs of the employment of four SCOERC workers until the funding ran out.

A major current difficulty with the SCOERC project has been the continuity of funding. In the last year, the project has experienced a 65 per cent cut in the level of grant coming in to the Co-operative Development Zone project.

> The difficulty is that of continuity of funding. There has been a 65 per cent cut this year in the funding for the Co-operative Development Zone project, and it is entirely because the European Social Fund was over-subscribed by applications. Not only from UK but from elsewhere and there are finite amounts of money that had to be distributed.
>
> However, the funding arrangements are such that a disproportionate amount of our time has had to be spent in trying to ensure overdraft guarantees. We have prepared our business plan for the private sector such as British Coal Enterprises; Vaux Breweries, and, the Co-operative Bank of course. We also sought the support of the

> local Council of Voluntary Services to convince them that we were an organisation worth backing.
>
> A lot of our time is taken up looking after our backs as well as trying to undertake present work and looking to the future.

The financial cuts and the resultant pressures on the project have also meant a reduction in the number of workers employed from a total of six prior to the cuts, to two after the cuts had been implemented.

SCOERC is now unable to sustain further losses in funding. Core funding support for SCOERC is therefore a priority for 1989-90.

The method of processing the European Social Fund applications has also been reconsidered. In future SCOERC intends to submit its application through the Industrial Common Ownership Movement (the federal body for workers' co-operatives in the UK) who will submit a European application for funding which will include Regional bids.

The changes in the financial situation of the project have also prompted the search for different sources of funding. To that end, the workers have set up Sunderland Resource Centre Ltd (SRC) a company limited by guarantee and with charitable status as an additional means of attracting resources to the agency. The SRC will act as a conduit for monies coming from other charities, foundations, philanthropic merchant bankers etc. The Directors have also converted the constitution of SCOERC from that of a company to that of an Industrial and Provident Society.

> We have converted our constitution from that of a company to that of an Industrial and Provident Society, because apparently the European Social Fund think that a Society is more concerned with the community than a company limited by guarantee, and, that a charity is even more concerned with the community than an Industrial and Provident Society. But, SCOERC cannot be a charity.
>
> It took six months to do the conversion.
>
> The change does not affect what we do, but, it is not just a name change. People have share certificates rather than guaranteeing a certain amount of money. The financial audit is also a little different from that of a company. So there are some constitutional differences, but, the actual powers of operation remain unchanged.

In many respects the project reflected a number of vicissitudes which confront other business ventures eg problems of cash flow and of maintaining customer confidence, which required a degree of business acumen on the part of the workers for the enterprise to pull through. This was reflected too in the workers' concern about the impact of increased interest charges which are not an allowable expense for funding purposes.

As part of the project's response to seeking to strengthen its financial base SCOERC has also recently undertaken short term consultancies.

A Further Development

The most important piece of consultancy being carried out by the SCOERC project involves that of a *co-operative village venture*. This venture is being funded by the Tyne and Wear Development Corporation and represents a further step in the development of the co-operative zone.

> The co-operative village project will be a £3-4 million project located just south of the Hendon area. The focal point of the venture will be 110 homes built by Banks of the Wear Co-operative Housing Services Ltd. However, it is already recognised

that whilst a new housing development provides some work, it does little for the local economy in the longer term. There has to be other aspects.

In this case there is going to be accommodation provided for people who have severe learning difficulties. Their care which is work, could be undertaken by an existing workers' co-operative that is already involved in 'care' and 'helping'. The new village also plans to provide for the building of a Social Enterprise Centre which would have rooms for offices which would house the housing co-operative, a credit union, the workers' co-operative and a large multi-purpose meeting room which would double up as a leisure facility for the local residents.

The plans for the Centre will also have space for hobby rooms, rooms where people who have particular interests and skills may want to develop their ideas along possible business lines and then possibly graduate on to a start-up unit.

The Workers' Skills

Reflecting back over the fourteen years of the project from its start as a housing association development through its succession of goals. John described the nature of the skills which are required by workers in that development process.

A willingness to fight for one's corner and an understanding of the realities of people's daily existence in hard pressed communities. To realise that the leap from unemployment to employment, coupled with the responsibilities of running a business is a quantum leap in the thinking and the action for people who have been unemployed and especially for the long term unemployed. To realise that a transitional bridging arrangement is perhaps required to help people move from unemployment to self employment, and, in the absence of that bridging arrangement, that an awful lot of after care support will be necessary. It is also necessary to recognise failure in trading enterprises and, also, failure in people. To be willing to change, be adaptable, be fluid. You have to have strength, a high level of lateral thinking. There is no point in focussing just on work activities or just on housing activities which compartmentalise the real life situation. A broad agenda is required if communities are to be turned around. And finally, to recognise that the process takes a long time and requires resourcing to do so. Being patient, having a sense of realism and a realisation that you are not going to change the world, but still keep that sense of commitment. To celebrate achievements even though these have been small. To be innovative and flexible.

Success

For John, there were several competing ideas on what constituted success in the Co-operative development area.

Success! There are two criteria of success. Jobs – which is the Urban Programme's criteria. With the European Social Fund – it is training. Both are very crude yardsticks. We are very successful in meeting these two targets; we achieve it by exercising a lot of energy.

In the Co-operative sectors success is that of personal growth. Success when people are able to work effectively and independently of the professional workers. When they stop coming in to see you, that's when you know it's a success.

Success for John was when people have learned about themselves and about one another and the situation in which they live through the process of working collectively. John stressed that in all local development, and not just economic development, the common denominator was the involvement of and the participation of people in schemes which are of importance to themselves and the local communities. Success lay in their energy and their willingness to participate in the openness of the democratic process,

> because it is the process that is important. It is the getting there and the learning experience which is important in measuring success.

The Future

John went on to express considerable concern over the social and economic future of the Sunderland area.

> I worry about the future of this town and this region which produces only 4.9 per cent of the gross national product. I believe the economy of Sunderland is in a terrible state. There are few large or medium sized local companies based in Sunderland. The owners are elsewhere. And there is problem of attracting inward investment.

With respect to the third sector economy, the prospects were equally unsympathetic.

> Politically, co-operatives are marginalised by local authorities. Here in Sunderland, the emphasis is more on welfarism rather than on developing the third sector economy.

Nevertheless, this somewhat bleak scenario, far from dampening John's spirits appears to give rise to an even greater sense of urgency and commitment to the value of empowering people and in seeking new alternatives to social and economic community regeneration.

> Freire used to say, and I will probably mis-quote him:
>
> > 'We should know of those forces that impinge upon our community.
> >
> > We should get to know those forces.
> >
> > And we should then be critical of those forces.'
>
> and I think that is community education and community work.
>
> In community development work we say 'We'll bloody well do something about it.'

Points for Reflection

- The role of the worker in exploring realities
- The range of educational opportunities
- The knock-on effects in the community and in the development of new initiatives
- The importance of after-care
- The issue of quality control
- Adaptability and changing goals

Part Three: Drawing the Threads Together

Introduction: The Need to Plan

> People didn't want to come to a club just to play pool and darts. They wanted real jobs. They wanted mine for a start, and at the end of the day they wanted paid employment; they did not want to continue to do volunteer jobs. People want salaries.

In this strong statement from Hazel McLeod, a community worker in Lothian, we observe the pressure on community workers to make a response to compelling community and group needs. The question is whether the worker turns away from such demands and syphons them off to other agencies, or whether she can summon the personal time, knowledge and financial resources that will enable her to take on the challenge herself and respond in terms of community development: educational, social and also economic development.

In the following discussion we shall explore how a role for community workers has been carved out of what might at first seem purely economic objectives. We shall base this discussion on our interviews both with workers directly involved in co-operatives and community businesses and also with other interested and supportive onlookers. Whereas in Chapter 2 we have described a 'community development' approach in somewhat theoretical terms, which have inevitably over-simplified the reality of practice, here we shall reflect, through the comments of our many respondents, the complexities, dilemmas and issues that daily confront the worker. We do not seek to arrive at specific prescriptions, but aim to chart some of the shoals, reefs and smoother waters for community workers setting sail on new seas.

The accounts we have presented are intended to enable workers to recognize similarities to their own situations and also to plan and prepare for future local development. As more and more community workers identify a role for themselves in social and economic regeneration in areas of high unemployment and social disintegration they should not have to go through the process without guidance. Reinventing the wheel is time-consuming and in Part Three we hope to bring together aspects of the development process in such a way as to reduce workers' need to learn by trial and error and to enhance their capacity to plan ahead.

Finding that community workers are too often described as 'track suited, bunch of keys, whistle wielding, community centre building-oriented managers' or, alternatively, as 'the guys that do the photocopying for you, or the guys that run the summer playscheme, or set up a class in dressmaking' we realised that some redefinition was needed, whether within the service or within the community, district or region. This redefinition includes a readiness to contribute to personal development, to increase the individual's (and the community's) ability to participate and understand what is going on in local and national politics, but also to take part in promoting a greater economic democracy. For this, as a planner put it:

> We want more people to participate in the economy, more people to discover and get the opportunity to develop new forms of creating employment for themselves. It is not just a nice, easy thing that would make the economy more effective if more people's talents were liberated.

Rather than concentrating on the social pathology of an area, on its poverty and deprivation and on individual dysfunctions, community workers with a developmental perspective may see themselves as contributors to enterprise initiatives and to the wider social and economic planning undertaken by both district and regional bodies. To contribute in this way, they need to widen their horizons, extend their skills and move out of the confines of the community centre 'and see themselves not only as service providers but initiators', (Senior Area Team Leader).

In order to help community workers to reflect upon their work in this field before entering it and during the process of development we have prepared our 5 Ks Questionnaire. This puts in question form some of the challenges faced by community workers who have already tried their hands at facilitating community enterprise. We hope it will alert readers to the issues. Forewarned is forearmed. You will find the questionnaire at the end of this book.

14 Raising the Question of Community Enterprise

'Enterprise' as such is a common enough term but its association with 'community' is relatively recent. This association and its potential for a locality with high levels of unemployment needs exploration, understanding and ultimately publicity. Here we examine the ways in which awareness gradually spreads from local decision-makers to the agencies, to the eventual participants and to community workers interested in a development approach. We also point out the relative elusiveness of the 'unemployed' and outline the means by which they have been contacted by those who have provided accounts of their work in this field.

A Developing Awareness

The Local Area

Community enterprises as a response to unemployment have only recently been on the agenda of local authorities and community groups. Frequently a process of realisation of the impact of unemployment precedes an active response. Recognising that large employers are unlikely to return seems to have been a crucial step for communities all over Britain. This realisation hits both individuals and community groups. As Mike Naulty of CEST told us:

> One of the first things people said: 'It's unlikely that we are going to get jobs round here. We can't wait for a big employer again like Timex or NCR because we can't see that happening, so how can we go about creating jobs for ourselves?'

This same view is reported by John McGhee, who found a local discussion group were compelled to address the problem of unemployment and seek means of job creation since they too were convinced the larger employers would never return to their area. Dwelling on the past and hoping, even campaigning for its return was seen as pointless. Such a feeling was fuelled by great disillusionment with companies such as British Leyland who pulled out in what were perceived as profoundly deceitful ways.

First then, we observe the growing sense of outrage and then the move towards a creative response. As Jim Hoseason, who began a community newspaper, put it:

> It was going to be about small groups of people like this group to get together, by their bootstraps if you like, to create opportunities for themselves, because there aren't the resources or, seemingly, the political will, to do very much at the moment in this neck of the woods, and we are all becoming quite concerned.

In West Calder, for instance, businessmen, local politicians, community leaders, and the community centre management turned their attention to what could be done and joined forces in a local employment committee. Similarly in another part of West Lothian, Armadale Community Enterprise (ACE) was formed to create jobs and 'have an impact on the town'. In both cases Community Programmes were used to produce immediate results, before more complex, self-initiated community businesses were started.

The rising tide of community awareness led, in some cases, to the use of community workers as resources. They had knowledge of committee work. They could draw up a constitution. They knew how to go about the task of setting objectives.

Furthermore, they could do the ground work for district and regional councillors and add their grass roots knowledge to the battle for resources. The community worker, in these circumstances, can act as educator of the local council and as a contributor to policy making, developing a critique of local authority decision-making where it by-passes the interests of the community and ignores the principles of justice and democracy.

Outside Agencies and Funding Bodies

Without outside agencies and the development support they bring there is little hope for community enterprise. They too have to feel the need to respond to unemployment. In the Scottish Highlands, for example, the HIDB only stepped in when it became clear that development was not taking place in some of the marginal areas within the Board's responsibility. The first reason for this was that, even if industries were persuaded to move there, they tended to fail because of distance from the market and distance from top management as well. Secondly, there were also very few local entrepreneurs to come forward for the grants that were available, and thirdly, in egalitarian rural communities, those people who did have ideas were reluctant to propose them for fear of resentment from their peers.

The Participants

The motivation to participate in establishing a community enterprise may come from a resolve amongst some unemployed individuals to take a pro-active role in response to their predicament. For others it is the awareness that living on benefits is becoming an ever more perilous way of surviving. As Jim Hoseason remarks:

> All the talk about change in the social welfare structure is beginning to get home to people, so they say that this word 'enterprise' must have some relevance to me.

In most cases those who feel that they themselves might take part in developing and running a business are community activists who have played an important role in local tenants' groups or other community organisations.

We are unable to devote more space to the important question of what motivates local people to participate in a community enterprise, but it is interesting to note Cliff Southcombe's generalisation from several different community co-operatives. He feels that the principal male activists are generally men with established positions in the local community who are consolidating their influence in local affairs. By contrast, he feels that many women get involved because they want to change their personal circumstances, and the community enterprise is a vehicle for them to do this. He observed that a very high proportion of women activists separate from their spouses following their participation in the enterprise, and many leave the housing estate (*see* Little Hulton).

There are various reasons why unemployed people might not want to participate in community enterprises:

> Some are happy to be made redundant or to become unemployed, because they have their own resources and their own interests, and for the first time they can survive on benefits. And they're not actually worried. I have actually come across quite a lot of happy unemployed people. (Christine Forrester, Voluntary Action Resource Centre)

We should also be aware of the fact that some of the registered unemployed are in fact at work in the informal economy, and have little or no wish to engage in legitimate but financially riskier ways of earning a living.

I know a lot of people who do work on the side. The key point is the feeling that the risk of being found out is lower than the risk of actually taking the plunge. (Development Worker in Wester Hailes, Edinburgh).

Furthermore, in Highland and Island communities though employment is often seasonal and sporadic there are few without some occupation, such as working on crofts, part-time work or 'helping out,' all of which conceal an underlying high level of formal unemployment. Again, not everyone wishes to be associated with a formal business enterprise. Nevertheless, community workers we have interviewed feel that if services, advice and opportunities are made available to people they then have the choice as to whether they formalise what they are doing into a community business or as sole traders.

The Community Worker

The community worker may arrive at the view that she must make a response to those who clamour at her door.

What we have is a massive problem with unemployment and poverty and to continue providing macrame and pottery is fine, but it's not going to meet the needs of our target group – the potential planning group of a community enterprise.

Indeed the way the community worker views community enterprise becomes the key to her response. If it is in the following terms then she may find ways to further community aspirations:

I believe that everybody is enterprising. It just depends on your definition of the word 'enterprise'. To some folk it means real go-getters that are going to make a million and fly off with lots of profits. I would rather think about it as Enterprise that people care about their communities, care about their society, are working towards the betterment of it in economic terms as well as social ones. That's the essence of Enterprise for me.

Many community workers involved in setting up community businesses have found themselves responding to groups which share these concerns. In fact, enterprising individuals who do not share this community orientation are likely to take another route into business, perhaps only using a community worker as a source of information on where to go next.

Organisational Context for the Community Worker

A little over half of the community education workers responding to a questionnaire we sent out in 1987 were working with the unemployed. Most of them found it only moderately rewarding because they lacked resources and knowledge, and most of their work was in the fields of counselling, social skills development, and recreational or adult education programmes.

When community workers find themselves part of an external drive to initiate community enterprises, for example as part of the major local authority initiative in Barrowfield, or as part of the Highland Region's strategic plan for facilitating community development, they are usually expected to fulfil a particular function. This is often to encourage the local population to contribute ideas, identify problems in community group functioning and enable the members to overcome them. Increasingly in Highland Region they may play a part in training management committees and boards of directors, in conjunction with ACEHI, if this is considered a priority area by the Department.

Contacting the Community

The Image of Community Workers

Community workers are frequently associated with centre based activity – with leisure and recreation, and with adult education classes rather than with outreach or community-wide initiatives. It seems that when big industries withdraw from a locality the redundant workers rarely turn to community workers for assistance. 'The majority of people hadn't needed those services before, and therefore they didn't know what was around and what to expect,' as one development worker put it. In fact, for the majority of local people the image of the community worker is more likely to be associated with youth work than with responding to unemployment.

This places the community worker interested in employment initiatives in the position of having to generate a new image, producing publicity that catches the attention of the community as a whole and the unemployed in particular. Unfortunately, much of the general publicity meets with a sour response. The unemployed may not wish to be associated with one another, they may not wish to recall the days of their employment which may be a source of bitter recollection, and they may not see themselves as having any future.

This raises two questions: firstly, to which sections of the unemployed population are community enterprises relevant and secondly, by what means might they be approached?

Initial Contact with the Unemployed

Whatever her interest in encouraging community enterprises, the community worker must first establish herself as an information resource. One development worker argues that she has to respond to a wide range of queries, whether on benefits, access to classes, or changes in legislation that affect the unemployed. If this first contact is unrewarding, community workers may not get a second chance. If, on the other hand, the community worker has the knowledge and skills to address an immediate problem which an individual (or group) has identified, then confidence is built and the community worker gains valuable credibility. This is crucial if she is to be approached for help with employment initiatives (*see* Armadale).

1 Other contacts may be made through the traditional leafletting, newspaper campaign and public meeting (*see* South Aston). This has been the approach adopted by the HIDB's development officers whose arrival on an island or in a village, is usually a well publicised event. Large numbers may attend, and new as well as well-seasoned community activists signal willingness to pursue the idea further. Other contacts occur through drop-in centres, or through the community centre acting as a Benefits office (e.g. Armadale and Bonnybridge, where it was possible for the workers to carry out a skills/needs survey amongst those collecting benefits).

2 Targetted Groups

Contact through pre-redundancy counselling can also form a useful means of developing an interest in employment initiatives. However, pre-redundancy courses must be approached with caution. When carried out in a large factory about to close they may focus on how to deal with redundancy payments and thereafter with benefits. But, since most of the workers will start making applications to other employers, they are apt to be deaf to statements that they are unlikely to find a job and need to think about setting up something for themselves. Nevertheless, people may be identified at this stage who, if offered the opportunity to look at self employment or community enterprise, may well be interested.

If the pre-redundancy courses are followed up, then, although most of the original list of workers will not turn up to post-redundancy recall meetings (as happened in West Lothian), a nucleus of individuals ready to invest time and energy in a collective future may emerge.

> There's a whole range of people. At one end there are the men who are now suffering quite severe depression and are on tranquillisers. In the middle, there are those who could benefit from being plugged into a District Council's recreational programmes and drop-in cafes. But at the other extreme there are men who are champing at the bit, ready to find a new lease of life and keen to get on and do something. (Development Worker).

It has, therefore, seemed important to be aware of impending closures. Through this the secondary purpose of encouraging individuals to consider involvement in employment initiatives may also be achieved (e.g. NUmac).

Another group of people who may become interested in generating jobs, but who set out with the intention of finding employment in traditional ways consists of those who sign up for Training Agency Re-Start Programmes (or their successors).

Community workers may find that these groups are alerted to the possibilities of moving on to community enterprises once their courses have finished. Of course, these may well not result in community businesses, but, if offered a supportive environment, may lead to individual self-help.

3 Door-to-door Calling on the Community

This form of contacting the unemployed has been tried, but is extremely time-consuming and not always welcome. Finally, it tends to draw very few into the services available.

In Blackburn, West Lothian, a different approach has been used. A volunteer who had been a shop steward in British Leyland before the factory closure, with local and personal knowledge of the workers, was enlisted as an animateur. He has increased the numbers making use of the services offered by the local school and the community centre, and from amongst these men a move towards employment generation is being made.

4 The Use of Existing Groups

Most employment initiatives appear to link into existing community groups. It may be a tenants' association as in Beechwood (Tayside), a housing action group (Renton), or it may be a local group which the community worker has already initiated (like the Adventure Play Centre committee in South Aston or the Kojak centre for people with a mental and physical disability in Castlemilk) or a Housing Association (Sunderland); it may be a voluntary group engaged in producing a community newspaper (Invergordon) or even an unemployed group meeting at a centre (Bingham, Edinburgh). In making a start with an existing group there are certain advantages:

> What you need to have if you are working in local economic issues is a local structure to link into, and you need to have actual physical resources which you can utilise, because any employment initiative you try to create in an area of deprivation is going to have a hell of a time getting off the ground. It's going to be at the bottom end of the market. It's going to be trying to employ people who haven't been employed for some time, if they ever have. It's creating work in an area which traditionally hasn't got an economy. So you're starting off with a series of

> disadvantages. One of the good things about building on existing resources, like centre projects, work schemes, whatever, is that they have already established themselves and they are credible, and they can afford to carry employment projects, perhaps financially, for a short period of time as well. So you're building these employment projects into a very supportive network.
>
> If you've got a lot of interest in an area, then a culture starts to emerge, and there are activists who start to come forward, who move on from being involved in a children's play scheme to a tenants' association, to a local enterprise group. There's a natural progression there. (Ex-worker in Castlemilk, Glasgow).

Together with the advantages of credibility, which may well help with later requests for funding, an existing group usually brings experience of management committees. This may be of great importance in enabling a group to move into the structure needed for a community business. Some of the essential committee skills may already have been acquired.

Furthermore, working with existing community groups allows the worker to take account of specific local needs and issues. The members of the group are likely to identify more accurately than the worker the need for e.g. a launderette, play group furniture, a newspaper, workspace, a bus service, a corner shop, an agricultural co-operative, or other community services or products.

Finally, an existing group makes it possible to reach more of the unattached unemployed than can be contacted through a community-wide or general project. Individuals have neighbours and friends who may provide links into the community. This becomes important when the aim is to spread the recruitment of an enterprise initiative beyond the first-comers, an issue for most community workers involved in such initiatives, and conscious of the need to counter the exclusiveness of the pioneer group.

5 The Whole Community

In setting up community co-operatives (Co-Chomunn) the HIDB has usually intended them to include the whole community. These communities are often isolated, not only from the mainland in the case of the island co-operatives, but also from the resources more easily available to less remote and sparsely populated parts of the country, whether it be contacts, funding, ideas, or demonstrations of possible business ventures.

Community workers working with ACEHI (the Association of Community Enterprises in the Highlands and Islands – part funded by the HIDB) may wish to use their knowledge of a locality and their interpersonal and training skills to assist with the development of large community-wide co-operatives (as well as enterprises which grow out of existing small groups).

Summary

In this chapter we have pointed out that community enterprises need to be underpinned by a wide spread consciousness and commitment to participation and funding. The possibility of community enterprise must be brought home to the local area at every level. The future workers and managers, as well as the support services, politicians and local authority officers should all share this consciousness and perceive community workers as potential agents in local regeneration. Last but not least, community workers themselves must view a role in community development as a challenge worth meeting. The difficulty of satisfactorily contacting the unemployed is just the first of many challenges. We have outlined a number of approaches to this complex task.

15 The Aims of Community Enterprise: Assessing Success

A quick calculation of the number of self-financing jobs created through community enterprises might suggest that these projects have had a very limited success, when seen in the context of 8.1 per cent unemployment (Unemployment Unit Index, December 1989). It is therefore important to begin this discussion of community workers' roles in employment generation by clarifying what the aims of community enterprises are. Almost everyone that we talked to involved in this field from a community education or community development background stressed the diverse objectives of community enterprises.

> '... the goals of community enterprises are never solely economic, nor are the goals solely social or cultural. Development must be integrated if it is to be effective. Community enterprises are organised in the interests of the whole community. Accordingly, their goals and strategies relate to the whole community – to its social and economic and cultural elements.' (Love 1985:2-3)

The only people interviewed who ultimately viewed success by the one criterion of job creation were a few (but not all) planners, and someone in a local economic development agency. For the vast majority of practitioners in this area their ambitions for community enterprises could be arranged in three broad categories: education, community development and economic self-determination, and job creation. We would not wish to prioritise these objectives, except to point out that the generation of employment is the essential characteristic of community enterprises that distinguishes them from other projects in which community workers might be involved.

An important point in considering aims and success is to acknowledge what the clients' perceptions of success are. These might bear little relation to the community worker's intentions, although one would hope that this was fully discussed. To be realistic, it is very likely that for participants in a community enterprise job creation (particularly for themselves) is the highest priority, the economic empowerment of the community is a welcomed side effect, and educational objectives are of minor importance. Most of the long term unemployed have had a great shock to their self-confidence and are extremely vulnerable to further failure, particularly if they invest a lot of energy into the project. As we emphasise elsewhere, it is imperative that community workers have a good understanding of what their clients' objectives are, that these are never allowed to become totally unrealistic, and that they are compatible with the community workers' goals.

Education and Personal Development

An educational dimension can permeate every aspect of establishing a community business. Some community education workers would go so far as to say that their aim is not so much to create jobs as to encourage a group to explore as wide a range of solutions to the problem of unemployment as possible (Kemp 1982:32-36). We would suggest that the educational potential of collectively examining an issue and exploring solutions should not be achieved at the cost of employment generation. But the two need not be in competition.

Building Up Confidence

Building up the confidence of the people one is working with was a recurrent theme for many of the community workers interviewed. Some felt that the process of exploring business ideas, learning new skills and trying to establish an enterprise is a means of regenerating the self-esteem of the unemployed in itself, while others thought it of paramount importance to build up the confidence of participants before attempting these things.

> I don't think you can go anywhere without enabling people to rebuild their own confidence in talking to and confronting other people. That may start from something as simple as... a drop in group. We have enabled them (the unemployed) to make contact with each other over a cup of coffee, and they have identified something that together they would like to do, which is painting. (Christine Forrester, Voluntary Action Resource Centre)

The group decorated the Centre's offices, but the important thing as far as Christine Forrester was concerned was that they made their own decisions about how to organise their work, what paint to buy, and so on. 'It's the first time in their lives, I suspect, anybody has given them the chance to determine how they plan their work.' Another suggestion for building up unemployed folk's confidence, and giving them the experience of team work, is to organise a skills survey of one's area. The slow, long term nurturing of people's self esteem, following the demoralisation of unemployment, is the kind of invaluable but unquantifiable work that justifies local authority spending on community workers, according to Councillor Tony Kinder (chair of Lothian Region's Employment Committee).

For community workers who are dealing with a pre-existing community group, building up confidence is generally much less important, since the fact that these community activists are already operating as a group means they have gained enough experience of group work, administration and decision-making to ensure a basic level of confidence. The consequence of not allowing time for everyone in the group to develop their self-confidence is demonstrated by the example of Ruchill, where several of those in the community business group dropped out as a result of the pressure to meet a six months deadline for its establishment.

Working towards a community enterprise not only builds up individuals' self-esteem but also boosts the confidence of the whole community. If a group comes to the understanding that it can create its own economic development, then it can have an enormous effect on the whole neighbourhood's perception of their ability to act on the world.

Working in a Group and Recognising Training Needs

Another advantage for the community worker of dealing with a pre-existing community group is that the individuals are likely to have already sufficiently worked out their personal relationships with each other to enable them to operate as a group successfully. Team work is one of the fundamental things that people learn in the process of establishing a community enterprise.

An important facet of working successfully as a group is the ability to explore which skills it possesses, and then to identify the training needed by the group. It is far better if the group themselves recognise their training needs, because then the motivation exists for those skills to be learnt. With a positive approach to learning community activists are less likely to leave areas of expertise to the professionals, absolving themselves of responsibility for things that they could learn to do themselves.

> The onus is on local people to do it themselves, nobody is going to do it for them. They'll do it with them, but not for them... the biggest understanding that any community group can have is that they create their own development, it's up to them... we can only help. (Mike Naulty, CEST)

Several development workers emphasised the value of people learning through experience rather than by being taught. Evidently this is far less feasible with specific business skills than with more general administrative expertise. With the latter it is often through the mistakes that folk make that they learn most and eventually develop confidence in their abilities.

Administrative Skills

Before a group is able to tackle establishing a community business a basic level of general administrative competence is necessary. Almost any activity carried out by a community group helps develop administrative skills, and it is important for the community worker to recognise that the administrative work she takes on herself is often at the cost of the group's experience:

> ... community workers must be willing to hand over and train individuals in the groups to take on tasks, rather than going away and doing it themselves. If... groups organise the five-a-side football or whatever, in scheduling the fixtures and booking venues there are organisational skills involved that an individual can take on and not only develop their confidence but develop their abilities and skills.
>
> (Christine Forrester, VARC)

The kind of jobs that can usefully be delegated to members of the group are minuting meetings, getting a record of decisions taken and checking that they are acted on by the relevant people. This develops a structured way of working which is an important skill for pursuing community enterprise ideas.

Effective decision-making is another general skill to be learned that is invaluable for a group embarking on setting up a community enterprise. This involves understanding how committees work, what the chairperson, secretary and treasurer's roles are, how different kinds of structures can assist or impede decision making, what a constitution is really about, and so on. The Falkirk Voluntary Action Resource Centre has designed a course to cover these topics, which is packaged to allow locally based community workers to use it. SCB also devotes the first course of its training programme to this subject.

It should be noted that Christine Forrester's approach of encouraging people to take on as much administrative work as possible themselves recognises education and personal development as one of the principal aims of community enterprises. Others, such as Glen Buchanan in SCB, have suggested that the community worker can usefully 'service' the group by organising meetings, taking minutes and so on, presumably to keep the momentum going and progress as rapid as possible. The relative merits and drawbacks of these different approaches are illustrated to some extent in the Armadale and NUmac case studies.

Management and Specific Business Skills

Skills in management seem to be far more difficult to develop than administrative skills, and several development workers interviewed identified this as a central problem in setting up community enterprises. In Castlemilk, Glasgow, the community activists who had been extremely successful in campaigning to establish the St Dominic's Centre found, by their own admission, that managing it demanded completely different expertise. Most community workers (and, perhaps, managers) would probably agree that one can get only an initial grasp of what management involves through classes, and that it really has to be learnt from experience. Since it is essentially about decision-making it follows that a substantial body of knowledge has to have been acquired before one can be a competent manager. Roy Pedersen, Head of the Social Development Section of the HIDB, felt that management skills were generally developed through crises:

> Almost every enterprise, once trading, goes through a crisis within say a year or two... and this is quite often to do with a manager not being up to the job, and then the committee has got to work itself up to firing this person or controlling them in some way. Often once that difficult decision has been taken that's when the management committee is welded into a fighting force able actually to run the business efficiently.

Despite the experience of such problems, however, many management committees do not develop sufficient management expertise to run community enterprises, according to Roy Pedersen. Consequently the HIDB has a Management Unit which helps committees of Co-Chomunns (Community Co-operatives) when in particular difficulties. The recognition of the need for management consultants in an area with perhaps the longest history of community enterprises, suggests that community workers should not be disappointed if the groups they are working with fail to become accomplished managers.

The more specific skills involved in running a business are less problematic for the group to learn, even though they usually know relatively little about business. It is unlikely that they will have much enthusiasm for learning about financial planning and cash flow forecasting in the abstract. But as soon as they set about developing a business plan the need for these and other skills becomes apparent.

A number of further education colleges provide relevant training in business skills, but for people with only a brief experience of formal education it is often less intimidating to arrange for tutors to come to them, so that lessons occur on 'their territory'. Community enterprise agencies, such as SCB and CESU, now provide specialised training courses for community groups, sometimes run centrally and sometimes with outreach workers travelling to the community. The SCB training programme for Spring/Summer 1988 covered the following topics: Effective Conduct of Meetings; Book-keeping for Community Business; Legal Responsibilities of Company Secretaries and Community Business Directors; An Introduction to PAYE and VAT; Financial Planning; Negotiation Skills; Health and Safety at Work and Time Management.

Breaking Down an Employee Culture

Whatever administrative or business skills a group learns in the process of trying to establish a community enterprise, at the least they should become more informed about their own capacities, about how to work with other people and about their condition as unemployed – the social factors which create unemployment and different responses to it. Participating in the development of a community enterprise, or even simply contemplating it, involves a move away from the cultural values associated with being an employee.

> I think that to go in and say to people, 'Let's get involved in setting up a community business,' or 'Let's get involved in looking at employment opportunities,' really is a frightening step to take, because employment is something which you go into, that is provided by someone else. In the main, for people in the communities that we are working in, they are employees, and their experience of work is as an employee. Work is not a career, it is a means of earning the money to provide you with the quality of life that you want, that gives you access to a whole range of things whether it be through union, social club, through having enough money to have a holiday each year, to buy a video or to run a car, or as an end in itself. Those of us who sit back, and particularly people who work in community based work, get very committed to what they are doing, tend to forget that for most people there isn't that commitment: it's a job. So the idea of making the commitment to becoming involved in something that creates employment is a very big conceptual step to get people to take. I think to see anything of that kind succeeding there has to be a lot of primary education in terms of getting people to take on board the whole idea that they can become themselves creators of work. (Christine Forrester, VARC)

Ideally the community benefits to be gained from a community business would make employees far more committed to their work and less alienated than most waged workers. Unhappily this is frequently not the case, and employees tend to treat their work as they would any other job. The workers of Flagstone Enterprises (Ferguslie Park) are a good example of this, while the Wester Hailes Cafe (Edinburgh) is a sad case of a community venture that failed through the absence of any community ethos amongst the workers: pilfering unfortunately occurred. Rather than despairing at such examples, some consider them a challenge for community education. Can community workers develop a new awareness amongst the participants of a venture?

Even in a community co-operative, where the members have a financial interest in the success of the business, developing new values towards work is an ambitious project. Chris Elphick spoke from his experience in Easterhouse, Glasgow:

> Where you find one or two people who are very much into the principle of co-operativism, they tend to underestimate that working in a co-operative way is pretty alien to most of us and most of our backgrounds, and most of our educational upbringing. It actually takes a long period of time to actually learn and develop an understanding of what it means to work as a co-operative... It wasn't enough just to create the structure, there had to be a whole sort of educational process that goes along with it.

The Sunderland experience bears this out.

Community Involvement and Economic Self Determination

The Ideal

Community enterprises are intended to be under the control and management of the local community, and accountable to it. Often community involvement is formalised through the enterprise's legal structure, with company articles specifying that membership comprise a majority of workers and/or residents drawn from the local area. Any profits that might be made by the business, and which are not needed for re-investment, are intended for the collective benefit of the local community. Many community enterprises have a policy of employing local labour, and in contrast to conventional businesses they are aware of the impact of employment on the community and so maximise their payroll. It is this community orientation that justifies the sustained involvement of the community worker.

Apart from the economic benefits to the neighbourhood, many people trying to establish community enterprises also have wider, less tangible objectives for the community. It is often hoped that a community enterprise could be the first step for a community to assert its ability to affect its own economic future. It might inspire enough confidence in local people for them to adopt an active, collective response to their economic problems. The formation of a community enterprise is also intended by many community workers to act as a catalyst for the development of community solidarity, (the Mossbank Co-operative, Shetland, being a prime example of this). For these wider aims to be achieved it is essential that local people feel they 'own' the idea of the community enterprise. They have to be involved in the initial discussions about the project from the earliest days, rather than be presented with someone else's scheme.

> I would argue that for the long term development of any area, the feeling of ownership of whatever goes on in the area by the local community is the most important thing. Economic development on its own is not the only part of the picture: social development, social welfare, the general well-being and happiness of the area come into that. The community worker could develop facilitation skills, and I think there are skills involved here, where he or she is looking at how groups that have been traditionally polarised against each other can work together around given issues. That's basically what we did eight years ago with this group in Easterhouse around economic development ideas. A lot of the groups didn't particularly like each other, but we knew they all shared a common interest: they wanted to create jobs basically. (Chris Elphick)

The Reality

As many of the case studies have shown, achieving wide participation in a community enterprise by local people is far from easy. This is partly due to the cultural values of employees, discussed earlier in this section in relation to educational objectives. The concept of owning shares or becoming a member of a local business is foreign to many working class people, and Strathclyde Community Business is well aware of the problems of persuading people to pay even £1 for membership of the business. Local membership of the management committee or board of directors is also problematic, in that local people generally have little management experience and so there is a tendency to bring in outsiders with some relevant professional expertise. Even when this does not happen, the management often lose touch with the local community in their desire to ensure the commercial survival of the enterprise. Local people can then become apathetic, or even hostile, feeling that it is a cosy organisation benefitting a few activists. Clearly good communication with the local population is essential to avoid this, and some enterprises have established regular newsletters or magazines that are circulated either to all the members of the enterprise or all local households depending on how representative the membership is.

Several community workers have come to the conclusion, after long experience with community organisations, that the search for representativeness is fruitless. Cliff Southcombe's explicitly undemocratic approach to the Little Hulton project is probably the most extreme example of this viewpoint in this book:

> I had a fairly scathing attitude towards mainstream community development, which is why I fitted easily into selecting a Steering Committee ... the democracy element would be built in at a later stage.

Glen Buchanan pointed out that one can never hope to represent everyone in a neighbourhood, since in any community people disagree fundamentally on many matters. All one can aim for is to have the support of the representative organisations in the area and the involvement of those activists who are committed to the community enterprise. From his experience in Easterhouse, Chris Elphick felt that trying to be representative and democratic can actually handicap the community worker:

> In my experience, the only way to develop these ideas is through example. If you get too worried about wanting to get at everybody straight away, wanting to be truly representative and democratic, I think you are going to get nowhere, and I think you are going to disappear. What tends to work is through people seeing their friends, neighbours, relatives, doing something that they hadn't thought possible. I don't think things work through committee, basically. I don't think things really go forward if you feel you've got to wait till you get everyone involved and on our side to do this...
>
> I don't think that community workers are about representing the wishes of the community, personally. Lots of community workers would tell you otherwise. I think they are about being a resource, one of many resources in an area, with a set of skills.

Job Creation

Creating employment is the objective that distinguishes community enterprises from almost all the other work that community workers do. In most cases it is also the prime aim of the participants in the project, who are usually unemployed and desperate for 'proper jobs'. The fact that jobs are not all evaluated in the same way means that success in generating employment should not be measured simply by the total numbers of people given jobs: a YTS place is very different from a self-financing long term job.

MSC/Training Agency Jobs

At the most modest end of the job creation scale have been MSC (now Training Agency) financed jobs, principally YTS and Community Programmes. The former were so low paid that few community workers dealt with them, but there was widespread involvement by community workers in Community Programmes (Clark 1987:86). These jobs lasted for a year and paid the rate for the job. Several community businesses have used Community Programmes as means (a) to establish a business with subsidised wages, (b) to train a work force, and (c) to select the best employees. As such the Community Programme was intended simply as a preliminary stage on the way to a self-financing business. Sometimes a community business emerged out of a Community Programme, when employees realised they would not be re-employed (see Renton), or the community enterprise was developed to provide more secure jobs than those on local MSC schemes (*see* Little Hulton). In other cases the Community Programme operated alongside the community business (eg, South Aston), and sometimes the community business acts as the administering agency. In the early 1980s two thirds of the community businesses in Scotland had MSC funding.

In September 1988 the MSC became the Training Agency and Community Programmes became Employment Training Schemes, with payment on the basis of 'benefit plus'. Many community workers feel that these have little to offer community enterprises, and some development agencies refuse to have any involvement with them (eg Greater Manchester Co-operative Development Agency).

Self-Financing Jobs

After the Training Agency, European Social Fund and Urban Aid grants constitute the main source of funding for jobs, both these bodies being far less restrictive about the wages paid and length of a person's contract. Nevertheless there is normally the expectation by the funding body that community enterprises will become self-financing after three years or so, and therefore ESF or Urban Aid jobs are never very long term. Clearly the greatest achievement in job creation is for a community enterprise to generate self-financing employment. Many community enterprises think this is a realistic prospect in the future, and a few have already created a substantial number of self-financing jobs. The most outstanding examples are usually where local authority responsibilities have been contracted out to the community business, as in Possil and Ruchill. Compulsory tendering of council services could provide many opportunities for community enterprises in the future, but in assessing success a clear distinction should be maintained between job creation and job substitution: to create jobs in one locality at the cost of local government employees in another locality contributes little to the overall problem of unemployment. In the Highlands and Islands the fifty-two full-time jobs (and 300 part-time) that existed in the various community enterprises in 1987 were created through a combination of locally raised funds (mainly through share issues) and matched funding from the HIDB.

If self-financing jobs were the sole objective of community enterprises it could be argued that they should be abandoned as a response to unemployment, and instead the resources they use should be allocated to co-operative development agencies or other economic development units. They often have a far better record for job creation. For instance, the co-operative development agency Bootstrap in London has a 50 per cent success rate for the businesses it assists (meaning that they continue to trade and repay their start-up loans entirely), while nine out of ten of those involved in the unsuccessful businesses go on to gain employment largely because of the skills learnt in the co-ops. However, this achievement has been possible largely because Bootstrap abandoned their original policy of targeting the most deprived in Hackney:

> We originally sought people with numeracy and literacy problems, and other social problems. Very often they didn't have any other support. We very quickly raised the levels in relation to who we would deal with . . . It was naive to assume that people with those personal and social problems were actually going to be able to be part of a team. They were so weighed down with their problems that they just didn't have any energy left. (Kevin Tunnard)

For many community workers, the personal development of such people is one of the goals of the community enterprise.

Spin-offs

Before concluding this section it should be pointed out that whatever the success of a community enterprise in creating jobs, there are often spin-offs from the initial project which themselves generate employment. People who contributed to the original enterprise may decide they need further education or training (having got the confidence to seek it), or they might set up their own independent businesses. The creation of only one or two jobs can have a significant impact in an economically depressed neighbourhood, and when a community business is successful in employing even one person full time it is often a great inspiration to others in the community (see Bingham). In Castlemilk, Glasgow, employees in the St Dominic Centre's Community Programme left to set up their own workers' co-op, while in Easterhouse the community business '41 Trades' gave rise to several developments:

> There have been two or three small businesses created as a result of them being in existence, purely through brothers and sisters of the people who work there, seeing them do it and recognising that it's not as alien as they thought it would be, and developing their own ideas. So I think that's a crucial role, and the community worker can support that, and they can develop this through individual contact, through talking to people, through pushing the ideas out. (Chris Elphick)

Summary

At the heart of community workers' involvement in community enterprises is their view of what will constitute 'success'. The view that enterprise activities provide a highly motivating opportunity for learning new skills and acquiring new understanding has been presented, with education and personal development accompanying an increase in administrative and business skills. Community involvement and economic self-determination though central to community workers' concerns are rarely fully achieved, partly because of the long history of local acceptance of the role of employee rather than community entrepreneur. Finally, job creation, and their criteria of success, vary according to projects and according to local authority support. Despite only moderate success in terms of the two last criteria there may be other unforeseen spin-offs in a community where a local enterprise has received wide publicity. Other potential recruits to self-employment or community businesses are heartened by what they see and contribute to the long process of redefinition of the community.

16 Revisiting the Role of the Community Worker

Community workers draw on a range of knowledge and skills in their work with womens' groups, groups of young people, the elderly, the disabled, those seeking adult basic education and those simply wishing to pursue leisure and recreational interests. They participate in and foster an educational process in all these, and many other settings. Using the account of our many informants as a base, we here draw together issues related to group functioning, to the political context, to networking and to funding that arise in every neighbourhood and demand what we have called generic community work skills. We go on to apply them to the community enterprise context.

Enabling and Directing

In Chapter 2 we described the community development approach to community work. One of the essential features of this approach, it is commonly thought, is that it is 'responsive to needs, rather than imposing viewpoints or strategies.' The convention is that the community worker should facilitate or enable local people to achieve objectives that they have defined themselves, not initiate or direct their projects. However, this 'bottom-up', educational approach to community development is often a very lengthy process, and if the project is intended to create jobs such a long time scale is often considered too high a price to pay. Many community workers therefore face a dilemma between gradually developing the skills and confidence of local people (but perhaps taking years to create any jobs), and being directive in animating people to participate in a community enterprise but perhaps losing the educational value of the exercise and leaving the group dependent on a professional outsider.

The Rationale of the Conventional 'Facilitating' Approach

> One of my colleagues and I were out at a meeting last week, in which a senior community education worker had more or less, as far as I could see, tried to hoist community business on what was not even a group, which is totally crazy. Community workers should only get involved in community business if people in the community are wanting that. It can't be you or me as the community worker, and we say 'We could really do with community business in this area': that would really be a top-down initiative. It should be me, as chairman of the tenants' association or something, having had wide discussions within the association, coming to you as the community worker and saying 'We've heard about this thing called Community Business', or 'We've heard about this thing called Housing Co-operatives, how can you help us get that set up?' (Glen Buchanan, SCB)

Once the initiative to develop a community enterprise has been taken by local people, they should be involved in the decision making, according to the conventional approach. They should not only share in the decisions but actually shape them, and be accountable to the rest of the community for their implementation, in so far as such participatory democracy is possible. The clearest example of a non-directive approach amongst our case studies is that of John McGhee in Armadale. One consequence of his not having directed the group to develop his personal ideas is that they feel the project is their own. If the community worker initiates the ideas and persuades the group to pursue them, ownership of the project will lie with the community worker, not the group. Christine Forrester, of VARC, is convinced that good community development depends on the group owning the project:

> To own the project they must understand, and not only understand but have taken on board, all the processes that need to be gone through to establish that project, whatever it is. I believe, from my experience, that groups can do it.

Another reason why many community workers are opposed to a directive approach is that, in their view, when professionals or agencies initiate action it generally does not act as a catalyst for local people but discourages them from taking the initiative. In Chris Elphick's experience, 'it tends just to add to the expectation that things will be done from the top.' This rationale for grass roots development makes some community workers very critical of recent moves to instruct their community education workers to become involved in community enterprises. It also explains the misgivings of several community workers in Strathclyde who have themselves been involved in community businesses but are wary of the way community enterprises have become 'flavour of the month' in the Regional Council.

The Rationale for a More Directive Approach

Even those workers who are committed to a non-directive approach to community development readily acknowledge that things take a long time to be done that way. In Armadale, for instance, there have not yet been any jobs created after eighteen months of meetings by the unemployment group. For many community workers this is too long to wait, and even those who argue that the community worker should not 'impose viewpoints or strategies' are prepared to advocate consciousness raising to focus attention on unemployment in ways hitherto unfamiliar to local people. Fiona Robertson, who was Senior Community Development Worker in Castlemilk, Glasgow, finds the debate between enabling and directing 'a sort of misnomer':

> I think workers do have a responsibility to raise issues with people, and I think we do have a responsibility to help people recognise options, to give information to people and for them to make decisions, and at times that may very well be seen as being directive, but the opposite of that is to be so non-directive in actual fact, that you're giving no guidance, and you're giving no input. Life isn't long enough. If you go into areas and you talk to people who are living in these deprived areas, where the spiral is very much a downward one, they're ready to be taking initiatives now.

Workers from development agencies tend to emphasise this need to provide a catalyst in the form of imaginative ideas. Reflecting on Community Routes in Hattersley, Cliff Southcombe said:

> You can't expect local people to have the vision to cross fertilise between enterprises because their breadth of experience isn't sufficient.

Kevin Tunnard, a worker in the co-operative development agency Bootstrap in Hackney, London, shares this view:

> We came to the conclusion very early on that you couldn't just sit and wait for people to come to you with business ideas. It seemed to us that the sorts of ideas that people were coming to us with were related to whatever skills or background they came from: industries in decline, basically. We didn't feel we had the competence to

> deal with the sorts of problems that would be thrown up... So we started looking for the ideas which we felt had some chance in being successful. They were really drawn from our own experiences at the beginning.

We have already observed that participants in the development of a community enterprise are likely to perceive success primarily in terms of job creation, so if after a year the business is not yet established there is a danger that the group will disperse, feeling nothing has been achieved. In Little Hulton the community workers felt that the group would have disbanded if funding had not been won in the first few months.

It is noteworthy that of the enterprises reported in the case studies, the two which were established fastest (Ruchill and NUmac) both had community workers who had no formal community work training. Greater Ruchill Community Business was established in six months, due to the need to meet the council's deadline for a security contract. Nevertheless Caroline Coleman, the community worker, was aware of the costs in terms of community development, such as members of the group dropping out because they could not keep up with the pace. NUmac Precision Engineering Ltd. (a workers' co-op) was trading within eleven months of being suggested. Paddy O'Brien, the community worker involved, was probably the most directive of those who have contributed their accounts. For him the opportunity of generating employment was too important for him to be inhibited from 'leading from the front'. The fact that these two successes (in terms of job creation) were both assisted by untrained, but experienced, community workers, raises the question of whether formal community work training inhibits people from taking initiatives.

Synthesising the Two Approaches

Very few of the practitioners that we spoke to thought it possible to advocate one approach to the complete exclusion of the other. The more experienced community workers suggested that both strategies can be appropriate at different stages in the development of an enterprise. Several felt that it can be constructive to take the initiative when the project is at its earliest stage, in order to generate enthusiasm in the group, and once the participants are motivated a less pro-active role can be adopted.

Even the community worker committed to a non-directive approach has her own values and expectations about what might be achieved through the project. It is much better if these are made explicit, rather than remaining a 'hidden agenda'. It is also helpful if the worker openly confronts the issue of how she prefers to operate with the group. Evidently if the community worker states what her hopes are for the enterprise it is unlikely not to affect the group's views on the matter, and thus it brings her closer to the position of animateur.

Some community workers acknowledged that you have to show people what the possibilities are for employment generation, but the way this is done is critical:

> Community workers have always had to tread this fine line between allowing things to emerge from within, and suggesting. I don't think that's an issue that is ever going to go away, and because you are dealing very often with a base of such low expectations, ideas have often got to be presented to people. Now I think it's the way that is done. I think if they're presented as a variety of possibilities, rather than 'this is the way to do it', then what you can create is the mechanism in which people can make choices. (Chris Elphick)

It is clearly impossible to be prescriptive about what approach community workers should take, particularly since situations vary so much with the stage of development of the enterprise, the group and the locality. Tor Justad's experience in the Shetlands led him to conclude that there was little need for animateurs in rural areas, since people there were usually good at initiating projects. The community worker's role was to help rural people acquire the skills to negotiate with the authorities.

In practice the approach eventually adopted by the community worker is usually determined more by the kind of work she is doing than by a distinctive personal style. Many of those interviewed mentioned that they had adopted a different approach to community development when involved in a different project, such as a tenants' group. The personal characteristics of those participating in the enterprise, the dynamics of the group and the nature of the business in hand are probably the most important factors influencing the community worker's position between a purely facilitative and an explicitly directive approach.

Generic Skills and Knowledge Necessary For Community Workers

The knowledge and skills that are valuable to community workers engaged in community enterprises can be divided into two categories: those which are useful in many different aspects of community workers' jobs, and those technical skills and knowledge which are specifically relevant to employment initiatives. We will first discuss the skills and knowledge of general use to community workers and go on to devote Chapter 17 to the more specific elements of this work.

Group Work

1 Group dynamics

Practically every community worker we interviewed emphasised how essential group work skills are. 'It's the group development process that's really the core to a community worker working with a local group that are interested in economic development,' (Mike Naulty, CEST). The essence of the group development is to enable the individuals to co-operate successfully, which means establishing a cohesive group that understands and is agreed on its aims. The participants must be encouraged to focus on issues rather than personalities, they should have some insight into basic interaction within groups and have an idea of how different kinds of structures can assist or impede decision making. Youth and Community Services in Central Region have produced and packaged a course on Decision Making in Your Group, available to locally based community workers. Understanding how committees operate is a further stage for the group in learning how to co-operate efficiently.

Group work skills are very important in facilitating effective group discussions, both in terms of helping to provide some focus to the proceedings and in helping to involve the quieter members of the group, who might otherwise easily lose out on early meetings and feel they have little to offer. Group discussion about how ideas for businesses are 'found' may be done by brainstorming, if the group have not already come prepared with ideas. Later the projects can be sifted through to identify the more viable ones that should be pursued in more detail. Brainstorming is a useful way for the community worker to observe how the group work together. General discussion as to why some ideas are more viable than others is also an informal method of discussing basic business concepts.

2 Recognising the time span

The setting up of a community venture is a long term commitment for those who are likely to become involved – not the least for the community worker. She needs to recognise that prospect and, if the project is taken up, retain that commitment. Equally important, local people must be made fully aware of the time-scale normally involved in establishing a community enterprise. Participants in the group must, at an early stage, address the question of whether they are prepared to devote perhaps five years of their lives to a project before it is financially viable.

A clear understanding of the time span helps avoid unrealistic expectations which can easily result in disillusionment when they are not fulfilled. For instance the group should be prepared to learn, months after they first started to prepare an Urban Aid application, that they have not been granted the money and must start again. The group should also be made aware of how the long development period could effect its membership, with new people joining, old members leaving, and possible changes in leadership.

3 Setting achievable short term targets

Several community workers have found that the best way to sustain the group's motivation during the potentially long period of development is by identifying short term goals which allow people to see things happening. Setting targets for each week or month also gives a framework for the gradual development of the group's skills and confidence. Organising trips to see other successful community enterprises is an obvious objective to fulfil early on: as Chris Elphick says, 'Very often people need to convince themselves it can be done, and the way to do that is to meet other people from a similar background and situation who've done it.' Other short term projects might include some kind of fund raising activity, or organising and attending training courses – anything may be used to keep the momentum going. Having several irons in the fire means that when one particular plan is held up, perhaps for a few months, other projects can be pursued to prevent enthusiasm flagging. The group can also be stimulated by the introduction of new ideas, new people or information that participants can relate to and which increases their own growth and development.

All the intermediate targets towards establishing a community enterprise can involve learning new skills and building up confidence, particularly in administrative work. Community workers have an important supportive role in this, acting as demonstrators of equipment or use of tools, offering constructive feedback on the level of work achieved, and so on. For example, they can draw members attention to simple maths or spelling errors, rather than letting these become public. Such occasions also help the worker to identify the particular learning needs of individuals. Many community workers felt that in supporting the group they should steer people away from tasks that they cannot attain, since the failure would be very damaging. However, others that we spoke to thought that failure was often valuable for the group's learning, and in their view it helped prepare the participants for the harsh business world.

4 Maintaining the group and encouraging self-appraisal.

Maintaining a group of people over a long period of time and despite set-backs is a challenging task for the community worker. Despondency is not the only problem that has to be faced: sometimes the enthusiasm to create jobs can lead to activists burning themselves out with self-exploitation or by exploiting each other. Chris Elphick suggests that the group should be made aware of this possibility:

> Perhaps the community worker has to develop some sort of basic idea of good management practice... that they don't work all hours of the day and night.

Another problem frequently encountered is the emergence of a core group of more confident activists who, either by default or by intention, begin to take the lead in activities and decision-making to the exclusion of other participants. A useful strategy to maintain group cohesion is to avoid delegating and, wherever possible, insist that the whole group attends meetings with council officials, goes on training courses, visits other enterprises and so on. This policy was adopted by the group campaigning for the St Dominic's Centre in Castlemilk, Glasgow, and proved successful in holding them altogether. Unfortunately the strategy is far less feasible when managing a project than when campaigning for it.

A method of identifying targets, establishing a time scale, avoiding undue expectations and holding a group together is to encourage the group to be self-analytical. There is a danger that participants may see the time spent on the project to have been wasted because they have their sights set on the main goal – a community business or jobs – which has not yet materialised. The community worker needs to help individuals and the group identify what in fact has been achieved, both by individuals and the group itself, throughout the period of their time together. Indeed, this reinforcement of what has been achieved should be an ongoing feature of the learning process. Such self-appraisal also allows the group to monitor whether they are on the course they originally set themselves, a task that Mike Naulty of CEST thinks essential to community development. 'Monitoring evaluation, is a very important part, and I don't think we do it nearly enough as community workers'.

5 Broadening involvement

A danger that community workers must be wary of is that the people who first initiate an enterprise project might come to feel they 'own' the idea to the exclusion of others in the community. In so doing they lose touch with the rest of the neighbourhood and the original objectives of a community business. This can be a particular problem when the community enterprise group has emerged out of another pre-existing organisation that had previously worked very cohesively, and which might not have had a goal of broad community participation. Mike Naulty, working in Beechwood, Dundee, found that it was not so much a failure to inform local people of what the community business group was doing that prevented it from expanding, but the group's exclusivity.

> Because it was a clique new people could sit for a couple of meetings and feel that they were a dead weight and move away again. The members of the committee were picking up and supporting each other and not allowing new people to speak. When that changed people did come in: they were more receptive to their needs and so they would stay. So that was the main factor that it increased from say six to fourteen.

> It was a friendship clique, and it was really working on that clique to say, 'Well, there is nothing wrong with being friends, that's a very important part of community life, but we've got all this work that we want to do and we can't get it done unless we have other folk'...It was quite painful and soul-searching for them because we embarked on a training programme. We went away and had a residential course in Edzell, and the whole issue was about increasing participation and how we were going to go about bringing other folk in. We had a good look at ourselves and how

> we operated, and how we excluded folk, and that was very hard, you can imagine. It was videoed as well, we played it back, we did group assessments, it was a very sensitive area that had to be done in a residential setting so nobody could run off or opt out. I think there were trouble spots, and there were sort of breaking points for folk, but it opened out and people could look more objectively, or stand outside themselves and say, 'Oh, is that what I am doing?'

It would, however, be naive to suppose that broadening involvement is always possible or effective. A group of activists, possibly originally trained in organisational work through their membership of tenants' groups, may remain central to the business. In Ferguslie Park, even when the business began to spawn subsidiaries, the initial activists were the ones on whom developments depended.

> When you talk about twelve on a committee you find that five or six of them won't have anything to do other than turn up and show an interest. It's the ones that have got something to do, who continue. I don't think generally it leads to a great mushrooming of interests... I doubt if we ever got more than thirty people at an AGM, and this was annoying when there were such important issues. (Neil Graham)

Neil, speaking of one of the best known community businesses in Scotland, Flagstone, reflected that realistically, 'If you were to walk out on the street and say, 'Is there a community business in Ferguslie?' folk would think you had just landed from Mars'. This was despite a strong publicity drive to obtain a wider commitment over the years.

It is therefore important for community workers to recognise that while they should encourage the initial group to enlist others, they may nevertheless have to invest considerable time and trouble in keeping up the spirits and commitment of those who have been active from the start and on whom the business may depend for long term stability.

6 Supporting the manager

Once a manager has been appointed by the Board of Directors he has, apparently, a clear mandate to manage. Where community businesses differ from other businesses is in the community orientation of the work and in attitudes to employment and profitability. Major conflicts of interest can develop (see Ferguslie) and the manager can find the internal politics of the group of directors, the lack of commitment of the workers and the financial pressures of a business that is often hardly viable extremely difficult to withstand. On these occasions, community workers may find themselves acting as sounding boards and consultants who sustain both the managers and the businesses. Tough decisions may have to be made over dismissal of managers, and here the community worker may play a part. But even more important is the process of selection (*see* Ferguslie for problems of selection). Mistakes made at this point seriously undermine the eventual chances of viability.

Knowledge of the Wider Scene

As part of her stock of knowledge any community worker needs to have a good grasp of the locality: the interest groups, the professional bodies, the provision available for leisure, welfare, and education and training. When it comes to launching into the world of business this knowledge has to be expanded. Christine Forrester of VARC lists the sort of local information she sees as essential:

> ... any schemes that are operating in their area and what is actually happening in terms of employment generally in their area. This needs to be very up-to-date. They should be in touch with local employers since there have often been long and close

> links between a firm and a specific local community. In the case of Grangemouth, where so many people who live in Grangemouth actually went there because of the petro-chemical industry, there are particularly close links between the community and the employers. These links must be fostered.

Contact with local employers may yield advance notice of impending closures and allow community workers to establish links with those about to become unemployed. Since contacting the unemployed presents major problems, targetting whole groups has obvious benefits (*see* for example, Armadale in West Lothian).

There is also a need to know about the local authority's interest and policies with respect to education, unemployment and housing. Such knowledge may well make it possible to enable a community group to generate a business idea, as for example in Ruchill and Barrowfield.

Planning departments in particular are concerned with employment generation. Knowledge of their intentions and co-operation with them in advance of decision-making may well enable community educators to engage in a strategic as well as a tactical role in the establishment of enterprise activities. However, there is often conflict and tension between Planning Departments and Community Education, with community work seen by other local authority departments as a luxury without obvious benefit to the community. On many occasions those we interviewed stressed the poor liaison and rivalry between different departments. As Chris Elphick put it:

> It's crazy that an obstacle for many community groups is the fact that the District Council doesn't liaise with the Regional Council, and one department doesn't know what the other department is doing.

In fact, complex political interests at a particular point in time can be a source of confusion and occasionally disaster for community enterprises, but advance knowledge may be turned to advantage. Where district and regional planning departments are both interested in a community business and both potential providers of funds their competitive feelings may be exploited. Indeed this has been the case at Pilmeny in Edinburgh.

Knowledge of these complexities is often haphazardly acquired, but the community worker may need to explore the situation systematically which may reveal strings attached to community development. This is often the speed forced on business start-ups, as in Livingston, West Lothian, where engaging large numbers of local people in development had to be sacrificed to the need for a quick response. In Stoneyburn, also in West Lothian, workspaces were supplied by the local authority but without adequate backup. The community business was informed that they had to manage it without helpers and with no manager.

Networking

No community worker is ignorant of the value of local networks. In the case of community enterprise the networks change somewhat. Here it becomes necessary to include in the network interested parties from the private sector eg firms ready to get involved with community enterprise – as well as from the public domain.

Schools appear to be increasingly keen on lifelong learning, and where space is available and staff are willing to join in adult education they can form a valuable link in the educational chain that leads to a community business. In Armadale (and in Blackburn, West Lothian) there are already strong links with the local secondary schools which have provided major technical skill support and development.

Colleges of Further Education are not immediately accessible to most of the unemployed, whether because of distance and the cost of fares or because of the didactic style of teaching. However, they may prove a useful second level of development, and plans are afoot to involve them in outreach work with community groups. This is only likely to be successful once these groups feel a degree of confidence in expressing their own desires and needs.

Other community groups that are already well on the way to establishing themselves as community enterprises are essential parts of the network. Contact with people who have been successful and can inculcate a belief in the possibilities of community enterprises creates the climate for personal, educational and business development.

In the specific field of community enterprise there is now an enormous range of agencies, from local Enterprise Trusts to Strathclyde Community Business to local authority agencies (see list at back of book). In Highland Region ACEHI has taken over many of the functions of the HIDB in advising and training new groups engaged in setting up community businesses. Development officers from these agencies are often vital for community groups to establish viable businesses. It is perfectly clear, for example in Ruchill, how important the training assistance given by Strathclyde Community Business was to the competence and confidence of the Board of Directors.

One of the comments made by the community workers we interviewed was that they had greatly enjoyed and benefited from the expansion of their networks. Where before they had been somewhat inward looking now they felt they had begun to see the wider regional, and even national context in which they were operating.

Formulating a Constitution

Community workers, as part of their normal training, learn the steps for formally constituting groups. This skill again comes into play when developing community businesses for the knowledge of writing constitutions is largely generic. However, the requirements of community businesses are more complex than most organisations and the assistance of development officers from enterprise units is important. Drawing up the Memorandum and Articles of Association for a community business is a matter for those with knowledge of the legal requirements.

Funding

We have mentioned sources of funding throughout the case studies. Community workers are already familiar with the necessity of writing grant applications. In the field of business the demands become even more exacting. As we learn from experience even registering the company require a care and attention to detail that does not come easily.

Our informants stressed that detailed knowledge of all the grant giving bodies was not essential, but an awareness that these bodies (a) had different criteria for awarding grants, (b) frequently changed their criteria, and (c) each needed their particular requirements to be met, was seen as fundamental. If community workers were unaware of this they were likely both to be disappointed and also to run the risk of seriously discouraging the group with whom they were working.

> Some kinds of funding are totally inappropriate for a group's needs, and again we come back to the question of how you keep a group together when you're not necessarily getting quick results from some of the work that you are doing? One of the worst things is where groups are encouraged to apply for inappropriate funding,

and I think one of the tasks of the community worker should be to sound out the different funding agencies, whether or not this kind of proposal would be acceptable. There is no point in sending certain kinds of groups off in pursuit of Urban Aid funding. A group that isn't in a defined Priority area, isn't going to get Urban Aid funding, there's no point in looking at it. And taking a group through all the hoops and hurdles and project development and so on, that can be a demoralising experience, so workers should know, and should learn the basic information on funding. (Christine Forrester, VARC)

Once again, recourse to the advice of specialised units was recommended. However, a naive dependence on such advice without some attempt to familiarise themselves with the funding bodies was felt to be counter-productive. In the offices of community workers we typically observed the well-thumbed tomes which specified the grants available to fledgling community groups and businesses. Decisions on which form of business to adopt depend on knowledge of the conditions which govern their funding. Roy Pedersen points out:

The advantage of a company limited by guarantee (a community business as opposed to a co-operative) is that you can get charitable status and that can be beneficial if you are raising cash from other charities. Charities can often only give to charities.

The HIDB has had a major part to play in launching co-operatives throughout the Highlands and Islands. They not only match the funds raised by the local community but also provide a management grant for a period of up to five years on a tapering scale. This is towards the administrative costs of the enterprise until such time as it is earning enough money to cover its costs. Lastly the Board pays the normal grants and loans for the various projects which the co-operative or enterprise starts to develop.

Raising share capital can present difficulties, though in the Highlands and Islands, this was not a problem. There appeared to be considerable sums available even in small communities. For example, Vatersay, with a population of just over a hundred raised about £6,000 in shares. A company limited by guarantee has no provision for raising shares, and can only get its money by an annual membership charge or by donations. In more urbanised areas this may be more appropriate. Roy Pedersen suggested this was so because:

There is less a feeling of community than you get in a small area, like a small island, where you often get the whole community subscribing quite substantial sums of money. There are pressures produced by the knowledge that everyone else has put in money.

It is also only fair to say that poverty is experienced and perceived rather differently in rural and urban areas.

Donations can act as a major resource for funding. The Helmsdale Heritage Centre, which draws a steady flow of tourists during the summer months, is a case in point.

Fiona Robertson, a senior community development worker, argues that:

Community workers must be trained to be resourceful, to recognise the main avenues of funding and the doors that need to be knocked on. I'm eleven years now in the field and I'm constantly coming across new pockets of money, and new sources of funding that haven't been used before. There's greater demands now on workers to do that because the old chestnuts of Urban Aid and the MSC are long gone, and we've got to be more imaginative than we used to be.

She feels that community workers should not rely exclusively on 'single door' funding agencies such as SCB, and in this she is in agreement with the development officers of community enterprise agencies themselves. Other avenues must be explored. She cites the two publications produced by the Directory of Social Change, the first on company funding and the second on charitable funding. She stresses the need to examine what the private sector will provide in cash, in kind and in sponsorship to local economic initiatives. Indeed, it has now become the policy of regional agencies to act as signposts to all types of funding, rather than remaining single minded advocates of Urban Aid or the European Social Fund.

Acknowledging the need for a new resourcefulness from community workers, she supports Christine Forrester's (VARC) view that the establishment of a local network that includes the private sector is an important element in community workers' professional equipment.

17 Expanding the Role of the Community Worker: Specific Knowledge and Skills

We now come to look at some of the knowledge and skills which community workers working in the field of enterprise have to acquire. Hitherto we have discussed the generic aspects of community work in all settings. Here we examine the more specific requirements of the role. We therefore define the varieties of enterprise in which a community group may engage from a simple bulk buying operation to a full-fledged community business. We provide an outline of the demands on Steering Groups and then debate the question of the degree of business knowledge required by community workers entering the field of community enterprise, given the new agencies supporting such developments. Lastly we turn to looking at the general problems facing those who embark on community development through community enterprises.

Knowledge of the Variety and Scope of Community Enterprises

We have emphasised the planning requirements in developing community enterprises. Planning and preparation are only feasible when some knowledge of possibilities is available, whether these concern funding, support structures or the forms taken by community enterprises. In this section we shall examine the knowledge about community enterprises that is thought useful for community workers by those who have been through the process themselves and those who occupy contingent positions in the districts and regions.

We have already mentioned the differences between the varieties of co-operative and community businesses with which community workers should be familiar (see Chapter 1). The importance of being able to introduce imaginative ideas for business schemes has already been discussed.

Despite the wide diversity of products and services in which community enterprises are engaged, it is possible to classify them according to the basis on which their workers are employed, though one form of activity does not exclude another:

i Temporary Employment and Training
ii Work-Space
iii Home Production
iv Commercial Trading Businesses
v Community Contracting for Council Work
vi Private Sector Involvement
vii Bulk Buying, Food Co-operatives, Credit Unions.

i Temporary Employment and Training

Community businesses have often been started up by community groups seeking to offer temporary paid jobs to unemployed adults and young people, making use of MSC (now Training Agency) funding. They had either YTS or Community Programme funding to underwrite the salaries and overheads of the business projects – albeit for a limited period only, as was common for all MSC-funded schemes. Local environmental improvement work, furniture recycling, energy conservation (putting draught excluders into old people's houses at cost of materials only) and gardening for the elderly and handicapped free of charge, were typical projects. The essential difference between community group use of such schemes and MSC schemes generally lay in the fact that the community group resorted to the method as a ploy. It was an expedient by which to gain expertise and experience in managing a business and a workforce, and a means to develop skills and technical knowledge through actually carrying out the work. It is perhaps for this reason that community workers' involvement in Community Programmes was widespread (Clark, 1987:86). A major difficulty, however, was that these schemes were not allowed to retain any profits made by the business, which might have been put into new ventures once the MSC funding expired. It was this transition from fully subsidised business schemes to independent business ventures that contributed to the failure of many schemes. Creative accounting sometimes assisted this transition.

In the short term however, such schemes offered services that reflected the needs of the local community, employed local people, encouraged the development of new skills and expertise and attempted to alter the thinking of the local community towards self-help and greater community participation. (Note the use made of the Community Programme by Armadale). Community Programmes had great potential for new styles of employment if the management committee so desired but this potential was rarely exploited because the members of the management committee were often uninformed, unimaginative or conservative.

An example of a general MSC scheme which did not seek to involve the community in this way occurred in Denny, Central Region, where environmental improvement was undertaken to landscape a small park and put in trees. Had they consulted the local community they would have been informed that what was being so attractively landscaped was the community's football pitch – and the means by which local youngsters amused themselves in their spare time.

Whether or not Employment Training, which replaced the Community Programmes in September 1988, can be used as a preliminary stage in community enterprises is not yet known.

ii Work-space: a Mini Development Agency

The term development agency is rather a grand title to give community businesses which are effectively only providing work-space for other commercial (private or community business) schemes. Apart from the physical facilities which community business work-space offers at a very cheap rent, a rent, incidentally, which neither the Council nor private factors would consider viable, the community business also typically offers commercial and clerical back-up facilities for users of their work-spaces. Unfortunately, local authorities have tended to ignore the potential of such cheap work-space provision for stimulating new sources of local employment in their community. Work-space provision indirectly offers employment prospects where previously few existed, and sometimes also generates additional income for the local community.

The concept of, and the stimulus for, creating work-space has often come from professional community business development groups such as Strathclyde Community Business. A few local groups have also been attracted to this idea as a form of generating 'seed money' for the less commercially oriented community business schemes. To the extent that the venture is successful in getting tenants for the work-space, they are able to generate a few permanent and part-time jobs associated with the management of the work-space and its services. However, not all community workers subscribe to this form of community business (*see* John McGhee), arguing that it is more supportive to private business than to the community and that it leads to few jobs.

iii Home Production

Home production provides both the labour and often the finished article for a number of community businesses in the Strathclyde area and for co-operatives in the Highlands and Islands – where it is rarely the only source of income (cp. Staffin in Skye).

The majority of people employed in what are usually craft industries are women (McArthur, 1985), for whom the work satisfies their obligation to look after children and home as well as to earn. However, for these same reasons continuity of production is difficult to maintain (Echlin, 1985). They are also unfortunately among the lower wage earners, for a number of reasons relating to part-time working, gender, and lack of organisation. The method of production – home based – may isolate or diminish support from other women. This is not, however, always the case. Educational opportunities for exploring women's role in society are generally difficult to create and sustain, and the concept of community business (or the co-operative) may be lost sight of by the single woman concerned with generating additional income for the home.

iv Commercially Trading Businesses

A number of these community enterprises operate out of shop premises, such as cafes or launderettes for example, whilst others make use of former local authority buildings, even former council housing, as the base for their activities. Unlike the MSC schemes, these community enterprises must attain economic viability or 'go under'. However, profit, where it is made, is not simply ploughed back into the firm in terms of higher wages, but used to finance other projects in the community or to support other fledgling community business initiatives. This formula is particularly apparent in the co-operatives of the Highlands and Islands, where the intention has always been to set up a multi-purpose business in which the more profitable elements support the less or unprofitable community services. The jobs are intended to be permanent part-time or full-time positions (e.g. Shetland).

v Community Contracting for Council Work

With the government's drive for the privatisation of the services of local councils, opportunities for communities to tender for contracts arise. Though there are objections on the grounds of one group of workers taking the jobs of another group, therefore producing job substitution rather than job creation, central government has some support for its privatisation proposals because:-

> Our service provision is not controlled by the workers and users. People see the slow, inefficient, bureaucracy and quite naturally think, therefore, that a community housing repair service would be more targetted and more efficient. Of course, any

privatisation which eliminates the possibility of public control can result in the lowering of the quality of the service, and almost certainly will result in fewer jobs and an erosion of conditions of employment ... but if privatisation goes ahead then certainly communitised provision is better than Wimpey or Barratts or something like that. (Tony Kinder, Lothian Regional Councillor)

The concerns expressed by community workers and this councillor (job substitution, possible job loss and loss of accountability and lowering of quality) are partially countered by the argument that there should be alliances between the local authority and community enterprises so that the needs of communities can be fulfilled. Some workers argue that compatibility between the aims of the local authority and the community enterprise can be negotiated, particularly if the local authority is sympathetic to community enterprise and willing to specify contracts that will be of interest only to small concerns as opposed to the big contractors. In Tayside the workers in community enterprise are keen to 'put in a marker' in the debate over privatisation, and ensure that the community enterprise dimension is voiced.

vi Private Sector Involvement

Community workers, looking for opportunities to benefit their localities should not turn away from the private sector nor from encouraging private sector businesses.

A community worker should know what private investment there is in his or her area. Maybe develop a relationship with some business people. Now there may be a problem there. Most business people I know are pretty hard and straight. Most community workers I know tend to be pretty waffly. We've created this Easterhouse partnership between the business community and the local community and the aim of that was that the local community should have access to the resources that the business community had. There were two big problems – it takes a long time usually for a community to get its act together, because there are lots of issues in communities that tend to drive them apart, but it seems a very legitimate area for a community worker to work in and develop skills in. The other issue is that the business community tends to get impatient. They want to see results (rather like politicians). (Chris Elphick)

This community worker (now working as a community development consultant) argued that the local businesses were keen to offer resources and that the role of the community worker might be to act as mediator during the slow process of development.

He also argued that alliances with such enlightened entrepreneurs as Anita Roddick of the Body Shop should be pursued. It is her intention, though basically a high street retailer, to set up smaller versions of her shops in less central areas even though they would not be expected to produce much or any profit. More important, however, is her consideration of plans to start a Body Shop factory in Easterhouse, a Glasgow council estate, not only providing desperately needed employment but also a percentage of profits which would go to community ventures. This is rather different from firms like Marks & Spencer who have a social responsibility department which funds worthy causes and seconds managers to help start up businesses. In short Chris Elphick stresses the need for community workers to keep an eye out for opportunities and not to limit their contacts to the professional support agencies.

My experience of a lot of community workers is that they're hooked into quite a bureaucratic style of thinking that actually prevents them thinking entrepreneurially and creatively.

A community business that was particularly creative was started in Walsall, where the group looked around their area and recognised that when people get married they need a variety of services, from organising the church, the band and the food to the invitations, the flowers and transport. They proceeded to develop a multiservice provision to meet the need for highly desirable stress-free weddings.

vii Exploring all Avenues: Bulk Buying, Food Co-operatives, Credit Unions

When the community worker presents these possibilities to a group it is important that all avenues be explored. The form of enterprise chosen may well be determined by the kind of support most readily available. The views of the professionals with whom we discussed business structures seemed to point to the managers' motivation, drive and vision being highest in small businesses and in workers' co-operatives, whereas the community's needs were best met by community businesses. On the other hand, the work force in community businesses is often alienated in the same way as it would be with conventional employment, and is therefore difficult to educate to a different role. (For a brief comparison of community businesses and community co-operatives see Chapter 1 and the section on Funding in this chapter).

Glen Buchanan of Strathclyde Community Business has pointed out that community businesses often take on the long-term unemployed and for them the different relationship with their employer may take some time to grasp. As employees they are working for a wage, but they need to understand that they are also working for the community, and, as part of the community, they share in the 'ownership' of the business itself.

This leads us on to observe that community enterprises are usually in areas where there is little demand for service provision and therefore ultimately they need to sell services outside the locality. This can, however, be counteracted by imaginative surveys of 'import penetration'. According to Chris Elphick, one community group 'did a survey of all the doorstep provision in their area – milk, bread, papers, fish and chips, all the things that serve the area and then went on to get an estimate of how much of the money was going out of the area to these businesses. They found that milk in particular was run by a city-wide, indeed, national, business. The community group started targetting these doorstep deliveries and produced their own 'Import Substitution Scheme' and now run a very successful milk round and deliver bread.'

Some of the businesses that have been described might well be considered over-ambitious as starter projects for newcomers to the field of enterprise. For this reason food co-operatives, bulk buying organisations and credit unions appear to offer a less intimidating and risky introduction to co-operative business activity. As Mike Naulty points out, a start should be made in a very modest way:

> Let's start with where the people are at, and so if they've assessed that there is a need for a bulk-buy scheme, that can be worked on, and the feasibility of developing it further into a full co-op can be looked at through that process. And that's the skill of the community worker – to be attuned first to recognising economic activity and then realising it can lead to further developments in the economic sense, and finally, starting to talk about possible routes to take where we might be able to help.

This brings us finally to consider credit unions from which other economic developments may stem. These provide the structure by which a local community can create their own bank and their own means of regular saving as well as a low rate of interest on borrowing. They also serve a valuable educational purpose in enabling the members to learn about the means of avoiding serious financial hardship. They have been remarkably successful in Ireland, and also where they have been developed around a single industry, such as Strathclyde Passenger Transport. They seem particularly likely to succeed where there is a core of common culture e.g. the Catholic culture of Ireland, a group of close knit families (as in Crownhill) or a particular industry. Credit unions are already quite widely established in England (eg, Scotswood Credit Union and East End Credit Union in Sunderland, and Little Hulton near Manchester) and are slowly taking off in Scotland.

The Community Business Development Process

Getting Started

On the evidence of our interviews few workers launch into community enterprises without having built up a considerable rapport with their groups, who have perhaps initially met together for entirely different purposes. The notion of self-employment or a community business of one kind or another may have been mentioned in general terms (e.g. in redundancy courses) but is often not the primary concern of an existing community group. The idea may grow out of the urgent need of group members, but it has to be fostered with care. It may be only one of a set of objectives that the group establishes for itself under the guidance of the worker.

Workers can facilitate discussions about employment initiatives by providing materials on written-up projects, pamphlets on self-employment schemes, on co-operatives and on community businesses, and most particularly by their own research. Research may lead them to existing community businesses willing to act as hosts and informants to their own group, it may lead to an awareness of local opportunities and it may indicate skills and competencies the worker and the group need to acquire. It will certainly reveal the appropriate network of informants and range of back-up agencies invaluable to the community worker nurturing a group with a business in mind.

The life-history of many groups indicates the importance of taking the group through what have been identified as the seven stages in developing a community business. In their Annual Report 1987/88, Strathclyde Community Business fills in the details of these seven stages. It is well worth consulting them.

In the early stages visits to other community businesses provide lively discussions with people who have gone through a similar period of doubt and uncertainty and have arrived at solutions. They also provide a series of activities for the group. John McGhee made it clear that groups of unemployed workers are demanding. Not only does the community worker need aims and objectives for her own work, but the group must be conscious of their own weekly objectives and be helped to achieve them. Setting targets puts the worker under strain but helps to maintain the group's interest.

A list of speakers who open up new avenues for exploration is recommended by many workers. The group itself needs to decide whether they are ready for such information and new contacts, and can then initiate the formal request (writing letters – asking a speaker to meet the group, or for permission to visit a project – form filling, requests for transport and so on). Such activities establish for the group at the outset that, whilst the community worker wishes to help and support them, the real responsibility for making things happen and getting things done rests with the members of the group themselves. The community worker's task is to try to ensure that they develop the skills and expertise necessary to further the project and their objectives.

Later developments are discussed at the end of this report and in much more detail in advice packages supplied by Strathclyde Community Business.

Business Skills

It should be clear from all the previous discussion that community workers in the field of enterprise need to draw upon and extend (often quite dramatically) many of their existing skills. Do they need to acquire a whole range of new skills, skills related to entrepreneurial activity? Do they need to have a businessman's knowledge at their finger tips? For the purpose of training management committees for their eventual role as Boards of Directors do they offer direct business education? Put briefly, the answer is no. Increasingly, there are development workers and consultants working in local authority agencies such as Birmingham City Council's Economic Development Unit, Nottinghamshire Council's Economic Strategies Team, Community Enteprise Lothian and so on (see the agencies listed on pages 179-81). There are also a growing number of support agencies operating outside the local authorities, several of which have already been mentioned: Greater Manchester Co-operative Development Agency, Strathclyde Community Business and the Association of Community Enterprises in the Highlands and Islands, amongst others.

Development officers in these agencies assist with the development of a business plan, with feasibility studies and with marketing, and with the training of the Board of Directors of the community business or co-operative.

These agencies realise that they cannot expect to develop and support hundreds of groups. Instead they look to community workers, whether employed by local authorities or by the voluntary sector, to provide the group work skill which enables communities to embark on their own redefinition, their own identification of needs, their own education and their own initiatives. Maintenance of groups cannot depend on the agencies but must remain with the local community worker until the groups become self-sustaining. It is essential that the community worker recognises when the group is ready for the services of a development worker. Involvement of outside agencies too soon can be counter-productive and some, but not all, groups have withdrawn with their confidence destroyed. Consequently, community workers should not undervalue their existing knowledge .

Nor, it must be said, should they fail to learn from each other, from development workers and from the publications of such bodies as Strathclyde Community Business, which supplies guidelines for the establishment of community businesses. Total ignorance of the steps in business development is destructive to the workers' and to the groups' confidence.

> While they don't need to be experts and know how to do it, they need to have some idea of what it entails so they can pass that on to people, partly so they don't raise expectations unnecessarily. They should know who has already done it so they can point people in the right direction and have some ideas themselves of what is possible. I think it's possible to develop an entrepreneurial spirit yourself. It's really a style of looking at the area in terms of what may be possible economically for that area. (Chris Elphick)

Neil Graham draws on his experience of the confusions created by ignorance to make a strong plea for business knowledge:

> There is the need to understand how a business works, first and foremost, because you can't take informed decisions unless you do know that. When we had our second manager appointed and he started to talk about business plans and introduced us to those concepts things began to fall into place, certainly for me.

Neil went on to say that he felt it was unlikely that the local people would have grasped the necessary business concepts if up to that time he himself had failed to understand them. He commented that the bank balance always looked good because 'we had large inputs of Urban Aid and MSC money, so we thought this is great, we are going well, but when we started to analyse it with our second manager we began to understand the situation more clearly'.

Selecting a manager for the community business also presents problems. Time and time again businesses suffer severe setbacks, if not liquidation because of the qualities of the manager that the committee has chosen. Even when outsiders are consulted mistakes may be made, as happened with Flagstone Enterprises when a personnel manager from a commercial firm assisted the committee's selection. Though it may become essential, sacking a manager goes against the grain in a number of ways – firstly, it offends the committee's commitment to deal with unemployment in their area, secondly it casts doubt on the committee's own capacity to take sensible decisions, and finally it is a painful process at a personal level. The selectors will find advice on this crucial issue in the pack of materials offered by Strathclyde Community Business.

Glen Buchanan of SCB confirms our view that community workers should also be capable of carrying out some form of macro-economic and political analysis, covering issues related to unemployment and economic regeneration. This, he suggests, should supplement knowledge of specific types of business of relevance to community enterprises.

Relationship with Development Agencies

As we have already pointed out, development agencies have a vital role to play, but they must be approached with caution with regard to timing and expertise.

Kevin Tunnard, of Bootstrap in London, is conscious that as soon as a specialist agency appears local people expect tangible results:

> You are immediately going in with some baggage, and the label on the baggage says 'We might be able to offer you jobs... So parachuting is very difficult. Whereas if you were working as a community worker on that housing estate, and in the course of normal conversation people express their worries about unemployment, you needn't respond in any other way than 'Let's investigate it a bit further.' You are not raising expectations.

Chris Elphick believes that the community worker should check out the sort of service the specialist agency is offering. As he puts it:

> If they send people off to an agency that can give them specialist financial advice and they find that they're getting talked to in a language they don't understand, or they're being intimidated, for whatever reason, I think the community worker has a role to go to the agency and say, 'Look, I sent someone from my area and they got completely bamboozled with what you were saying. How can we rewrite the things you offer in a language that people can understand?'

More than one community worker and member of a community business has commented negatively on their interactions with development agencies – largely on the grounds that the language and concepts were inappropriate for the group at that point in time. Also, on occasion, the advice has seemed to be offered without sensitivity to the particular economic opportunities and political complexities of an area. Renton Regeneration provides an example of how a development agency can actually prevent local people from pursuing a very feasible business idea, through its control over capital funds. Consequently, community workers should approach the agencies carefully and, of course, constructively. They have much to offer.

Training and Assisting Steering Committees and Boards of Directors

Community workers have considerable experience in enabling local group members to acquire the skills of committee work, whether it be as chairperson, secretary, treasurer or ordinary committee members. In establishing community enterprises the same experience must be drawn upon. As Christine Forrester says:

> Most people's work experience is of somebody else telling them what to do. It is a very significant learning experience if you are going to move people on to looking at creating their own employment and taking decisions which involve other people.

Committee structure and committee procedures all have to be learned. The provision of agendas, the writing and presentation of minutes, the voting procedures, and the means by which other interested parties can be involved are aspects of the development of a community business with which community workers should be concerned. They may play a useful part in writing clear job descriptions for members of the management committee, as Paul Reid of Grampian Region points out. There is no question that the knowledge already acquired by community activists through their membership of tenants or other organisations can be of fundamental value to the business.

More specific training for an eventual Board of Directors is also required:

> In order to get a business onto a sound footing we have to get training in – in basic business management techniques, both to the committee members, who at the end of the day are those that are in charge and responsible for determining the policy and direction of the business, and also to the staff, who are there to carry that out on a daily basis. So we are looking at everything from training in financial control and even in understanding basic business accounts. So many committees are presented with management accounts and they sit there and simply turn them over. They have no idea what they are looking at; no idea whatever. People need to be trained to understand a balance sheet, read off profit and loss, and how to organise and run a business. (Iain Clark, Director, ACEHI)

Without claiming that community workers should take on this training, Iain Clark does see a function for the community worker in drawing new members into the enterprise as previous committee members drop out. There is a high turnover and replacements are often needed.

John MacDonald, in Skye, stresses the help that community workers can give in the wake of official development workers. Business concepts may remain hazy and not fully understood. The worker who is continually present in the community can be of value in clarifying concepts as well as issues. Without this sort of clarity management committees cannot appropriately take decisions.

Lastly, and by no means least, community workers are expected to be able to tackle the local hostilities and the conflicts which emerge in the development of a community business. Development workers will rarely stay long enough to enable the community to confront what are often damaging and self-destructive activities on the road to a community business. By facilitating this the community worker lays the foundation for development.

Implications for Training of Community Workers

In the last year support groups have mushroomed for community enterprises. They offer valuable consultancy advice, often given by development officers who have themselves gone through the experience of community business development. In Lothian, consultants within the Community Education Department itself have been appointed. They have, in many cases, learned by trial and error but now can help prevent much of the uncertainty and even anguish that accompanies launching into the unknown.

As Cailean McLean, once a community education worker involved in the development of Staffin Community Co-operative in Skye, remarks:

> If I could have done it again I'd have every stage in the process worked out before I started. I was starting on this venture without knowing how the thing would go. In the youth clubs there is an amount of money involved but it's not going to make the difference between someone's having or not having a job... something not to be treated lightly. Looking back on it, I was not really aware of the responsibility attached to getting into that field, nor of the long term commitment to a crucial aspect of the community, one in which people's money is involved.

Cailean makes it clear that work in this field must be treated very seriously. In previous pages we hope we have mapped out how community workers can contribute to community development and individual growth, through initiating and/or maintaining an idea for community enterprise.

We have drawn attention to the following main areas which training should address:

1 Understanding unemployment and the processes of economic regeneration;

2 Developing generic skills which bear on community enterprise
- Planning
- Group work (over a long time span)
- Support and Maintenance
- Identification of Community Needs
- Skills Audits
- Exploration and understanding of local political and economic situations
- Establishing Networks
- Funding – grants available, applications, sequencing
- Writing Constitutions
- Training for Committee Work;

3 Developing a Specific Knowledge Base and Skills
- Knowledge of the different forms of community enterprise
- Knowledge of forms of support available
- Some familiarity with the steps in planning from feasibility study to trading
- Awareness of which business skills are involved in community enterprise, if not actual knowledge of skills themselves, eg. accounting, market research, personnel management
- Training and Assisting Management Committees, Boards of Directors and in some cases Managers.

Problems for Community Workers Involved in Community Enterprises

The accounts given by the community workers we have consulted, and the reflections of others associated with their work, make it clear that work in this field is both challenging and problematic. Here we shall draw attention to four main areas of difficulty: (l) the unique stress on accountability, (2) the support offered to community work involvement, (3) the political situation affecting the work, and (4) the community group. All of these matters have been touched on elsewhere and are simply drawn together here for final emphasis.

1 Accountability

Nearly every informant stressed how conscious they were that where people's jobs and money were directly concerned they felt under great pressure to be both careful and knowledgeable. Amongst the pioneers in this work the strain as businesses came to the point of trading and, in some cases, to the point of liquidation, was intense. Hopefully as more consulting agencies enter the field the burden may become less. However, the community worker will probably still remain the front line worker who maintains the group, confronts them with the problems, and endeavours to move them away from personalities to issues.

2 The Support System

Some community workers are well supported by their local regions, are offered consultancy back-up, and are encouraged. Others find themselves precipitated by their local authority into community businesses and 'the flavour of the month', without adequate training or understanding of the complexity of the work. Funding to attend conferences and courses, to visit others who have already gone through many of the stages in enabling community groups to form businesses, and to buy the necessary information packages becomes essential. Funding for the support units must also be sustained at a high level if individual community workers are to embark on this work.

Perhaps even more important is that within neighbourhood teams there needs to be a commitment to this type of work. This may be difficult to obtain since it is exceptionally time consuming and deals with a relatively small section of the populace. Teams have to understand what is involved when they assign individuals to this work.

Amongst the team there may be those who regard the whole activity as wasteful and pointless, making few inroads on the massive problems of poverty and unemployment and often leading to disillusionment and failure. Furthermore, community enterprises might be thought to distract attention from vital political campaigning in areas of despair and deprivation. To some extent these arguments can be met by pointing to the businesses that have made a direct impact and have affected the local consciousness even when on a small scale (e.g. Bingham). We have yet to evaluate the effects of the support agencies which may serve to reduce error and unprofitable use of time. The arguments can also be addressed in the terms of Graham Robertson (Livingston Development Corporation):

> Community business raises understanding and skills, and it raises the ability to tackle problems in the community rather than simply diverting people from fighting for their rights. Furthermore, it tries to provide a model employer, humane and sensible conditions of service, reasonable wages, and treatment of people with respect and dignity.

3 The Political Context

The Conservative government has encouraged the break up of local authority service provision. One result has been for some local authorities to force community business ideas on groups who are far from ready to embark on business start-ups, seeing this as a preferable alternative to privatisation. Officials, councillors and representatives of the local community may want things to happen overnight. Conflict with those who wish to impose a top-down approach on a group drawn in urban areas from the psychologically demoralised and least skilled at managing their own affairs is inevitable. The objective is a highly ambitious one – to move members of the mass of unemployed into non-alienated, self-directed employment – and unseemly speed, under the pressure of particular forms of funding and of local authority departments, is unlikely to lead to successful, sustainable community businesses amongst this group. The community work role in these circumstances is to advise on time scales, and warn of the need to create organisational and legal structures as well as develop ideas on types of product or service.

4 The Group

Informing, organising, motivating and enabling a group to educate themselves in the ways of community business and community development is a demanding task. The task becomes even more demanding when the group is likely both to become over-dependent on a professional – knowledgeable or not – and at the same time to feel resentment of that professional's salary and full time employment. The long-term development of the group and the group's ideas into a Board of Directors who appoint a Manager to run a company is often beset with rancour, individual corruptibility, and very moderate levels of commitment. Yet it also depends on months if not years of voluntary effort before any pay-off to individuals or the community is obtained. However, maintaining this group, widening it, and enabling it to achieve its ambitions is made worthwhile not only by the creation of jobs but by the very real personal development that participants report.

We quote from Paul Reid, a participant in the Balnakeil Craft Village Co-operative development:

> Why was it worthwhile? It was the effect on a core of people. It was the experience of a voluntary association making, or attempting to make, substantial changes in the economy of the village. We felt we were playing for high stakes, and that our own activities would have an effect on our own and our neighbours' well-being. It was a feeling like no other. These were life and death issues – giving people the opportunity to make decisions, and gaining an incredible amount of skills.

References

Barr A 1982 Practice Models and Training Issues. In Bidwell, L and McConnell, C (eds) *Community Education and Community Development*. Dundee College of Education

Barr A 1988 *Community Work and Community Business.* CB News 25: 18-19

Clark C 1987 Unemployment, Day Care and Community Development. In Horobin G (ed) *Why Day Care? Research Highlights in Social Work*. Kingsley, London

Community Business Scotland 1986 *Community Business in Scotland: 1986 Directory.* CBS

Community Business Scotland 1987 *The First Ten Years: A Decade of Community Enterprise in Scotland*. CBS and ACEHI

DES 1982 *Experience and Participation: Report of the Review Group on the Youth Service in England*. (Thompson Report) HMSO Cmnd 8686. London

DES 1983 *Draft Circular to all Local Education Authorities and National Voluntary Youth Organisations: Youth Service.* London

Dinham B and Norton M 1977 Education and Play. *In The Directory of Social Change Vol 1.* Wildwood House, London

Echlin L 1985 Setting Up and Running a Community Business. In Inglis M and Kramer S (eds) *The New Economic Agenda*. Findhorn Press, Forres

Gulbenkian Foundation 1986 *Community Work and Social Change: A Report of a Study Group on Training* (Younghusband Report). Longman, London

Head W A 1975 Community Development in Post-Industrial Society. In D A Chekle (ed) *Developmental Theory of Method of Planned Change*. Vikas, India

Kemp T 1982 Participation and Community Education. *Community Development Journal*, **17** (1) 32-6

Love N 1985 Let's do it Ourselves. *Community Enterprise* **1**: 2-3

Lynch B 1986 Education at Work. *Times Educational Supplement Scotland* January 17 1986 p 22

Lynch B, McMichael P & Buchanan G 1986 The Making of a Course on Community Business. *SCAN*, June/July 1986 p l5

MacFarlane R 1989 *Communities in Business: The Process of Development* CDS Training Ltd, Liverpool

McArthur M 1985 *The Community Business Movement in Scotland: Discussion Paper No 17*. Centre for Urban and Regional Research, Glasgow University

McConnell C 1982 Definitions, Methods and Paradigms. In Bidwell L and McConnell C (eds) *Community Education and Community Development*. Dundee College of Education

McMichael P and Sommerville T 1986 *Opportunity Knocks: A Review of the Leith Pack of Enterprise Materials*. Moray House College, Edinburgh

Smith P W 1983 *Intervention. Un/Employment:* 2. Department of Youth and Community Work, Durham University

Acronyms

ACE	Armadale Community Enterprise
ACEHI	Association of Community Enterprises in the Highlands and Islands
CELL	Community Enterprise Lothian Limited
CEST	Community Enterprise Support Team (Dundee)
CESU	Community Enterprise Support Unit (Stirling)
COWL	Community Opportunities West Lothian
CP	Community Programme
ESF	European Social Fund
HIDB	Highland and Islands Development Board
LEAP	Local Enterprise Advisory Project (precursor of SCB)
MSC	Manpower Services Commission
RHAG	Renton Housing Action Group
SARC	Scottish Action Resource Centre
SCB	Strathclyde Community Business
SCDC	Scottish Co-operatives Development Council
SCOERC	Sunderland Common Ownership Enterprise Resource Centre
SDA	Scottish Development Agency
(F)VARC	(Falkirk) Voluntary Action Resource Centre
YTS	Youth Training Scheme

Resources

Community Workers

John Blackburn, Hendon Co-operative Centre, 44 Mowbray Road, Hendon, Sunderland, SR2 8EL.

Alma Caldwell, Sunderland North Community Business Centre, Winchester House, Baxter Road, Sunderland, SR5 4LW.

Caroline Coleman, Social Work Department, 3 Arnold Street, Flat 1, Ruchill, Glasgow, G20. Tel 041-946 6904

Neil Graham, Strathclyde Sub-Regional Office, Cotton Street, Paisley, PAl lLA. Tel 041-842 5000.

Dan Hamill, Barrowfield Project, 79/85 Stamford Street, Glasgow, G40 3QY. Tel 041-556 2731.

Jim Hoseason, Community Education Office, South Lodge School, Castle Road, Invergordon, IV18 OLW, Ross & Cromarty. Tel 0349 852718.

Tor Justad, Community Enterprise Support Unit, Unit 35, Stirling Park, Kerse Road, Stirling, FK7 7RP. Tel 0786 50969.

John MacDonald Community Education Office, Elgin Hostel, Portree, Isle of Skye, IV51 9HA. Tel 0478 2386.

John McGhee, Community Education Centre, North Street, Armadale, West Lothian, EH48 3QB. Tel 0501 30708

Hazel McLeod, Sighthill Community Education Centre, Sighthill Wynd, Edinburgh 11. Tel 031-453 6078.

Karen Minnitt, Salford Council for Voluntary Service, c/o TUC Centre for the Unemployed, 84-86 Liverpool Road, Eccles, M30 0WZ. Tel 061-787 7795.

David Mitchell, 171 Main Street, Renton, Dumbarton, Strathclyde. Tel 0389 58593.

Paddy O'Brien, Musselburgh Unemployed Workers' Centre, Brunton Hall, Ladywell Way, Musselburgh, East Lothian. Tel 031-665 8858.

Julia Preece, TVEI Project Officer, Mini-Enterprise in Schools Project, Centre for Education and Industry, University of Warwick, Westwood, Coventry, CV4 7AL. Tel 0203-523951.

Phil Quinn, Barrowfield Project, 79/85 Stamford Street, Glasgow, G40 3QY. Tel 041-556 2731.

Selected Advisory Agencies

Scotland

Lothian

Community Enterprise Lothian Ltd (CELL) 37 George Street, Edinburgh, EH2 3HN. Tel 031-220 2201 (Helen Presland)

The Centre for Employment Initiatives, 29 Queen Street, Edinburgh. Tel 031- 225 3144

Bathgate Area Support for Enterprise, 19-21 North Bridge Street, Bathgate, West Lothian. Tel 0506-633906.

Central

Community Enterprise Support Unit (CESU), Unit 35, Stirling Enterprise Park, Kerse Road, Stirling, FK7 7RP. Tel 0786-50969. (Unit Manager – Tor Justad)

Scottish Enterprise Foundation, University of Stirling, Stirling, FK9 4LA. Tel 0786-73171. (John Munro, Dept. of Business and Management, Ext. 2269).

Highlands and Islands

Association of Community Enterprises in the Highlands and Islands (ACEHI), 3 High Street, Dingwall, IV5 9HL. Tel 0349-64020 (Director – Iain Clark).

Highlands and Islands Development Board, Bridge House, Bank Street, Inverness, IVl lQR. Tel 0463-234171 (Head of Social Development Section – Roy Pedersen).

Fife

Community Business Fife, 43 High Street, Kirkcaldy. Tel 0592-642115.

Strathclyde

Strathclyde Community Business Ltd. 6 Harmony Row, Govan, Glasgow, G51 3BA. Tel 041-445 6363.

Scottish Co-operative Development Committee Ltd., Templeton Business Centre, Templeton Street, Glasgow, G40 lDA. Tel 041-554 3797 (for Workers' Co-operatives)

Tayside

Tayside Community Enterprise Support Team, St Mary's Centre, Leonard Road, Dundee, DD3 9HQ. Tel 0382-816769. (Co-ordinator- Mike Naulty)

Grampian

Community Business Group Ltd. Granitehill Enterprise Centre, Granitehill Road, Aberdeen, AB2 7AX. Tel 0224-684308 (Manager).

Dumfries and Galloway

Support in this region is channelled through Community Business Scotland Ltd. and Solway Community Business Ltd. Community Business Scotland Ltd., West Calder Workspace, Society Place, West Calder, EH55 8EA. Tel 0506-871370 (General Secretary).

Credit Union Agencies

Credit Union Development Agency, 95 Morrison Street, Glasgow. Tel 041-429 2100. (Mary Ferris/Jennifer Lees). 21 Lawmoor Road, Glasgow. Tel 041-420 1699. (John Wilson)

Credit Union Development Agency, Atlantic House, 38 Gardners Crescent, Edinburgh. Tel 031-228 5239. (Declan Jones).

England

ABCUL (Association of British Credit Unions Limited) Unit 307, Westminster Business Square, 339 Kennington Lane, London, SE11 5QY. Tel 071-582 2626 (Contact Roger Lewis)

Bootstrap Enterprises, 18 Ashwin Street, London, E8 3DL. Tel 071-254 0775 (co-operative development agency) (Kevin Tunnard, Helen Evans, Julian Putkowski).

CDS Training Ltd, 36 Slater Street, Liverpool 1 4BX or 41 Bold Street, Liverpool 1 4EU.

The Centre for Employment Initiatives, CEI Consultants, Room F38, Euston House, Euston Street, London, NW1 2ET.

Community Economy Ltd, Essex House, 375 High Street, Stratford, London E15 4QZ. Tel 081-519 6447 (provides research, training and consultancy for public, voluntary and private sectors to further community based economic development in disadvantaged communities).

Cornwall Enterprise Board Ltd, Trevint, Strangways Villas, Truro, TR1 2PA. Tel 0872-223883.

Economic Strategies Team, (Nottinghamshire County Council) 2nd floor, Castlegate House, Castlegate, Nottingham, NG1 7AT. Tel 0602-587397. (Andy Muter and Mark Hume).

Employment Initiatives Unit, Birmingham Voluntary Services Council, 138 Digbeth, Birmingham, B5 6DR. Tel 021-643 4343. (Jane Mills and Rosemary Porter).

Fairshares Community Development Team, Townhall, Halifax, HX1 1UJ. Tel 0422-357257 x 3099. (Bob Hayfield)

Greater Manchester Co-operative Development Agency, 23 New Mount Street, Manchester, M4 4DE. Tel 061-833 9496.

Hendon Co-op Centre, 44 Mowbray Road, Hendon, Sunderland, SR2 8EL. Tel 091-565 0476. (John Blackburn, Kevin Marquis).

Industrial Common Ownership Movement, The Vassally House, 20 Central Road, Leeds, LS1 6DE. Tel 0532-461738.

London Co-op Training Ltd, Bootstrap, 18 Ashwin Street, London, E8 3DL. Tel 071-254 7051.

National Federation of Credit Unions, 13 Fairfax Crescent, Bierley, Bradford, BD4 6BP. Tel 0274-687692. (Joseph Yewdall).

Wales

Community Projects Foundation, Wales. Tel 0792-798973.

The 5 Ks Questionnaire for Community Workers in Community Enterprise

Know Yourself, Know the Group, Know the Context, Know the Resources, Know about Enterprise

We refrain from prescribing but suggest an alternative. Before committing yourself to a community enterprise and during the process of development ask yourself these questions. They have all been derived from the accounts in the earlier part of the book and from the comments and advice offered us by others associated with the development of community enterprises. We believe that they will help you to appraise your work as you progress through the stages of development.

Know Yourself

How do you cope with **working with adults** – male and female?

What views have you got of the **unemployed's capacities** and future?

What is your view of the concept of '**enterprise**'? Is it compatible with working with an unemployed group towards a community enterprise?

Have you an **opportunistic approach to life**? How have you shown this so far?

Can you spare the **time**? Are you willing to give many hours a week to the group in the early period of skill development and later at times of crisis?

Would you feel comfortable as a **catalyst** within a group **OR** are you more comfortable as an **enabler**?

Do you know **when to quit**? What might lead you to leave the group?

Team Support

Is your team ready to allow you the time and resources you will need for a commitment to enterprise development?

What resources does your department offer?